Achieving

QTS

meeting the **professional standards framework**

Learning
and Teaching
Using ICT

in Secondary Schools

John Woollard

LearningMatters

First published in 2007 by Learning Matters Ltd

British Library Cataloguing in Publication Data
A CIP record for this book is available from the British Library.

ISBN 978 1 84445 078 7

Cover design by Topics – The Creative Partnership
Project management by Deer Park Productions, Tavistock, Devon
Typeset by PDQ Typesetting Ltd
Printed and bound in Great Britain by Bell & Bain Ltd, Glasgow

Learning Matters Ltd
33 Southernhay East
Exeter EX1 1NX
Tel: 01392 215560
info@learningmatters.co.uk
www.learningmatters.co.uk

Contents

The author

John Woollard is a lecturer in information technology education at the School of Education, University of Southampton. He was teacher-in-charge and head of special educational needs in three different Hampshire schools before becoming teacher adviser for IT and SEN. During the early 1990s John held a variety of positions as consultant, adviser and inspector. He now teaches on the MSc computer-based learning and initial teacher training programmes and completed his PhD in 2004. John's research focus is pedagogy and the teaching of difficult concepts in and with computers including e-learning and computer-assisted learning.

Dedication

My thanks go to my colleagues, past and present, in my earlier schools and the advisory service. In particular, my thanks go to teachers and my trainees working in partnership schools of the School of Education, University of Southampton. They have given me a wealth of good ideas and have helped make this writing possible.

This book is dedicated to my family, Heather, Mattie and Becky.

Introduction

Motivated by the conviction that information and communication technology (ICT) should be used as an effective tool, this book shows how it can support teaching and learning in the classroom and in the virtual world of school intranet, websites and learning platforms. Classroom examples and practical applications demonstrate how imaginative use of the technologies can promote creative and enthusiastic teaching, as well as enable new approaches to teaching and learning. It includes lesson plans and structured approaches to follow or adapt, together with guidance on the software, and activities to engage students in their own learning.

This book is designed to support you in your initial teacher training (ITT) to achieve Qualified Teacher Status (QTS) as a secondary school teacher. The most important function is to ensure that you meet the Training and Development Agency for Schools (TDA) requirements with regard to ICT (DfES, 2006). However, the activities will also support your professional development in a number of other areas and a number of the other requirements. For example, when using ICT to support your professional development, you may also be meeting the requirement to be familiar with the key stage strategy and able to make the lessons more motivating. Throughout the book, the examples are taken from all subjects of the National Curriculum and they have been carefully selected to ensure that the most effective use of ICT in your curriculum area has been included. The appendix contains a description of the use of ICT in the different subjects providing a succinct overview. However, it is more valuable for you to treat each chapter as an important area of your development as a teacher and perhaps identify examples of ICT work that are most appropriate for you personally or the particular training school in which you find yourself.

The title, *Learning and Teaching Using ICT in Secondary Schools*, indicates its three areas of focus: teaching, learning and ICT. Obviously, this book will identify good ICT practice but teaching can only be good if learning takes place. Teaching, learning and ICT are therefore equal partners in this approach to teacher training and development.

Teaching has four aspects: teaching is about organisation of resources; management of people; planning of the curriculum; and dealing with the students. These are reflected in every chapter of the book and each chapter can contribute to your growing skills and knowledge as a teacher. Through this book, you will 'know how to use ICT effectively, both to teach [your] subject and to support [your] wider professional role' (DfES, 2002, p9).

Learning is the key to your success as a teacher. Through the informed implementation of the skills and crafts of teaching, students will learn. Throughout the book, there is reference to the current research on learning and how it can take place more effectively or efficiently. There is reference to further reading to support your understanding of the learning process. Developing ICT is just one of four school-wide initiatives being introduced nationally. They are ICT Across the Curriculum (ICTAC), Assessment for Learning (AfL), Leading in Learning (LiL) and Literacy Across the Curriculum (LAC). Your placement schools will be receiving local authority support for one or more of the initiatives.

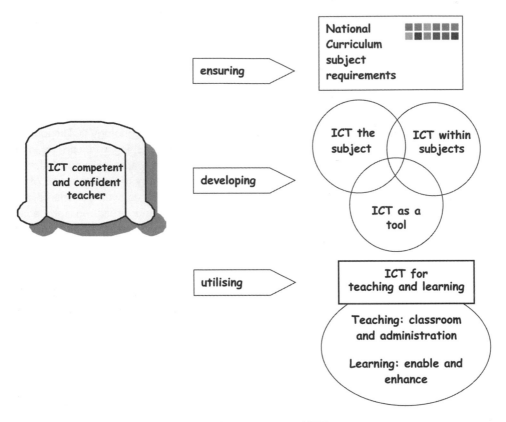

Fig. 1. Competences of ICT

ICT in teaching has three facets.

1. ICT is a vehicle for teaching and learning and, through the examples described in the book, you will be able to identify how ICT activities support your teaching in the classroom. To meet the standards and the needs of our students, you must be effectively and discriminately teaching with ICT. Also, you must 'use ICT effectively in [your] teaching'. There is also a responsibility to teach the skills, knowledge and understanding of ICT that under the National Strategy is called 'capability'.

2. 'All those qualifying to teach a subject at Key Stage 3 must be able to use the cross-curricular elements set out in the National Strategy for Key Stage 3, in their teaching, as appropriate to their specialist subject' (DfES, 2002, p12). This book clearly identifies those appropriate areas for developing students' ICT capability.

3. ICT is a part of each subject of the National Curriculum. For example, in mathematics it includes charting and graphing programming, in PE it is the use of stopwatches with lap recorders linked to data-collection devices to analyse and evaluate performance. In design and technology, it is identifying relevant sources of information and using a range of resources including ICT. Through reading and carrying out the activities of this book you will learn and understand the contribution ICT specifically makes to your subject area.

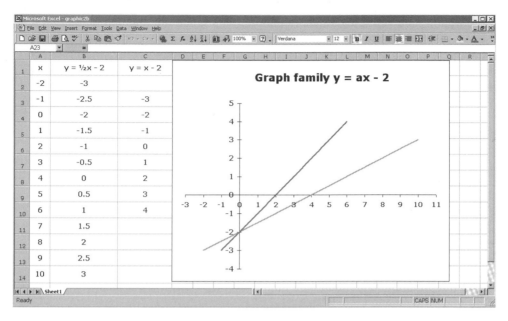

Fig. 2. Graphing using a spreadsheet

Becoming an ICT-competent teacher

If you are training to be a mathematics teacher you have 4,000 years of recorded and celebrated history on which to base your pedagogy. Teaching with computers began in the 1970s and is therefore not serviced with such a richness of ideas that have been trialled and improved upon. For everyone, including those specialising in the subject, the teaching of ICT skills poses challenges because we are still learning how to teach ICT.

Moreover, ICT is not a trouble-free zone. Indeed, in many respects computers add a further layer of complexity to the teacher's role in the classroom. The issues that have to be dealt with raise many questions to challenge whether our teaching with ICT is effective.

The gender divide exists in ICT; when teaching with ICT you have to consider whether the apparent differences between the genders are significant in your teaching and the learning taking place.

There is a technology breakdown syndrome; as technology develops it seems as if the ICT-centred disasters are greater. As you learn to become an effective and efficient teacher with ICT you will also be learning how to solve or work around the technical problems as they arise.

You need to consider why some groups of students are more successful while others are more enthusiastic and yet others positively 'geekish' towards using ICT. Good teaching harnesses the energies of enthusiasm and nurtures small successes to build competence through confidence.

ICT can have a personal impact upon the students. You must consider how to safeguard them from the physical hazards of computers and personal hazards associated with the internet and inappropriate relationships with adults.

The current initiatives in education, including Building Schools for the Future (BSF), School Workforce Remodelling (SWR), the Disability Discrimination Acts, the Special Educational Needs Code of Practice (DfES, 2001), the guidance on safeguarding children (DfES, 2005) and *Every Child Matters* (ECM) all have significant implications for why, how and what we teach with ICT.

There is a fashion trap. You need to consider whether, by using the young person's interest in modern technology, are you denying the traditional values of established pedagogy?

BECTa	British Educational Communications and Technology Agency
DES	Department of Education and Science (1964–1992)
DoE	Department of Education (1992–1995)
DfEE	Department for Education and Employment (1995–2001)
DfES	Department for Education and Skills (2001 onward)
DEFRA	Department for Environment Food and Rural Affairs
GTCE	General Teaching Council for England
OFSTED	Office for Standards in Education
QCA	Qualifications and Curriculum Authority
TDA	Training and Development Agency for Schools (2005 onward)
TTA	Teacher Training Agency (former name of the TDA)

Fig. 3. There are a number of organisations and areas of government that are having an important influence upon the direction and speed of change in education. You will come into frequent contact with these abbreviations and acronyms

How to use this book

It is the intention of this book to equip you with the knowledge and understanding of the ICT curriculum and processes so that you can hold better-informed opinions on the role of ICT in education and the value it has to students, schools and society as a whole. It is divided into four sections. The first deals with the generic skills, knowledge and understanding of ICT and identifies the key concepts of ICT that you, as a subject teacher, need to know about and understand. The second section deals with how you use ICT to enhance your teaching and the issues of lesson planning, managing the resources and managing the students within an ICT room. The third section focuses upon the students, their learning and the progress you enable them to make. The final section considers the wider implications of ICT in the emerging curriculum, community and society and the wider world. There is an important chapter about ICT-enhanced research and the role of the teacher. The final chapter also considers the more recent technologies that are likely to have an impact upon your early years as a teacher.

Although there is a progression of ideas through the book, it is not necessary to deal with the issues in the same sequence. It is important to identify your own training needs and priorities in consultation with your mentors and tutors. It is through the setting of targets, reflecting upon your own performance, reading about the issues and researching within the classroom that you will become a competent and confident professional ICT-enabled teacher.

Note about URLs. All URLs quoted in this book were valid at the time of going to press. However, the provisional nature of the internet almost guarantees that some will be changed in the near future ('provisionality'). If you cannot locate a resource using the URL quoted then read the advice on 'Searching the web' and 'The wrong URL' in Chapter 15.

Professional Standards for QTS

Each chapter is headed with a short paragraph describing the QTS standards (DfES, 2006) that are relevant to the activities within the chapter. Many ICT-related activities support the standards but the most important ICT standards are:

Q8 Have a creative and constructively critical approach towards innovation, being prepared to adapt their practice where benefits and improvements are identified.

Q16 Have passed the professional skills tests in numeracy, literacy and information and communication technology (ICT).

Q17 Know how to use skills in literacy, numeracy and ICT to support your teaching and wider professional activities.

Q23 Design opportunities for learners to develop their literacy, numeracy and ICT skills.

Q25 Teach lessons and sequences of lessons across the age and ability range for which you are trained in which you: (a) use a range of teaching strategies and resources, including e-learning, taking practical account of diversity and promoting equality and inclusion. (DfES, 2006, pp5–6)

REFERENCES REFERENCES **REFERENCES** REFERENCES **REFERENCES** REFERENCES

Building Schools for the Future (BSF) **www.bsf.gov.uk**

DfES (2001) *The special educational needs code of practice.* London: Department for Education and Skills.

DfES (2002) *Key Stage 3 National Strategy Framework for teaching ICT capability: Years 7, 8 and 9.* London: Department for Education and Skills.

DfES (2005) *Statutory guidance on making arrangements to safeguard and promote the welfare of children under section 11 of the Children Act 2004.* London: Department for Education and Skills.

DfES (2006) *Professional standards for qualified teacher status.* London: Department for Education and Skills. **www.tda.gov.uk/partners/ittstandards**

Disability Discrimination Act (2005). **www.opsi.gov.uk/acts/acts2005/20050013.htm**

Every Child Matters (ECM). **www.everychildmatters.gov.uk**

School Workforce Remodelling (SWR). **www.remodelling.org** also **www.teachernet.gov.uk/wholeschool/remodelling**

The Children's Act (2004). **www.opsi.gov.uk/acts/acts2004/20040031.htm**

Part 1

Generic skills, knowledge and understanding

1
The skills of ICT

By the end of this chapter you should:

- be more confident in being able to lead a computer-based lesson in your subject;
- have a better understanding of students' ICT capability;
- have identified the areas in which to develop your ICT capability;
- be aware of the importance of ensuring your students stay safe on the internet.

Professional Standards for QTS

Q3, Q6, Q16, Q17, Q21a, Q23, Q33

This chapter introduces you to the ways in which you can use ICT to support your wider professional activities as well as develop your students' ICT skills. Both collaboration and working with other classroom colleagues are identified as ways in which you enhance student learning. Three current legal requirements relating to the use of computers are identified. Advice is provided with regard to the professional skills tests.

Introduction

When you are introducing students to ICT in your subject area, you will most likely find yourself needing to support students in their ICT development – you will have to teach ICT skills. For example, you may have to explain to students how to copy text from one document to another or how to copy an image from the internet to their own work. This chapter focuses upon basic aspects of teaching generic ICT skills and windows navigation. A generic aspect of computing we will consider is the teaching of keyboard skills. The first topic discussed is **help** – the strategies for supporting students in their learning.

Getting help to your students

Taking a class of students into a computer room for the first time can be daunting. Teaching with and about ICT has all of the same issues as traditional classroom teaching but with that added element of complexity – the computer. Watch an ICT teacher supporting students at the computer; they do not constantly look at the student. They listen but they are gazing at the screen; they are trying to work out how the student got to where they are so that they can best frame a response to the student's query. The student frequently says, 'it isn't working' or 'it has gone wrong' or 'I don't know what to do (now)'. A successful ICT-based lesson is made more likely if there are good strategies in place to enable students to get help when they 'get stuck'.

The following strategies are designed to ensure that students become independent users of computers and will give you more time to look at students and not screens.

What I'm looking for (WILF)	Make sure that the students know what they are doing and how to do it. Make it clear at the start of the lesson 'what I'm looking for'. Many ICT lessons begin with a demonstration of the techniques. This can be useful for the visual or auditory learner but needs supporting resources to help the kinaesthetic learner. Students can benefit from written guides that illustrate the key stages or identify the steps to be taken. These may be presented on the network in the class's shared area.
Monitors/ helpers	Identify the most able students to act as monitors. Give them direct instructions to move around the class looking for good examples. This strategy focuses upon the positive aspects of celebrating students' achievements but invariably means that help is being given informally.
Traffic lights	In the 'traffic light' system students identify themselves as needing help by placing a red cube on top of the computer monitor. A yellow cube indicates that they have finished their work and a green cube means they are going well. A quick scan of the room indicates the level of difficulty being encountered and the probable need for your intervention with the whole class or a small group of students.
Mile- stones	When planning an ICT lesson consider what you would expect to see on the screen of successful students as the lesson progresses. Each stage of the activity will have a different image. With these in mind, a quick scan of the computer screens of the class will reveal the level of progress in general and also identify those falling behind. Your help can therefore be strategic by talking to individuals or small groups. For example, students making slow progress might be given permission to miss out steps or be given a solution so that they can start the next stage. Those students making the best progress can be given enrichment or extension activities.
Help menu	There are several ways in which to filter out some of the queries that you have to answer. Insist that before putting their hand up to ask for help, students first seek help through the Help menu of the software. This is a powerful technique because it benefits the student in other lessons and when they are working on their own. Being skilled in using Help supports independent learning.
Ask a friend	Encourage students to work in pairs or threes; allow students to talk to the person next to them. Make it clear that they should ask the student next to them for help before putting up their hand for help from you. This means that when you do give help then it is to at least three adjacent students, making your explanations more cost-effective.
Rations	Ration your help – encourage the students to be strategic when seeking help by limiting questions to two per student per lesson.
Teaching Assistants (TAs)	Ensure your planning includes the briefing of classroom assistants and specific instructions on how you would like them to support the lesson. Good advice is contained in the publication *Working together: teaching assistants and assessment for learning* **www.standards.dfes.gov.uk/keystage3/downloads/ afl_ws109905wkg_ta_afl.pdf**. On page 4 are some quotes from teaching assistants – use those to make an *aide-mémoire* or set of prompts for yourself to make your briefing of TAs more effective.

Fig. 4. Getting help to your students

Teaching the basic skills

It is an often-made observation that teachers teach the way they learn. It is the sign of a good teacher that he or she teaches to meet the needs of different learning styles. When teaching ICT you need to be aware that you might be teaching the way you do it and perhaps not the way in which students learn. For example, there are three typical ways of interacting with and using a windows-based computer characterised by the dominance of keyboard short-cuts, or the use of contextual menu or the use of drop-down menus.

Consider how you copy a block of text from one part of a document to another part of the same document.

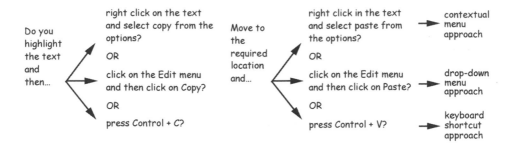

Fig. 5. Copy–paste styles

Competent and experienced computer users develop their own style that may be a hybrid of techniques swapping between mouse and keyboard. Some tasks favour a particular approach. For example, while word-processing it is likely that keyboard shortcuts will be deployed. On the other hand, when using a painting program a mouse-based approached is likely to be used.

PRACTICAL TASK PRACTICAL TASK PRACTICAL TASK PRACTICAL TASK PRACTICAL TASK

Consider this scenario: you are going to take your class to the ICT room as part of the preparation for an extended project. One activity that will last for ten minutes is for students to gather a small collection of images from the school intranet (learning platform), the internet (world wide web) and some locally installed programs. Write down the description you will give of the three methods of how to copy images from a web page into their word-processor document. These two graphics may help to illustrate your prose.

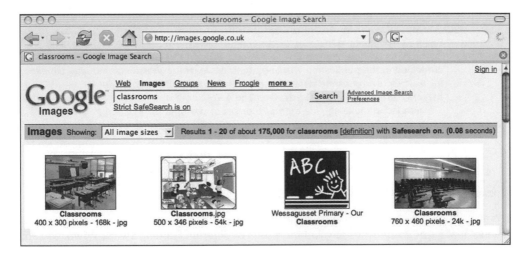

Fig. 6. Image search using Google

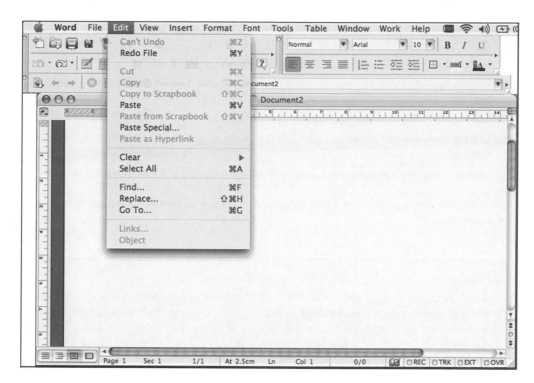

Fig. 7. Microsoft Word

Animation

Animation is the technique that combines several images into one image, which when saved and rendered as a GIF image (bitmap) jumps from one image to the next in the form of an animation. Animation is also possible in many vector-based programs. For example, Macromedia Flash generates moving images that are driven by an underlying script of instructions. One feature is called *tweening*. The user creates two similar, but distinctly different images, and the computer calculates and then renders all the in-between drawings. These are then played as an animation. Some packages do the same with bitmap images. For example, in Kai's Goo the user chooses two different images and marks common points in both. The software calculates in-between images; when the sequence is rendered as a cartoon, one image appears to change into another. This is called 'morphing'. Other techniques to enhance images range from the idiosyncratic and specialised such as sepia, which makes any image look as if it was a photograph taken 60 years ago and then faded through time. Others are universal such as Gaussian blur and invert (negative photographic image). The image manipulation functions include: skew, rotate, distort, flip, reflect and image size.

Another technique is to apply pixelation to part or the whole of the image. A low-resolution screen has 640 by 480 pixels in it. Individual pixels can be seen by the naked eye but the general image appears without distortion. A pixelated image is generated by taking every 10 by 10 area of pixels and rendering it as a single (average) colour. It is used on films to obscure the identity of an individual. The pixelation removes the detail without hiding the overall picture.

PRACTICAL TASK PRACTICAL TASK **PRACTICAL TASK** PRACTICAL TASK **PRACTICAL TASK**

- Use the Google search engine and click on 'images'. www.google.co.uk
- Use the keywords 'ICT' and 'mathematics'. Mathematicians are guaranteed to find something of interest.
- Now search using 'ICT' and your subject as the keywords.
- Use the keywords 'animation' and 'mathematics'. Many of the images cited will have an animation effect.
- Search for images and animations relevant to different aspects of your subject.

Consider what the pedagogic value is of moving images in terms of motivation, interest and clarity of the subject content.

TECHNICAL TIP

Google Images is available on most computers by accessing the webpage **www.google.co.uk/images**. *However, some schools employ systems to protect the students from inappropriate material and also prevent them accessing certain web pages. One method is to employ a proxy server to filter requests to the internet. In one LEA, the filter blocks any search which includes the word 'image'. Although you would be able to do the work on your computer, you may not be able to on the school computers.*

Until you are confident that you know the foibles of your school's computers, always check out well before the lesson the activities you or your students will be using.

TEACHING TIP

Use your ICT experience of successful and less successful use of ICT to advise students.

Your worldly experience of success and perhaps failure with ICT makes you a better judge of the potential and probable value of trying out a particular strategy. Even when you are working with students whose ICT capability is more advanced than your own, you can give helpful advice regarding strategies. But you must enable students to become worldly-wise by allowing them to choose and also learn through trial and improvement.

The National Curriculum requirement is that 'they select and use information systems suited to their work in a variety of contexts' (QCA, 1999, p41).

Keyboard skills – touch-typing versus 'search and peck'

Touch-typing is a much-debated point and it appears that the issue is not going to leave us in the near future. Increasingly, students are using computers from a very early age, and by the time they reach secondary school, they need to be proficient at inputting data by the use of a keyboard. The argument expressed by some is 'to be really efficient as adults, they must acquire touch-typing skills at some stage'. At present, it is not common in schools to teach touch-typing although there are celebrated instances when it does take place. Where touch-typing is an established part of the curriculum it is associated with skills-based courses such a pre-vocational education and GNVQ.

PRACTICAL TASK PRACTICAL TASK PRACTICAL TASK PRACTICAL TASK PRACTICAL TASK

Investigate the following and then make an informed professional and personal decision as to whether to learn to touch-type.

- **Does your school have touch-typing as part of the curriculum?**
- **Are touch-typing programs available to students?**
- **Search the internet and discover more arguments for and against structured touch-typing instruction.**
- **Clarify whether you think students should be taught to touch-type.**
- **Make the decision to learn to touch-type or not.**

Being safe on the internet

'Hardly a week goes by without some reference within the media to the dangers of the internet. Such is the fear raised, that the temptation is to pull the plug and return to life before the PC. This is, of course, a ridiculous and extreme reaction, but nevertheless we have to weigh up the enormous opportunities that the internet can bring against the dangers' (BECTa, 2006, p1).

The traditional health and safety approach is to identify the hazard and assess the risk and then to eliminate the hazard or reduce the risk. The hazard is enormous: there are those who would use the opportunity to approach, groom, solicit and physically harm students and we cannot eliminate the hazard. The strategy has to be one of risk reduction. Many millions of internet activities take place daily, students learn a great deal through the internet, they have many appropriate and supportive social interactions and activities previously impossible can take place. Those activities will and must take place. To reduce the risk you have to ensure that students behave so that they do not expose themselves to the activities of those who would cause them harm. In all you do, you must acknowledge that the welfare of your students is paramount. However, because many students are using the internet at home for homework it is vital that good, safe school use of the internet also promotes good, safe home use.

It is natural for students to trust the printed word. We put much faith in books and that trust is frequently transferred to other media such as television and the internet. Students must be discerning and we need to reinforce the importance of making judgements. Friends made on the internet may not be as they appear to be – students need to be aware of internet 'avatars'. An avatar is a personality or character on the internet that in reality can be something quite different.

For example, in 1988, using the Times Network for Schools e-mail service, Key Stage 1 and 2 students in Hampshire schools could e-mail Santa and receive back personal responses. Santa in this case is an avatar representing a group of advisory teachers encouraging e-mail activities. Nowadays, there are many opportunities for students to 'ask an expert' by e-mail or even in chat rooms. The Askanexpert site connects you with hundreds of real-world experts, ranging from astronauts to zookeepers – **www.askanexpert.com**.

However, there is the danger that your students follow leads to websites that are not authoritative and perhaps have avatars that have not gone through the same vetting as teachers. Students may be tempted to reveal more about themselves than is advisable. Just three clicks from 'ask an expert about the internet' and a student can be entering into a conversation about sustaining online romantic relationships.

Category: How to Have an Online Relationship		Sort By: Knowledge
Name	**Expertise**	**Status**
vanessa View Profile	I love helping people and and some may say that I am a very chatting and friendly person. I can offer advice to people who are in long distance or a different cultural online relationship as I have experienced both. I know how hard it can be and how heartbreaking it can be but I also know how rewarding they can be.	**Available** Ask A Question View Past Answers

Fig.8. This might lead to inappropriate material

The hazards we have to protect students from are: exposure to inappropriate material; physical danger and psychological danger, for example, cyber-bullying and grooming. The strategies in place are: internet filtering, clear advice, codes of conduct and pastoral support.

An avatar is more than just an icon. Avatar is the whole personality that the icon represents. Our avatar is who we think we are when we are in a particular environment. More accurately, our avatar is the impression we wish to give of ourselves when we are in different situations. For example, on an education bulletin-board you would display your (student-like or teacher-like) academic skills yet in MSN-type chat you would act in a more personally reflective/affective way. An avatar can be malicious (paedophiles representing themselves in icon and word as empathetic). The avatar can be professional (a market researcher gaining a reaction to a new proposal or a teacher/tutor seeding conversations on a weblog or bulletin board). The avatar can be frivolous (an otherwise sensible person acting out a part while playing poker).

PRACTICAL TASK PRACTICAL TASK PRACTICAL TASK PRACTICAL TASK PRACTICAL TASK

Consider the hazards associated with students' online activities and list those you think are most pertinent in your teaching and in your placement school. Scrutinise the PSHE programmes to identify activities that would help protect students, including being taught how to deal with abusive behaviour and cyber-bullying. Discuss the issues with your subject mentor and arrange to discuss them with an ICT specialist teacher or ICT technician who has a responsibility for online security or technology monitoring students' access to the network. If possible, obtain a copy of your school's internet safety policy. Are there systems in place to keep data about students secure? Is there a code of practice for teachers?

Use these keywords in your discussion with ICT staff: proxy server, online filtering, walled garden, logon and user identification/authorisation/authentication, individual history caches, code of conduct and parental permission.

Many of these issues arise from the Every Child Matters agenda and your 'duty of care' to promote your students' safety and well-being.

Other considerations for students' online activity

Students do not always behave well in the classroom and outside. The same is true when they are online. Similar strategies of behaviour management and behaviour modification need to be in place. Students need to be taught how to behave online so that they do not appear to be rude, intolerant, unkind, insensitive or inconsiderate. When online, they also need to use appropriate netiquette.

Students should also be aware that their online actions might have legal and financial considerations. For example, there are many websites that offer both free and chargeable services associated with music, mobile phone services and competitions – students may not be aware when the product they request is free and when it is chargeable. They will all receive 'personal e-mails' suggesting that they can gain large sums of money by giving just a little or even just bank account details. Students need good advice given in a supportive, empathetic and professional way. They should be advised not to disclose personal details and be sensitive to signs of inappropriate requests for personal details.

Students need to be aware the ethical aspects of online activity including: the school code of conduct, the ISP regulations and the laws of data protection, computer misuse and freedom of information.

Data Protection Act 1998	There are eight principles, including: Principle 4 – data must be accurate; Principle 7 – data must be secure	you must not record inaccurate or ambiguous records on students; passwords must be used to protect access to databases; computers must be protected from theft.
Computer Misuse Act 1990	The offences are unauthorised access to: programs or data; support further crime; modify computer material.	you must not allow students to: download software; gain information/images for illegal use; hack into systems or make programs/computers faulty.
Freedom of Information Act 2000	The Act creates a general right of access, on request, to information held by public authorities with numerous exemptions.	a parent can see all documents relating to the process of education; the Act does not cover personal information about the student.

Fig. 9. The law and ICT

TEACHING TIP

The three laws relating to the use of ICT have implications for your training and work as a teacher. You must ensure that:

- students' records are accurate and secure;
- you do not download software and install it on school computers unless authorised to do so;
- you keep separate the information about 'what you are teaching' from that about 'who you are teaching'.

FURTHER READING   FURTHER READING   **FURTHER READING**   FURTHER READING

It is a BECTa recommendation that 'e-safety training be embedded in all initial teacher training (ITT) and continuing professional development (CPD) courses for teachers' (BECTa, 2006, p3).

The following publications provide a detailed description of the issues and solutions that are currently adopted by schools:

Safeguarding children in a digital world is published by BECTa and provides a strategic overview of e-safety issues to policy-makers; it makes reference to the technological and infrastructure requirements and is more suited to the needs of ICT specialist trainees.

E-safety – Developing whole-school policies to support effective practice is published by BECTa. Internet safety in the classroom is discussed and the booklet proposes a useful model of student awareness and how you should deal with groups of different experience and expertise. It also describes the roles of different members of staff in school.

Signposts to safety – Teaching internet safety at Key Stages 3 and 4 is the most useful publication for you to read. It contains a lot of practical advice, a number of useful websites and reference to teaching materials. It is freely available from **www.becta.org.uk/corporate/publications/publications_detail.cfm?currentbrand=1&pubid=194&cart**   or locate it using a Google search for 'signposts to safety becta'.

Know IT All – What you need to know about internet and online safety is an educational resource pack especially designed for secondary schools published by Childnet International containing references to materials for students and teachers **www.childnet-int.org**. They also publish 'Jenny's Story'.

'Jenny's Story' is a hard-hitting film based on the true story of a young teenager who chats to a stranger online. The film shows how through online chatting, Jenny reveals personal information that results in her being contacted in real life, and ultimately hurt. The film aims to challenge young people about the dangers to chatting to strangers on the internet, but also help them reflect on important issues such as trust, flattery, personal information and how they can develop strategies to avoid being manipulated or feeling 'trapped'. The teachers' resources will help you prepare this as a classroom activity for secondary school students from Key Stage 3 upwards. A preview is available at **www.childnet-int.org/jenny/video.html**. This resource is highly recommended.

Albion.com is a useful site to brush up on your own netiquette as well as introduce some of the issues to the students. There is an interesting quiz as well as links to other resources – **www.albion.com/netiquette**. The ThinkUknow website is controlled by the Child Exploitation and Online Protection (CEOP) Centre and contains a lot of information on how students can stay safe online. Topics covered include mobile telephones, blogging and gaming sites with the invitation for students, if they feel uncomfortable or worried about someone they are chatting to online, to contact them – **www.thinkuknow.co.uk**

TEACHING TIP

If you are planning an internet-based lesson, ensure that you know what guidelines and support are available to your students and incorporate some reference to those guidelines in your lesson. The six tips provided by Thames Valley Police for students to become web-wise are:

1. Do not give out personal details, photographs, or any other information that could be used to identify you, such as information about your family, where you live or the school you go to.
2. Do not take other people at face value – they may not be what they seem.
3. Never arrange to meet someone you have only ever previously met on the internet without first telling your parents, getting their permission and taking a responsible adult with you. The first meeting should always be in a public place.
4. Always stay in public areas of chat and where there are other people around.
5. Do not open an attachment or download a file unless you know and trust the person who has sent it.
6. Never respond directly to anything you find disturbing – save or print it, log off and tell an adult.

The world wide web is a wonderful place full of information, entertainment and a new way of making friends. The internet has opened up a completely new world in cyber space, where you can communicate with people you may never meet face to face. From an early age, we are taught about the potential dangers posed by some strangers and ways to avoid getting into harmful situations. Unfortunately many children and teenagers do not use the same caution when using the internet. (TVP, 2006)

ICT skills test for QTS

www.tda.gov.uk/skillstests.aspx

The ICT skills test ensures that you have a good grounding in the use of ICT in the generic applications:

- **word processor;**
- **spreadsheet;**
- **database;**
- **presentation;**
- **e-mail;**
- **web browser.**

It does not use the conventional Microsoft, Linux or Apple windows environments but like the Key Stage 3 online assessments, it uses an idiosyncratic interface. **www.tda.gov.uk/ skillstests/practicematerials/ict/features.aspx**

Passing the QTS skills test for ICT does not mean that you meet the ICT-related standards. It is simply a minimalist assessment of ICT skills. It does not ensure that you have:

- **the knowledge and understanding of the ICT specific to your subject;**
- **the ICT skills specific to your subject;**
- **the knowledge of how to teach ICT within your subject;**
- **the opportunities for ICT to meet the administrative aspects of your work.**

The advice is to use the practice material available online, book a test early in your teacher-training programme and, if necessary, take advantage of the limitless retries. **www.tda.- gov.uk/skillstests/practicematerials/ict/practicematerial.aspx**

The QTS skills tests helpline is 0845 450 8867; it is not possible to book tests by telephone.

A recommended book to support your preparation for the test is: *Passing the ICT Skills Test (Achieving QTS)* by Clive Ferrigan (2005).

A SUMMARY OF **KEY POINTS**

> **Set yourself clear targets for developing your ICT competence.**

> **Focus your ICT competences upon those areas of ICT that will enhance your teaching (presentation of information) and make your administration more efficient (data handling and storage).**

> **Be aware of the ICT that is particularly important in your subject area.**

> **Ensure that you use your competences confidently in class to develop the students' ICT capability.**

> **Include in your ICT development the skills of using hardware that will support your presentation work, including: cameras, scanners, MP3 audio recorders, digital video cameras and CD writers.**

REFERENCES REFERENCES **REFERENCES** REFERENCES **REFERENCES** REFERENCES

BECTa (2006) *Safeguarding children in a digital world. Developing a strategic approach to e-safety.* Coventry: BECTa.

Childnet (2007) KnowITAll for trainees. London. UK: Childnet International. **www.childnet-int.org.uk/KIA.**

Ferrigan, C (2005) *Passing the ICT skills test (Achieving QTS).* Exeter: Learning Matters.

TVP (2006) *Chat safe.* Oxford: Thames Valley Police. **www.thamesvalley.police.uk/chatsafe**

2
The knowledge of ICT

By the end of this chapter you should:

- **know the place that your subject-specific ICT fits in the framework of ICT in general;**
- **have a better awareness of the importance of your ICT in developing the ICT capabilities of students;**
- **be more aware of your preferred learning style;**
- **understand the principles and motivations of the minimalist approaches;**
- **know how to construct an ICT learning activity within your subject area.**

Professional Standards for QTS

Q7, Q9, Q22, Q23, Q25d

This chapter introduces you to the ways in which you can develop your students' ICT skills. Importantly, it enables you to identify your own personal professional needs with respect to ICT, suggest that you consult with and then respond to the advice of mentors, indicates how you can manage the learning of individual students through the design of ICT-related teaching materials and how to plan lessons.

Introduction

This chapter is concerned with the subject knowledge of ICT. It is concerned with those aspects of the use of computers with which you should be familiar and with which you are able to work competently and with confidence.

Kelly's construct theory

George Kelly was an American psychologist born in 1905. Espousing on the axiom 'Man is a scientist', he developed an approach to understanding based on the idea that we all individually and collectively strive to make sense of the world as we experience it. We do this by constantly forming and testing hypotheses that he called *constructs*. These build to a very complex model of the world and our place in it. Kelly's theory of personal constructs (Kelly, 1955) includes considering whether and how we modify our constructs when we are faced with contradictory information and whether some constructs are immutable, even in the light of apparent contradictory evidence. Constructs therefore serve two purposes – they represent the view you have constructed about the world; they also indicate how you are likely to construe the world as you view or perceive new experiences.

A table can be used to represent a construct. The table below contains, in the central column, a construct of ease-of-use and usefulness of different forms of ICT. The most useful or easiest to use are near the top; the more difficult or less common are near the bottom. Before using the list to plan your targets and the subsequent strategies to develop your ICT skills and knowledge, it is useful to discuss the construct with peers, tutors and mentors to establish how they feel about the relative positions of the ICT activities with regard to your subject.

- **Are some items more easily achieved? Are some items more useful for your subject? They can be moved up the list.**
- **Are some items less easily achieved? Are some items less useful for your subject? They can be moved down the list.**

Because it is a mental construct built up of the author's experience, it is likely to be at variance with other similar constructs made by trainers, tutors, mentors and teachers. Indeed, you may feel that the relative positions of some items should be different. Developing constructs is a useful exercise to help your students understand complex issues.

The construct becomes interesting when an item is more useful than represented yet more difficult to achieve. It may be necessary to change the representation from a single line to a two-dimensional display. Those items require more discussion with mentors and tutors before setting targets for action.

PRACTICAL TASK PRACTICAL TASK **PRACTICAL TASK** PRACTICAL TASK **PRACTICAL TASK**

Using Figure 10 on page 21, identify the extent of your ICT knowledge. Copy the table and shade in those areas where you know what the ICT activity entails and you can work with some confidence. Then identify what the next step is in developing your ICT awareness. It is likely to be a balance of generic (central) areas and aspects of ICT that make a specific contribution to your subject. Now discuss your conclusion with your mentors and tutors. They may have a different perspective and can better advise you about your ICT development. It is a required standard for QTS that you act upon advice and feedback. Ensure that your ICT targets are clearly stated in terms of outcomes. Write down what the evidence will be that you have met the targets within a set period.

Setting SMARTER targets in ICT

Specific – targets should specify what they want to achieve – the strategies are how they will be achieved.

Measurable – you, your tutors and your mentors should be able to tell whether they have been met.

Agreed – you should discuss your targets with your tutors and mentors.

Realistic – ensure the targets are realistically achievable with the resources and facilities available.

Timely – targets should be appropriate to the stage of your training and with set limits.

Exciting – targets should be challenging, stimulating, motivating and interesting to encourage achievement.

Reviewed – targets should be reviewed within a reasonable time and if necessary modified.

examples	examples	ICT function	examples	examples
DT gathering information	Hi, Gg and RE internet searching	**internet browsing**	RE raising belief and faith awareness	Gg using mapping sites
MFL raising cultural awareness	Eg internet reading			Sc viewing experiments
Hi, Gg and RE exploring curriculum material		**using multimedia**	MFL raising cultural awareness	Sc simulation software
En writing web pages		**presenting information**		Mu creating scores
Ar creating collage				
En and MFL e-mail (asynchronous)	En and MFL chat rooms (synchronous)	**communicating information (cmc)**	En emoticons En texting	En bulletin boards/forum
Ma modelling		**number manipulation (spreadsheets)**	DT modelling time and cost analysis	
Ma manipulating shapes	Ma geometry packages	**image manipulation**	Gg map annotation	Mu sequencing and editing scores
Ma LOGO				
Ma and Sc data analysis		**information analysis**		Sc analyse data (search and sort)
Ma and Sc charting data		**data presentation**		Mu sequencing
Ma graphing				
MFL making podcasts	Ar creating interactive installations	**authoring multimedia**	Ar creating vodcasts	En Kartouche
Ma graphic calculators		**video/sound manipulation**	Mu editing recordings of performances	MFL making listening resources tapes, audio files, CDs and DVDs
Ma for handling information	Sc for analysing results	**creating databases**	Hi for analysing data	DT to analyse materials and their properties
Sc sensing and timing equipment	Gg weather station	**sensing**	Mu recording MIDI music	PE pulse rate monitors
				Sc sensing
		control		DT controlling artefacts

Fig. 10. Construct of ICT with subject-based activities

The minimalist approach

One well-discussed approach to the design of instructions is the *minimalist* framework. It is particularly applicable to computer training materials. The critical idea of minimalist theory is to minimise the extent to which the instructions obstruct learning. Instead, the focus of the design is on activities that support the learner's ownership of the learning process and support learner independence.

The theory suggests that:

- **all learning tasks should be meaningful;**
- **the tasks should be self-contained activities;**
- **learners should be given real activities;**
- **instructions should permit self-determined reasoning;**
- **learners should be encouraged to devise their own learning tasks;**
- **handling errors is important.**

Like the work of Carl Rogers' client-centred or non-directive approaches (Rogers, 1961), the minimalist theory emphasises the necessity to build upon the learner's experience. John Carroll states, 'learners are not blank slates; they don't have funnels in their heads; they have little patience for being treated as 'don't knows'... New users are always learning computer methods in the context of specific pre-existing goals and expectations' (Carroll, 1990, p11).

Out of the work of minimalists come principles for the design of teaching materials. In an experiment described by John Carroll, instead of using a large manual to teach word processing, the learners were issued with a small number of cards. Each card had a meaningful task to complete and was self-contained. Importantly, each card contained error recognition and error recovery information. The cards did not contain step-by-step instructions but only the key ideas and hints on what to do, yet proved more successful than the more prescriptive manuals (Carroll, 1998).

TEACHING TIP

There is a tension here between pedagogy and classroom management. If learners determine their own route they are more likely to meet dead-ends and need support. Because they are working individually, they are less likely to be able to obtain help from peers. It is more likely that you will not be able to quickly identify their error and put them back on a more fruitful route. Consequently, teaching the class starts to become unmanageable and fraught. When planning lessons, there has to be a compromise between the principles of student self-determination and the pragmatics of classroom management.

Consider this classroom example: you need the students to create a presentation or piece of prose about themselves, a character from fiction, a personality from the media, a person from history or a famous scientist, musician or technologist. The didactic prescribed approach would specify the books to consult, the exact format for the presentation and the questions to be answered.

The minimalist approach would be to give a structure that does not limit, as illustrated by the following cards.

Card 1	Card 2	Card 3	Card 4
Read about your character by exploring the world wide web using Google and Wikipedia. Write a list of the interesting facts as you find them. Read your list and cross out the facts that are not relevant or interesting or do not fit in with what you want to say.	Using the slide presentation software, design an appropriate background (master slide or template). Make a list of slide titles that includes slides for the credits, introduction, main work, summary, conclusions and references.	Look at your list and decide which slide each fact should go on to. Enter the text into each slide. Paste images in appropriate places.	Remind yourself of the design guidelines. Scan your presentation and make a list of improvements and revisions. Ask a friend to evaluate your presentation. Make any necessary changes.

Fig. 11. Carroll cards

There would need to be a backup set of cards called: 'copy and pasting images', 'starting a presentation', 'design guidelines' but these would be available on request. Chapter 1 described ways for students to receive help. Look back at the strategies and consider how they can be incorporated into this approach to teaching.

PRACTICAL TASK PRACTICAL TASK **PRACTICAL TASK** PRACTICAL TASK **PRACTICAL TASK**

If you have not created a slide presentation before then choose an educationalist that you think is influencing the way in which you are becoming a teacher. Perhaps that is John Carroll and the minimalist approach; Benjamin Bloom and his cognitive hierarchy; Lev Vygotsky and the concept of social constructivism; or George Kelly and his construct theory. Follow the steps in the cards above and create a short presentation suitable for a colleague teacher to see the pertinent aspect of the theoretical model and the implications for your teaching (Carroll, 1998; Bloom, 1956; Vygotsky, 1978; Kelly, 1955).

If you are competent in using presentation software then analyse with a colleague the value and limitations of the example above and devise your own instructions for, say, creating a data file of students and marks and analysing results in terms of 'average', 'min', 'max', assigning grades and other analyses that would be useful to teachers.

The cards fulfil the minimalist theory framework in that they are self-contained, meaningful, and self-directed. Together, the cards can be used to teach an overall process (skills), raise awareness of the subject matter (knowledge), develop concepts (understanding) or enable reflections and opinions (attitudes). The cards facilitate the learner's reliance upon him or herself to construct their understanding of the situation (Bruner, 1966; Piaget, 1999).

Gagne's approach focuses upon the context and describes the events that provide the necessary conditions for learning as the basis for designing instruction and selecting appropriate media (Gagne et al., 1992). A significant aspect of Merrill's instructional model, the Component Design Theory (CDT) framework, is learner control. However, unlike the Carroll model where the learner chooses how to go about the learning process, the more recent framework (Merrill, 1994) has instructional transactions with the trainer or teacher at the centre of the process.

> **TEACHING TIP**
> When creating learning activities in your lesson planning, ensure that the self-contained tasks are drawn from real life and are meaningful to the students. The intentions should be clear and unambiguous, encouraging the students to devise their own learning tasks. Ensure that there is sufficient support including physical resources and strategies for help (see Chapter 1).

PRACTICAL TASK PRACTICAL TASK **PRACTICAL TASK** PRACTICAL TASK **PRACTICAL TASK**

The preceding text has made the case for a particular approach to constructing learning materials, the learning environment and the order of learning. Reflect upon how you go about learning in a new area. How did you learn to word process or use e-mail for the first time?

Warning – because you learn best in a particular way it does not mean that all of your students will learn best in that way. Importantly, it does not mean that your preferred learning method is your best teaching method. You are now at the point where you need to identify your personal learning construct and separate it from your professional teaching construct.

Re-read the preceding text and try to identify the hints that an alternative approach might be more suitable for your teaching of ICT. Explore another learning, teaching or instructional model to further develop your own professional teaching construct.

A useful starting point is TIP, the Theory Into Practice Database (tip.psychology.org). TIP is a tool intended to make learning and instructional theory more accessible to educators. The database contains brief summaries of 50 major theories of learning and instruction.

A SUMMARY OF **KEY POINTS**

> **You must set yourself clear targets for developing your ICT knowledge.**

> **Focus your ICT on those areas that best support your subject.**

> **Ensure that you use your knowledge confidently in class to develop the students' ICT capability.**

> **Develop your awareness of learning theories (epistemology) and continually reflect upon your teaching style.**

> **Develop your awareness of teaching and instructional theories (pedagogy) and continually reflect upon your planning of learning resources, activities and procedures.**

REFERENCES REFERENCES **REFERENCES** REFERENCES **REFERENCES** REFERENCES

Bloom, BS and Krathwohl, DR (1956) *Taxonomy of educational objectives. Handbook 1: Cognitive domain.* New York: Longman.

Bruner, J (1966) *Toward a theory of instruction.* Cambridge, Mass.: Belknap Press.

Carroll, JM (1990) *The Nurnberg funnel. Designing minimalist instruction for practical computer skill.* Cambridge, Mass.: MIT Press.

Carroll, JM (ed) (1998) *Minimalism beyond the Nurnberg funnel.* Cambridge, Mass.: MIT Press.

Gagne, R, Briggs, L and Wager, W (1992) *Principles of instructional design.* Fort Worth: HBJ College Publishers.

Kelly, GA (1955) *The psychology of personal constructs. Volume 1: A theory of personality. Volume 2: Clinical diagnosis and psychotherapy.* New York: Norton.

Merrill, MD (1994) *Instructional design theory.* Englewood Cliffs: Educational Technology Publications.

Piaget, J (1999) T*he Construction of reality in the child* (International Library of Psychology). London: Routledge.

Rogers, CR (1961) *On becoming a person: A therapist's view of psychotherapy.* London: Constable.

Vygotsky, L (1978) *Mind in society.* Cambridge, Mass.: Harvard University Press.

- **Initial teacher training (ITT)** www.tda.gov.uk/partners/ittstandards **(DfES, 2006)**
- **ECDL** www.ecdl.com
- **Microsoft software training accreditation** www.microsoft.com/trainingandservices

These represent the major contributions to teaching with and about computers but the most recent developments of note are:

- the **Key Stage 3 Strategy for ICT capability, which is designed through specialist-taught, one-hour-a-week lessons to systematically give the skills of ICT ('knowing how'), combined with the knowledge of ICT ('knowing what') and the concepts of ICT ('understanding what') (DfES, 2002, p9);**
- the **ICT across the curriculum initiative describing the integration of ICT into all subjects of the National Curriculum and RE: '... statutory responsibilities within the National Curriculum for teaching ICT in schools at Key Stage 3. Schools need to ensure that all pupils are ... given opportunities to apply and develop their ICT capability through the use of ICT tools to support their learning in all subjects' (DfES, 2004a, p9).**
- the **introduction of digital applications, to replace GNVQ, followed as a single, 2 or 4 GCSE equivalent courses (QCA, 2005, p3) that are being provided by Edexcel called Award, Certificate and Diploma – AiDA, CiDA and DiDA respectively.**

ICT: integration of technology and curriculum

This analysis of the concepts of ICT is based around six aspects. They reflect both the technical aspects as well as curriculum aspects of teaching about and with computers. The rigour of this analysis is limited by the vocabulary and it may mean that the six areas are not mutually exclusive. Indeed, the overlap and tensions arising draw emphasis towards those more important areas of the curriculum that have an influence in many fields (Woollard, 2001).

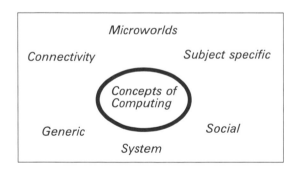

Fig. 12. Concepts of computing

The systems aspect of ICT encompasses the technical aspects of the computer; it includes the hardware components and the types of microprocessors. There are concepts based upon size and speed. The standard units of the computer world are the byte; the rate, Hertz; and the quality, dots-per-inch. Children aged 4 have to understand the concept of size – the disc apparently does not run out of space when saving typed work but it will only hold two pictures. 'System' is part of the computer paradigm of continual change in specification and improvement of performance. Even with broadband access to the internet, the size of a file is important – a normal e-mail seems to go immediately. An e-mail with an attachment of a 5Mb image can, in the least well-designed software, cause the program to freeze. Better software causes it to appear in the Outbox and not appear in the Sent Items folder for a little while. During that time, all the worries of a the computer having crashed or losing your typing go through your mind. Being aware of the concepts of size and bandwidth avoids the many ICT tensions.

Computer systems are not isolated; *connectivity* is the interaction of computers. Much is encompassed under the terms internet, intranet and extranet, but it also includes, for example, the transfer of data from laptops, tablets and PCs to PCs and the printing from graphic calculators. The technologies include remote infrared connections, Bluetooth^{TM}, docking, file transfer protocol (FTP), wireless technology (WiFi) and mobile telephone connections (GPRS) and so forth.

The three traditional generic packages are word processors, databases and spreadsheets. These have been joined, because of the development of what-you-see-is-what-you-get (WYSIWYG) and windows/graphic user interfaces (GUI), by drawing and painting packages, desktop publishing (DTP) and presentation tools. The web browser has become ubiquitous. Recently there has been an integration of the functionality of the generic packages. Applications now exist with the combined features of all. Your students' understanding of what is generic may mean that you have to describe the individual functionality: for example, the difference between word-processor functionality and full DTP functionality and which may best meet the needs of the task in hand. An important phrase in some subjects is 'fit-for-purpose'. In ICT, you have to ensure the students are enabled to choose and make fit-for-purpose decisions.

Generic software can be used in a range of contexts. The complementary term is 'subject-specific'. It is also known as computer-assisted learning (CAL) or across the curriculum ICT (ICTAC); it is the use of software to teach or train an individual in a specific skill, knowledge, understanding or attitude. An example of each is:

- **a talking word processor to teach the skills of spelling or grammar;**
- **a music notation program to present knowledge;**
- **a graphic tool to help manipulation of geometric shapes to aid understanding of the concept of area; and**
- **an unwanted pregnancy scenario used to consider and discuss the use of contraceptives to change attitudes.**

The aged term 'microworlds' refers to microcomputer-based environments that can be explored. They can be based upon real, imaginary or conceptual environments. Microworlds, which include models and simulations, are used where the exploration of the real environment would be too expensive, difficult or dangerous. Students cannot explore a blast furnace in the classroom, follow a fox through an urban environment or spend thousands of pounds on the Stock Exchange. Airline pilots are trained on simulators and their emotional reaction to mistakes is paralleled in the engagement you see the students making with the subject material of a simulation. Imaginary situations are found in adventure games such as SimCity, Civilization and Capitalism (**simcity.ea.com**). The conceptual microworlds are those based upon shape, spatial features and numerical representation. LOGO and spreadsheets are their representation in the National Curriculum. The features of microworlds are the freedom for the students to explore, a clear set of rules of engagement and their representation of boundaries or limits.

The social, economic, ethical and moral aspects of the pervasive use of computers have featured in the curriculum from the earliest syllabus. The growing emphasis on political awareness and the implications of the pervasive use of computers within our lives is a part of the ICT and PSHE curriculum. Also, the value judgements relating to quality and appropriateness and the measure to which the use of ICT enables and enhances learning and life.

The National Curriculum Programmes of Study (2000)

There are four areas or themes in the ICT National Curriculum:

1. finding things out;
2. developing ideas and making things happen;
3. exchanging and sharing information;
4. reviewing, modifying and evaluating work as it progresses.

As written, these statements reflect higher-order skills of analysis, synthesis and evaluation, relating to Bloom's taxonomy. It is important that you are aware of the skills, knowledge and understanding of ICT that students will arrive with from their primary schools (Bloom and Krathwohl, 1956).

During Key Stage 1 students explore ICT and learn to use it confidently and with purpose to achieve specific outcomes. They start to use ICT to develop their ideas and record their creative work. They become familiar with hardware and software. The first part is headed '1. Students should be taught how to:' Other areas of knowledge, skills and understanding that the students should be taught focus upon 'use', 'try', 'present', 'review' 'describe' and 'talk'.

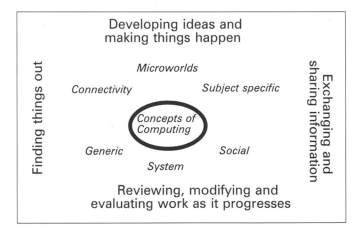

Fig. 13. Concepts of computing and the themes of ICT

A similar analysis of Key Stage 2 shows that students are expected to use a wider range of ICT tools and information sources. They should begin to question the plausibility and quality of information that introduces higher-order concepts; what 'plausible' means and what the judgements of quality are.

The 'Developing ideas' section relies heavily upon the skills of using the programs in a predetermined way. Only the more generalised skills of identifying patterns and relationships move the targets from mere skills to requiring a level of understanding. In the rest of Key Stage 2 the concepts of 'quality', 'needs of others', and 'effectiveness of their work' are alluded to. These, with the concepts associated with 'selecting suitable sources', 'classifying' information and interpreting information to identify patterns and relationships are the important aspects of effective use of ICT.

PRACTICAL TASK PRACTICAL TASK PRACTICAL TASK PRACTICAL TASK PRACTICAL TASK

If possible, carry out this task during a Key Stage 1 or Key Stage 2 placement. If that is not possible, then arrange to meet with some Year 7 students. It may be possible to organise this during an ICT lesson by saying you want to withdraw all of the students (paying due recognition to equal opportunities) in groups of five for five minutes each.

Devise a schedule of questions that will tease out the students' understanding of the ICT concepts. The list below may help but you will need to make a judgement about the general ability of the students and also listen to the advice of the teachers. It is important that you are confident in explaining what the words of the questions mean. They are all drawn from the National Curriculum. You could ask if they have:

- **created tables, images and sound;**
- **created, tested, improved and refined a sequence of instructions to make things happen (perhaps using a programmable toy like a Roamer);**
- **monitored events using a sensing box or a set of sensors;**
- **used a simulation program to explore an imaginary or real situation;**
- **changed the values in a spreadsheet to see what happens;**
- **used e-mail in school;**
- **created on the computer a display, poster, animation, web page or piece of music;**
- **compared computer work with that prepared by traditional methods;**
- **collected data to put into the computer;**
- **obtained information off the internet; and**
- **designed something on the computer.**

You could ask the students:

- **Do you know what being 'sensitive to the needs of the audience' means?**
- **Have you been asked to review your work and consider how it could be improved?**

Try to ascertain their understanding. If the students appear to have a good understanding, then try to pose questions that allow them to apply their understanding. If the students appear to have less understanding than you expect, then try to take their ideas further with discussion and questioning. Think about the questions you asked and the discussion you had.

- **How closed or open were the questions?**
- **Did the students seem to understand the questions?**
- **Did you reinforce good ideas?**

- Did you give positive or negative feedback?
- Did the students have opportunities to ask questions?
- Was the level of understanding what you expected?
- Did the discussion appear to help the students' understanding?

You may wish to follow up this task with other students. It is also useful to carry out an observation of other teachers' questioning of individual students. You may be wondering why teachers ask so many questions – Socrates reflected some 2,400 years ago that teaching is the art of asking questions. The late Ted Wragg proposed a theoretical model of three types of questions to ensure learning (Wragg and Brown, 2001): empirical (based upon facts), conceptual (based upon understanding, definitions and reasoning) and values (personal beliefs, moral issues and ethical grounding). There is another sort of question that is procedural or functional and relates to classroom and behaviour management.

National Curriculum ICT at Key Stage 3

During Key Stage 3 your students become increasingly independent users of ICT tools and information sources. They have a better understanding of how ICT can help their work in other subjects and develop their ability to judge when and how to use ICT and where it has limitations. They think about the quality and reliability of information, and access and combine increasing amounts of information. They become more focused, efficient and rigorous in their use of ICT, and carry out a range of increasingly complex tasks.

In Key Stage 3 there are a larger number of concepts that students need to understand. You should be supporting your students to:

- be systematic;
- produce information well matched to purpose by selecting appropriate sources and questioning the plausibility and value of the information;
- construct efficient procedures that are fit for purpose;
- create good-quality presentations in a form that is sensitive to the needs of particular audiences and suits the information content;
- exchange information effectively;
- reflect critically on their own and others' uses of ICT to help them develop and improve their ideas and the quality of their work;
- understand the significance of ICT to individuals, communities and society;
- judge its effectiveness, using relevant technical terms.

The 'breadth of study' suggests that the students should be taught through working with a range of information to consider its characteristics, structure, organisation and purposes. This is a rich ground of concepts of ICT.

In the teaching of ICT there is an understandable emphasis upon skills teaching. Your students have to be able to use the software before they can learn through using the software. Many lessons in computer rooms are based on skills development. However, it is recognised that to develop ICT capability (DfES, 2002) you need to extend the students' knowledge and application of those skills. Importantly, you need them to understand the concepts behind those processes.

Here is an example of a concept in ICT. The National Curriculum level descriptors have the statement 'know that information exists in different forms'. This is level 1 and is an expectation for children who are five years old but it is an important concept even with adult computer users. The different forms that information takes are: the written word, pictures (signs and symbols) and the spoken word (instructions and descriptions).

- **How do you describe the different forms that information takes in the technological world?**
- **Should you differentiate between the different media like the floppy disc, CD-ROM, EPROMs (cartridges for games machines or data cards for cameras)?**
- **Should they consider which is volatile and which is non-volatile?**

Obviously, this is outside the experience and necessary understanding of most five-year-olds. But all computer users do need to know when they can switch off the computer and not lose their work. They do need to know that the information they have just typed is not safe. It is in an electronic form but not saved. They need to understand the concept that information can exist temporarily and that it can be made permanent. An analogy I have seen used with young students is to say 'your work is not safe unless it is put into your tray or in my [the teacher's] tray'. Saving the work into your 'tray' makes it safe. If you leave your work out then it might be knocked on the floor and lost, or the cleaner might pick it up and put it in the bin. This leads to the use of the desktop metaphor – talking about the recycle bin, files of work that are placed in folders and the students' understanding of more complex concepts is beginning to build. This is an example of metaphor being used to help students understand.

PRACTICAL TASK PRACTICAL TASK PRACTICAL TASK PRACTICAL TASK **PRACTICAL TASK**

Consider the concepts identified in the National Curriculum for ICT and identify those that have direct parallels with aspects of your subject's National Curriculum programmes of study:

- **know that information exists in different forms;**
- **organise and classify information;**
- **understand the need for care in framing questions when collecting, finding and interrogating information;**
- **understand how ICT devices with sensors can be used to monitor and measure external events;**
- **identify the advantages and limitations of different information-handling applications;**
- **design ICT-based models and procedures with variables to meet particular needs;**
- **consider the benefits and limitations of ICT tools and information sources and of the results they produce;**
- **they use these results to inform future judgements about the quality of their work;**
- **in informed discussions about the use of ICT and its impact on society;**
- **design and implement systems;**
- **make appropriate use of feedback;**
- **evaluate software packages and ICT-based models;**
- **social, economic, political, legal, ethical and moral issues.**

Your list will be identifying where your subject teaching can best exploit ICT to develop the students' ICT awareness and National Curriculum attainment. This is very different to identifying the ICT activities that best support teaching and learning in your subject area.

These descriptions of concepts present a challenge. From the list of concepts, you can see that by level 4 most students leaving primary school should understand how ICT devices with sensors could be used to monitor and measure external events. This is not simply doing it once but having developed the understanding such that they can apply it to novel situations. A critical question could be:

There is a computer in the pedestrian crossing – how does it make the lights work?

The response that 'it switches them on and off' is not level 4. They need to understand and therefore express the relationship between the outputs (the lights) and the inputs (sensors in the road, buttons for pedestrians to press) and use words such as 'sequence', 'program', 'sense', 'control', 'input' and 'output'.

Younger students are required, within ICT, to organise and classify information. In science at level 3 they have to classify changes that take place in materials; in mathematics they classify at level 2 with one criterion. What are the criteria for that classification and what are the objects to be classified? A clear solution is to set this ICT activity within the context of another subject. However, you could enhance the students' ICT knowledge and understanding by setting the classification in terms of ICT and getting them to describe different types of programs, different uses for computers or the range of everyday objects that have computers in them.

There are many more concepts of ICT introduced in the higher levels of the National Curriculum, including the technological and sociological and those considered to underpin good learning in all subjects. What is society and what are the social, economic, political, legal, ethical and moral implications of the use of ICT? They are expected to understand what a model is, benefits and limitations, feedback, variables, procedures, system design The challenge to you is how to incorporate ICT into your lessons so that it:

- **meets the need for students to understand ICT concepts;**
- **as well as teaching the necessary skills of ICT;**
- **as well as exploiting ICT to support teaching and learning in general;**
- **as well as teaching the knowledge and understanding of your own subject.**

Teaching: high status, high standards

Ten years ago, there was a different teacher-training curriculum. The role of ICT in training was described by Annex B of DfEE Circular 4-98. The focus on understanding of ICT is exemplified by these phrases that describe the skills, knowledge, understanding and attitudes that all trainees were expected to possess:

- **employ common ICT tools;**
- **can use a range of ICT resources;**
- **know how to use ICT to find things out;**
- **know how to use ICT to try things out;**
- **know how to use ICT to communicate and exchange ideas;**
- **how to use ICT to improve professional efficiency and to reduce administrative and bureaucratic burdens;**
- **use computers to make things happen. (DfEE, 1998, p17)**
  www.dfes.gov.uk/publications/guidanceonthelaw/4_98/annexb.htm

PRACTICAL TASK PRACTICAL TASK PRACTICAL TASK PRACTICAL TASK PRACTICAL TASK

With two or three colleagues, look through the list of concepts and match them against the descriptions. You could introduce competition to enhance cognitive engagement. Alternatively, you could create a game of dominoes by copying and cutting up each line.

predicting patterns	having information and actions that are not apparent to the user viewing the screen
automatic functions	drawing conclusions about the future based upon changes in the past, using charting
compression	describing software that can be used in a variety of ways and different contexts – it is not subject specific
dynamic linking	organising the resources on a hard drive, memory stick or website into folders (directories) and sub-folders for ease of access
ethics	being non-permanent, changing over time and in response to changes of input – for example the ever changing content of some web pages
file managementc	changing of values, properties or output without the direct request of the user – the best example is the automatic calculations of a spreadsheet each time a value is changed
generic	protecting the computer from unauthorised access by people of software including viruses, worms and Trojan horses
interactivity	describing data that are not only true but also appropriate to the needs of the activity
invisibillty	describing the right behaviour based upon rules, laws or codes of conduct – for example, you are guided by the Children Act and the Education Reform Act and the code of conduct of the General Teachers' Council
models	representation of a real-world situation by variables, formula and relationships, usually in a spreadsheet
provisionality	making a connection between two files so that updating one file changes the content of another – for example, linking a word processor to a database file to produce personalised letters (called mail merge)
range	describing the source of data as being always present (but not necessarily constant) – for example, the BBC weather forecast site
reliability	handling and exploring large amounts of information including the challenges of data overload, the skills of scanning and affordances of seeking patterns and making sense
security	responding to the inputs of the user through buttons, text entry or dragging
validity	reducing the space required to store resources

Fig. 14. Match the word to its meaning

A SUMMARY OF **KEY POINTS**

> Ensure that you talk with individual students and find out about their ICT experience and understanding.

> Identify the themes of ICT that best relate to your subject.

> Read the ICTAC document for your subject and make sure you understand the concepts so that you can develop the students' ICT capability.

> When working in the key stages above and below your training range, identify the students' understanding of ICT as well as their skills.

REFERENCES REFERENCES **REFERENCES** REFERENCES **REFERENCES** REFERENCES

Abelson, H (1982) *Apple Logo.* BYTE/McGraw-Hill.

Acorn Computers (1993) *The Horizon project.* Winchester: Hampshire Microtechnology Centre.

Bloom, BS and Krathwohl, DR (1956) *Taxonomy of educational objectives. Handbook 1: Cognitive domain.* New York: Longman.

Bull, J and McKenna, C (2004) *Blueprint for computer-assisted assessment.* London: Routledge-Falmer.

Conole, G, Dyke, M, Oliver, M and Seale, J (2004) Mapping pedagogy and tools for effective learning design. *Computers and Education,* 43: 17–33.

Cunningham, M and Harris, S (2003) *The ever-open classroom: Using ICT to enhance communication and learning.* London: National Foundation for Educational Research.

DfEE (1998) *Annex B of DfEE Circular 4-98.* London: HMSO.

DfES (2002) *Key Stage 3 National Strategy Framework for teaching ICT capability: Years 7, 8 and 9.* London: Department for Education and Skills.

DfES (2004a) *Key Stage 3 National Strategy ICT across the curriculum.* London: Department for Education and Skills.

DfES (2004b) *Progress towards a unified e-learning strategy.* London: Department for Education and Skills.

DfES (2006) *Professional standards for qualified teacher status* London: Department for Education and Skills. **www.tda.gov.uk/partners/ittstandards**

Hope, M (1986) *The magic of the micro: A resource for children with learning difficulties.* London: Council for Educational Technology.

Kennewell, S, Parkinson, J and Tanner, H (2003) *Learning to teach ICT in the secondary school.* London: RoutledgeFalmer.

Papert, SA (1980) *Mindstorms: Children, computers, and powerful ideas.* Boston: Basic Books.

QCA (1999) *The National Curriculum Programmes of Study and Attainment Targets.* London: HMSO.

QCA (2005) *GNVQ successor provision: alternative qualifications (final update).* London: Qualification and Curriculum Authority.

Williams, D, Wilson, K, Richardson, A, Tuson, J and Coles, L (1998) *Teachers' ICT skills and knowledge needs: final report to SOEID.*

Wood, D (1998) *The UK ILS evaluations final report.* Coventry: BECTa.

Woollard, WJ (2001) *Concepts of ICT InteracTive #32.* Birmingham: Quest Publishing.

Wragg, EC and Brown, G (2001) *Questioning in the secondary school.* London: RoutledgeFalmer.

Part 2

Supporting teaching
and classroom management

4
One of those days in the ICT room

By the end of this chapter you should:

- **feel more confident to take your class into the ICT room;**
- **know more classroom, curriculum and resource management strategies;**
- **be aware of the impact of resources, computers and the curriculum on the behaviour of the students.**

Professional Standards for QTS

Q3, Q10, Q30, Q31

This chapter addresses the issues of behaviour management in the ICT room. The QTS standards require you to be aware of the policies and practices of the workplace. The chapter raises issues relating to behaviour management strategies, establishing a purposeful and safe learning environment and implementing a clear framework for classroom discipline.

Introduction

This chapter is about how you can deal with those crisis issues that arise in the ICT classroom. How do you deal with 'no I won't', 'you are a...', 'I'm leaving', 'f*** o**' and physical violence against property, another person or yourself.

Everyday life in the ICT classroom

Everyday life in the ICT classroom is a balance between:

- **class management (say, ensuring safety and resource availability, keeping computers working, ensuring students can log in);**
- **pedagogy (ensuring you are teaching the right things, teaching them in the right way and that students are learning the curriculum);**
- **behaviour management (ensuring that student conduct is as you expect).**

Each aspect has an influence upon the others. Schools have a characteristic balance between each and individual teachers have their own balance between each. Some of us manage the behaviour of the students through persistent and assertive techniques to establish a good working atmosphere, while others may hold the control and interest of the students through the management of the curriculum and the teaching approaches used. The same teacher will use different techniques with different classes. Importantly, for you in your placement schools, some techniques are appropriate in one school and not in another.

Your teaching experience will be in more than one school. You will see that different schools have different balances between behaviour management, environmental issues and pedagogy. Teachers in the more challenging schools are forced to spend a greater proportion of their efforts in the management of the students' behaviour while less challenging schools are freer to give more attention to the environment and the curriculum. In the win–win situation of our more successful schools, the students will behave better because of the improving environment and curriculum. In our failing schools, teachers are forced to succumb to time- and resource-demanding behaviour management and can pay less attention to the environment and the curriculum.

PRACTICAL TASK PRACTICAL TASK PRACTICAL TASK PRACTICAL TASK PRACTICAL TASK

Carry out an observation of a lesson in a computer classroom. Preferably, this is in your own subject but if necessary, it can be of another subject or even an ICT lesson. Make notes about the factors that influence behaviour and try to spot the precedents of bad behaviour incidents. If there is an incident then make clear notes of the strategies the teacher adopted to deal with the incident. Design your observation sheet to capture the following information:

Date, time, year, subject, class size, comment on the physical environment.

Describe the classroom entry procedures and computer log on.

Describe any teacher presentation of skills or knowledge: time, content, use of questioning.

Describe how the ICT equipment was used to enhance the exposition.

Describe the behaviour of students during 'hands-on' parts of the lesson: permitted talking, on/off task behaviour, collaboration, and co-operation.

Describe the sequence of events near the end of the lesson: logging off, printing, plenary, exit.

Living graph to represent behaviour and stress

'Living graphs' and 'fortune lines' are described in the *Leading in Learning* thinking skills materials: **www.standards.dfes.gov.uk/keystage3/respub/ws_lil_ts (DfES, 2005).**

The following 'living graph' shows the lower wavy line of the ups-and-downs of normal classroom interaction where long-term strategies of behaviour modification, good behaviour planning or assertive discipline come into play.

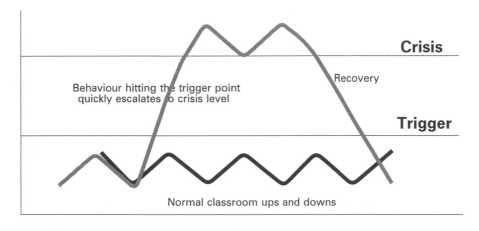

Fig. 15. Living graph showing trigger, crisis and recovery

However, the upper line shows the consequence of when an 'up' reaches the trigger level for a crisis. That crisis might be in the form of refusal to carry out an instruction, direct verbal abuse, leaving the ICT room without permission, swearing, damaging property, threatening or actual physical harm to another student or yourself.

TEACHING TIP

When you are in that situation, it is of little value to know that skilled and successful teachers in challenging schools recognise that they have passed the trigger point and immediately change the strategies they deploy. Those teachers also recognise the signs of getting near the trigger point and what triggers individual students or groups within a particular teaching group. However, every crisis you experience is another opportunity to learn how to handle crises and, importantly, time to reflect upon the signs of that crisis emerging.

The number one rule for dealing with crises is to reduce conflict. It is the only way of bringing the tension line down into the recovery area. The key phrases are 'low arousal', 'low key', 'laid back', 'cool' and 'deep breath'. It is not the time for sanctions, threats, rationalisation and reminders of consequences. Those are the strategies, behaviour modification or assertive discipline, you employ all of the time to avoid the crisis.

Importantly, as a trainee teacher, you will normally have a teacher responsible for the class nearby; it is not necessarily your responsibility to deal with the crisis.

Here is a vignette of an ICT room crisis experienced by a trainee. It is written in the first person as he described it.

'Sally is always a bit touchy but she can work quite well and her printout file is always up to date. I told her to stop talking and go back to her computer. With that, she told me that she wouldn't, pushed passed me, and ran out the door. I followed and was met with a lot of abuse. As she tried to run along the corridor I put my hand out to stop her...'

After the event, you can rationalise a number of explanations of Sally's behaviour. Perhaps you might have sensed the reasons in the classroom. You might have been aware that the tension had reached the trigger point. When the crisis occurs the 'low arousal' activities should come into play: avoid the chase; stop using the loud or assertive teacher voice; use an intermediary; avoid conflict. Perhaps a simple 'Jenny, go and find out what is troubling Sally' might have resolved the situation.

'I put my hand out to stop her' draws our attention to that decidedly tricky topic of physical intervention. Teachers and other staff do have the right to use reasonable physical force to restrain students in certain circumstances. Any form of physical punishment of students is unlawful, as is any form of physical response to misbehaviour unless it is by way of restraint (DfES Circular number 10/98).

When the crises occur, you have to concentrate upon managing the crisis instead of managing the behaviour. You have to deal with the individual while being fully conscious of our responsibility to the rest of the ICT room. When tensions are at the crisis level, the more you intervene the more likely the crisis will continue. Your first priority is to bring that tension into recovery and then you can use your conventional behaviour management techniques to maintain the calm.

Here is some advice from the Association of Teachers and Lecturers on managing conflicts. 'You don't solve conflicts by sweeping them under the carpet' and 'you don't solve conflicts by force'. They offer further advice on how to deal with classroom conflicts. These can be interpreted to help resolve the conflicts you find yourself in:

- **talk to the student quietly and do not talk over the student – take it in turns to speak;**
- **distance yourself both physically and in time – 'let's deal with this later' – and do not stand over them;**
- **get the student to make suggestions for how to resolve the situation;**
- **treat it as a practical problem-solving exercise rather than a moral lesson – 'what can we do to solve this' rather than 'I want you to apologise right now';**
- **be clear in your statements of what you want;**
- **listen to what the student has to say – they may have the solution.**

After the lesson has ended, you have a responsibility to yourself to talk it through. This debriefing is not the official reporting of an incident but the colleague-to-colleague conversation that helps you come to terms with the emotions that these incidents generate.

There is a good book on dealing with managing challenging behaviour edited by Bill Rogers in which he outlines the principles of good practice. Here is a brief selection:

- **avoid confrontation (most of the time);**
- **use non-intrusive interventions;**
- **be assertive, not aggressive;**
- **keep the corrective language positive (wherever possible);**
- **keep a fundamental respect for the students – it is the action not the child that is bad (Rogers, 2004).**

Because you have less familiarity with students, the crises can occur because you have not sensed the trigger points and you continue to use the assertive and forceful techniques that you have been encouraged to adopt to establish your presence in the classroom. You, perhaps, have neither the confidence nor the mandate to act in a more relaxed 'low arousal' way to soothe the atmosphere. Successful teachers are those who change their strategies to meet the more demanding situations in which they find themselves.

Classroom layout and teaching strategies

As a trainee teacher, you will have little control over the layout of the computer rooms and the location of computers in your classroom. It is important that you become aware of the difficulties that some room layouts present. This section will help you identify the potential problems and then give some strategies for overcoming them. Where you do have the opportunity to rearrange facilities it is even more important that you do not introduce further difficulties in establishing good classroom and behaviour management and supporting teaching and learning.

Computers tend to dominate the lesson when they are present and used within a lesson. It is recognised that portable equipment can be less distracting but that too has associated problems. It is a challenge to ensure that the benefits ICT can bring to teaching and learning are not undermined by the distractions and difficulties of management they create. Some classroom layouts facilitate particular teaching strategies and styles. Some layouts have challenges, and alternative strategies must be established to compensate for the problems arising from the layout.

PRACTICAL TASK PRACTICAL TASK PRACTICAL TASK PRACTICAL TASK PRACTICAL TASK

Consider the situation in the room where you can teach using computers. Make a simple sketch of the room, marking in these important aspects:

- **the position of the computers and the direction the screens face;**
- **where you consider the front of the class to be;**
- **where the whiteboard for writing (if available) is positioned;**
- **where the whiteboard/screen (if available) is positioned;**
- **where the projector (if available) is positioned;**
- **the computer that is connected to the projector;**
  (will you have to take your own laptop to conduct the lesson?);
  (may you take your own laptop to conduct the lesson?);
- **the main exit/entrance to the room;**
- **the important resources for use in lesson time, for example, printer/scanner.**

The following questions will help you determine where the challenges exist and how your lesson planning can help avoid the worst situations.

- **Can you see all the students' computer screens when standing at the front?**
  (Is there 'network management software' to allow you to view students' screen on your computer?)
- **How far do you have to walk so that you can have viewed all the screens?**
- **When the students are working at the computers, can you physically move to each and every computer?**
- **Are there areas of the classroom that are not readily accessible?**
- **When the students are at their computers, can they see the projector screen?**
- **Is there space to move the students closer to the screen?**
- **When controlling the projector's computer, can you see the screen and see the students?**
- **When controlling the projector's computer, can you move around the room?**
- **Is there an interactive whiteboard? Is there furniture obstructing the front of it and can you reach the top?**
- **Will it need calibrating before you start? Is it necessary for the lesson you plan to teach?**
- **Where do the students line up at the start of the lessons? Is there a place for students to store coats and bags?**
- **Are they allowed to enter without waiting for the teacher?**
- **Can they log on immediately or are they expected to wait? Once logged on, can they access the internet?**

You will be expected to write some of these details in the context section of your lesson plan. Other answers will have an impact upon the chronology of the lesson – in particular, how long you have to plan on the start and end routines of the lesson. Obviously, the resources available in the classroom may have an impact upon the curriculum content of the lesson as well as any assessment procedures.

TECHNICAL TIP

Computer projectors are becoming very common in classrooms and the main means of displaying teaching materials. Ceiling-mounted projectors need a remote (usually infrared) controller. Always point the remote controller at the screen, as most projectors sensors are at the front and they will receive the signal reflected from the board.

Computer room layouts

There are some common or typical layouts for rooms. These are represented here diagrammatically. The video screen projector is becoming increasingly popular – consider where the projection point is and which computer will be used by the teacher/trainer. The room layout has implications for the style of teaching that is facilitated. Small clusters of computers encourage collaborative work because they divide the class and can aid differentiated input (differentiation by grouping).

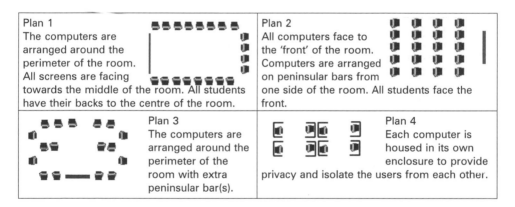

Fig. 16. ICT room layout

Plan 1
The computers are arranged around the perimeter of the room. All screens are facing towards the middle of the room. All students have their backs to the centre of the room.

Plan 2
All computers face to the 'front' of the room. Computers are arranged on peninsular bars from one side of the room. All students face the front.

Plan 3
The computers are arranged around the perimeter of the room with extra peninsular bar(s).

Plan 4
Each computer is housed in its own enclosure to provide privacy and isolate the users from each other.

PRACTICAL TASK PRACTICAL TASK **PRACTICAL TASK** PRACTICAL TASK **PRACTICAL TASK**

With two or three colleagues, choose one of the room layouts above and identify the challenges and some possible strategies to meet those challenges. Decide upon your personal preference for ICT room layout and your reasons. Which model best describes the situation in which you are teaching? How can you adapt the environment or style of teaching to best suit your current placement?

Models of interaction and the implications for teaching

The way in which teachers use computers when demonstrating new skills and knowledge has an impact upon the teacher–student relationship and the sense of ownership the students may have about their learning. Consider the four models of interaction described below. Which one best represents the relationship between you, the computer and your students when you are teaching with ICT?

The tutor is acting as a 'gatekeeper' between the students and the computer. Control of the computer is in the hands of the teacher/tutor. Imagine giving a demonstration of a skill with all the students gathered around.	The tutor is acting as an 'enabler', providing the focus for the work but not directly controlling the computer. The computer is the focus of attention and carries the message of the lesson.
The tutor is acting as a 'supervisor', observing the process, giving guidance but allowing the process to proceed under the control of the students. The tutor/teacher is free to intervene but in the main remains in the background to the teaching process.	The tutor is acting as a 'partner' in the teaching process. Both the teacher/tutor and the student body can take control of the computer. Interaction between all three aspects of the situation is enabled.

Fig. 17. Tutor/teaching styles

FURTHER READING   FURTHER READING   **FURTHER READING**   FURTHER READING

BECTa (2005) *What the research says about ICT and classroom organisation in schools* is available at **www.becta.org.uk/page_documents/research/wtrs_classroom.pdf** Effectively organising the ICT room can make a significant impact upon the ease of teaching and the quality of learning taking place.

'Government acts on cyber-bullies' is a BBC news article dated 26 July 2006 published on the Behaviour4Learning website, and is available at **www.behaviour4learning.ac.uk/viewArticle.aspx?contentId=12651** It raises many of the issues that you need to be aware of when using the internet in your teaching.

How to manage children's challenging behaviour by Bill Rogers (2004) is a recommended read.

Improving behaviour in schools; positive behaviour equals success is published by the DfES and is available online at **www.dfes.gov.uk/ibis**

Managing classroom behaviour is available from the Association of Teachers and Lecturers (free to members): **www.askatl.org.uk**

The 'Behaviour and attendance' section of the TeacherNet website is a useful source of information.

Getting the buggers to behave 2 has useful tips for behaviour management (Cowley, 2003)

The use of force to control or restrain pupils, Section 550A of the Education Act 1996, is a DfES Circular which is one of many legal documents of which you should be aware.

TEACHING TIP

Be prepared for the inevitable – computers fail to work. Do not panic but be prepared with a 'lesson in the back pocket', that is, an activity you can do with the students without the use of electricity and without a hesitation. Here are three different examples:

Resources required	Activity	Examples
Sheets of A4 plain paper (taken from the printer tray).	Divide the class into groups of four pupils and ask them to produce a diagram collaboratively:	to represent the set-up of sensing/music/control/turtle equipment with instructions for making the connections; of the layout of a three-fold A4 pamphlet with a front page, reference page, back page and an A4 spread on a specific topic (En, Hi, Gg); describing a possible website to represent the content of the current curriculum topic including: home page, four content pages and a references (links) page showing the navigation button design.
Ten different A4 colour-printed and laminated web pages relevant to your subject area.	Divide the class into groups of four, give one sheet to each, after three minutes move the sheet on to the next group:	making a note of three salient facts from each web page, after seeing the examples plan a single web page to contain the 15 most important facts identified; from each web page identify three different ways of moving from that page (button, hypertext link, drop-down menu ...) then produce a guide to web page navigation; examine the images on each web page, after seeing the examples plan a single graphic to illustrate an aspect of the current curriculum.
You and your exposition.	Talk to the group for five minutes about an ICT-related aspect of your curriculum subject then chair a class discussion or manage small group discussions	

Fig. 18. Lesson in the back pocket

A SUMMARY OF **KEY POINTS**

> **Be sensitive to the mood of individual students, groups and the whole class and deploy the appropriate and recommended strategies to avoid crises.**
> **If crises occur, deal with them through low-arousal techniques.**

> Check the layout of the rooms in which you teach to foresee and plan for the challenges they present.

> Consider your style of teaching in the ICT room; identify the affordances and limitations of that style.

REFERENCES REFERENCES **REFERENCES** REFERENCES **REFERENCES** REFERENCES

ATL (1997) *Managing classroom behaviour.* London: Association of Teachers and Lecturers.

BECTa (2005) *What the research says about ICT and classroom organisation in schools.* Coventry: BECTa.

Behaviour4Learning (2006) *Government acts on cyber-bullies.* Press release 26/07/06. London: BBC.

Cowley, S (2003) *Getting the buggers to behave 2.* London: Continuum.

DfES Circular number 10/98 (1998) *The use of force to control or restrain pupils*, Section 550A of the Education Act 1996. London: HMSO.

DfES (2005) *Leading in learning: developing thinking skills at Key Stage 3. Handbook for teachers.* London: Department for Education and Skills.

Rogers, B (2004) *How to manage children's challenging behaviour.* London: Paul Chapman Publishing.

5
Enhancing class teaching with ICT

By the end of this chapter you should:

- **understand the value of remote pointing devices to support your teaching;**
- **have determined your potential use of an interactive whiteboard;**
- **be aware of the relative costs of ICT equipment and the source of funding;**
- **be aware of the use of tablet PCs and classroom performance systems.**

Professional Standards for QTS

Q8, Q12, Q17, Q24, Q28

This chapter reinforces your knowledge of ICT to support your teaching and wider professional activities. The ICT-based practical tasks, as with all ICT, should be carried out with an attitude of a creative and constructively critical approach. The ICT issues relating to assessment, guiding learners, homework and out-of-class learning are considered.

Introduction

This chapter identifies the teaching affordances of the interactive whiteboard, remote pointing devices, projection, tablet PCs and class performance systems.

Interactive whiteboard

> *An interactive whiteboard is a dry-erase whiteboard writing surface which can capture writing electronically. Interactive whiteboards require a computer. Some interactive whiteboards also allow interaction with a projected computer image ... are used in one of two ways: to capture notes written on the whiteboard surface using dry-erase ink or to control (click and drag) and/or mark-up (annotate) a computer-generated image projected on the whiteboard surface from a digital projector.* (Wikipedia, 2006)

There are different types of interactive whiteboard (IWB) based on different technologies for detecting where the pen (or finger in some cases) is touching the board. They include the electromagnetic, where wires in the board detect the magnet in the pen; touch-sensitive (soft surface) boards which can be operated with your finger; and the least expensive, audio/infrared clip-on alternative.

Interactive whiteboards are largely taking over from blackboards and whiteboards. They work as a large computer screen by projecting the computer image onto the board via an external projector and the computer can be controlled via the board. There are sensors on the board that, when activated, move the cursor.

PRACTICAL TASK PRACTICAL TASK PRACTICAL TASK PRACTICAL TASK PRACTICAL TASK

If you have an IWB in one of your teaching bases, carry out the following checklist survey. Then decide the steps you must take to enable you to successfully incorporate the IWB into your regular classroom practice. Finally, identify the affordances of the IWB that are most likely to be important in your future classroom practice.

- **Is the IWB connected to the teacher's computer?**
  Can it be connected to your computer?
  Is the IWB software installed in the computer?
- **Is the board calibrated?**
  Are the pens present and working?
- **Is the projector present, working and connected to the teacher's computer?**
- **Can you reach the top of the board?**
  Can your students reach the top of the board?
  Can the students get to the board easily?
- **Are there obstructions in front of the board preventing you getting close enough?**
  Is the floor covering in good condition?
  Are there tripping hazards?
- **Is one side of the board clear of obstruction so the presenter can stand to the side yet still reach and point?**
- **Is the surface of the board clean?**
  Is the surface of the board non-reflective or is there a blind spot caused by the glare of the projector?
  Is the image clear?
  Is the projector focused?
  Is the projector bright enough for the light conditions in the room?
- **Is there curriculum-specific IWB software available?**
  Can you install and use it on your own computer?
  Does it match the topics you are required to teach and the ability of the students?
  Have the students used it previously?

Some questions suggested by BECTa include: Can students get to the board easily and quickly through their desks or tables to help maintain the pace of a lesson? Is there a sign making it clear to all users that no one should stare directly into the beam of the projector? Is all cabling safely secured for the entire length of the cable? (BECTa, 2006)

Having considered the points raised above, decide what steps you must take to ensure that you could use the IWB in your teaching. Then decide which of the following affordances of IWBs most particularly apply to your teaching.

- **navigate through a slide presentation;**
- **demonstrate how to use some software;**
- **highlight important aspects of the display;**
- **enable students to present their ideas/thoughts/answers;**
- **move objects across the screen;**
- **write on the board and record the work for later.**

> ### TECHNICAL TIP
> *If the classroom projector is ceiling mounted or screwed to a fixed plinth/stand, then using an IWB poses fewer problems. However, if the projector is on a tabletop or moveable stand then the IWB will need calibrating every time the projector is knocked or moved. Practise calibrating the IWB as part of your preparation for the lesson. You may need to do it in the middle of the lesson in front of the students.*

Remote pointing devices

In 1970, Douglas Engelbart received a patent for the wooden shell with two metal wheels (U.S. Patent # 3,541,541) describing it in the patent application as an 'X-Y position indicator for a display system'. It was nicknamed 'the mouse' because the tail came out the end. Nowadays the mouse is ubiquitous. All students and teachers are proficient with it or an alternative such as the tracker ball (particularly useful for those with physical disability or spastic-type conditions), touch pad (found on many laptops), toggle stick (also a laptop device) and the light pen (used to touch the computer screen). However, all of these devices, like the IWB, tie the user to the computer and they tie the teacher to a particular spot in the classroom. Remote pointing devices give freedom for the teacher or student to access the computer from any point in the room.

PRACTICAL TASK PRACTICAL TASK **PRACTICAL TASK** PRACTICAL TASK **PRACTICAL TASK**

Reconsider your responses to the previous task, where you considered how you would use an interactive whiteboard.

Look at the items that you responded positively towards. Could you perform those activities as effectively or more effectively with a remote keyboard and mouse?

- **navigate through a slide presentation;**
- **demonstrate how to use some software;**
- **highlight important aspects of the display;**
- **enable students to present their ideas/thoughts/answers;**
- **move objects across the screen;**
- **write on the board and record the work for later.**

Tablet PCs

A tablet PC is similar in shape and size to a conventional laptop but the screen surface is hard and is touch-sensitive. A stylus (digital pen) is used to enter text (handwriting recognition) and navigate around the windows environment. There are two types: slate and convertible. Slate versions do not have an integral keyboard but an external one can be attached for extended typing. Convertible versions are essentially laptop computers with a hard-faced, touch-sensitive screen. An important classroom issue is that the stylus contains electronics and is expensive to replace – some tablet PCs have a tethered stylus.

The growing popularity of tablet PCs is associated with some of the more flexible uses they enable. However, as a device to support you and your presentations to the class, its mobility

Device	Approximate cost	Features
mouse	£5	commonplace, reliable, inexpensive; tied to one spot in the classroom
keyboard	£10	commonplace, reliable, inexpensive; tied to one spot in the classroom
tracker ball	£15	skills need to be acquired but considered to be more ergonomic; tied to one spot in the classroom; special needs application
interactive whiteboard	£1300	supports visual-kinaesthetic teaching and learning; puts the teacher at the focus of attention and the centre of the subject matter; expensive and tied to one spot in the classroom
remote keyboard (and mouse)	£40 (£50)	easy-to-use and relatively inexpensive; allows student interaction without physically moving about the room; does not tie the teacher to one spot
graphics tablet (wireless)	£50 (£150)	skills need to be acquired but allows good fine-motor control; tied to one spot in the classroom; special needs application (allows student interaction without physically moving about the room; does not tie the teacher to one spot)
remote keyboard and mouse (Bluetooth)	£100	Easy to use and relatively inexpensive; allows student interaction without physically moving about the room; does not tie the teacher to one spot; good physical range and some have gyroscopic function
tablet PC + remote projector adaptation	£1400 + £200	powerful technology that meets the requirements of all curriculum software, classroom teaching, administrative software and personal applications but relatively expensive and some security issues allows student interaction without physically moving about the room; does not tie the teacher to one spot

Fig. 19. Remote pointing devices

is as limited as a conventional PC unless there is a wireless network (to access resources, students' work and the internet) and a wireless projector to display the tablet PC's screen.

Many students were reported as finding tablet PCs easy to use and as being motivated to work using them. Teachers cited this as a significant factor in students' academic progress, most frequently with regard to handwriting. (Sheehy *et al.*, 2005, p9)

PRACTICAL TASK PRACTICAL TASK **PRACTICAL TASK** PRACTICAL TASK **PRACTICAL TASK**

First, recall a lesson you have recently taught where you have used the screen to display information. That can be through conventional 'chalk and talk' (whiteboard and marker pen), audiovisual (using slides, video tape, television), verbal exposition supported by paper-based pictures, diagrams or wall displays, a computer slide presentation or the demonstration of computer software.

Assume for the next step that you have a tablet PC with your software installed, a proficient wireless network and a remote projector and screen that all the students in the class can see.

Now consider each of these declared advantages of tablet PCs. Identify which of these are likely to apply to your lesson and which are likely to apply to your style of teaching. Against each item, you should be able to describe how the tablet PC provides support for your lesson or why it is not supportive:

- **mobility – the tablet PC can be taken to any spot in the classroom and used to present off the projector screen;**
- **engaging individuals – the tablet PC can be passed to a student, who can then present or demonstrate to the whole class;**
- **it is a professional device – you can take it home and do all your administrative and personal work on the same device as you use to conduct your lessons (issues of security and backup are important);**
- **sketching and handwriting directly onto the screen is more akin to the traditional teaching methods of board writing;**
- **in art lessons, the mouse is not particularly useful device for fine-motor control and drawing with finesse;**
- **tablet PCs improve handwriting (Sheehy *et al.*, 2005, p2);**
- **tablet PCs are highly portable – most are lighter than laptops, can be held with one hand while navigating/writing with the other, and they can be used standing up while also being vigilant of the class;**
- **navigating the screen is quicker with a stylus than a mouse because it is a 'point and click' (described technically as an *absolute device*) rather than a 'keep pushing until you get there then don't move until the button is pressed' (described technically as a *relative device*);**
- **student note-taking – the tablet PC makes it possible for students to take handwritten notes and make sketches during the lesson for processing later (there are special education needs opportunities for those who find a keyboard difficult to use);**
- **eliminating keyboard tapping – handwriting is almost silent (tablet PCs have a virtual on-screen keyboard if necessary);**
- **battery life is extended – usually tablet PCs can last longer before recharging than their laptop counterparts.**

The educational motivation to introduce tablet PCs into schools is to support and improve traditional school tasks and to extend practice and introduce new ways of enabling learning. Some of the newer practices include:

- **discouraging keyboard use and encouraging pen input in order to develop handwriting skills;**
- **the electronic exchange of assignments between students and staff;**
- **using electronic 'reward stickers' to annotate work during marking;**
- **both teachers and students adding written comments to documents;**
- **teachers adding handwritten notes to homework received electronically;**
- **annotations to journal and office documents and returning them to the students;**
- **students acting on teachers' comments and then remove the comments, leaving a 'clean' final product;**
- **the use of 'Track Changes' to enable a 'dialogue' between the teacher and student as work develops;**
- **accessing materials such as video, web links or worksheets in small groups;**
- **being used with data projectors in place of interactive whiteboards; and**
- **students moving around to collect data.**

Tablet PC evaluation

In 2003, BECTa commissioned the Open University to conduct a substantial piece of research on the use of tablet PCs in schools both in learning and teaching, and school management. The research also considered the differences in use and benefits of tablet PCs compared with other technologies such as laptop and handheld computers. There was general agreement that wireless networking was essential for effective tablet PC use. Two-thirds of the schools thought that data projectors were also very important. There was general agreement that a tablet PC plus data projector with wireless connection was better and more cost-effective than an interactive whiteboard or a laptop plus data projector.

FURTHER READING FURTHER READING **FURTHER READING** FURTHER READING
Tablet PCs in schools: A review of literature and selected projects. This review highlights key findings from a literature search and review of projects using tablet PCs in English schools (Sheehy *et al.*, 2005)

Tablet PCs in schools: Case study report. This review provides an analysis of tablet PC use, based on case studies from 12 English schools (Twining *et al.*, 2005)

Graphics tablets and remote keyboard

You have just read about two significant and expensive technologies (tablet PCs and inter-active whiteboards) that have become popular during the last few years. Their popularity in most part is because of the ease of computer access they give to the teacher. They enable student interactions, whole-class display and, in the case of tablet PCs, portability of the computing power.

You are now going to discover two technologies that are inexpensive and yet offer signifi-cant advantages in enabling computer access, student interaction and control of the whole-class display.

Graphics tablets consist of a flat surface on which the user draws using an attached stylus. The action can create a drawing on the screen or it can simply be moving the pointer (just as a mouse does). Tapping the stylus or holding it steady has the same effect as left and right button clicks on the mouse. Less expensive versions have to be attached to the USB port of the display computer, while others are wireless (RF or WiFi). The wireless versions enable you to take up any position in the classroom to control the computer display. They also enable students to interact with the display without having to leave their seat.

Remote keyboards and mice act and behave just as conventional keyboards and mice but there is no wire attaching them to the computer. With a remote keyboard and mouse, you can move to any spot in the classroom and control the display on the screen.

With graphics tablets and remote keyboards and mice, you can sit among the students or sit behind them so that you can scan the classroom as well as concentrate on the screen display. The remote keyboard can be given to a student to demonstrate to the rest of the class. Students can be involved in talking about and demonstrating their achievements without the emotional or physical issues of having to go and stand in front of the class. As your confidence grows, you might let a student use the mouse and keyboard to carry out the computer operations as you give your exposition from the front of the class. This gives some students a sense of responsibility and you greater freedom to concentrate upon your exposition or management of the class. The general approach meets with the desires of student centredness or personalisation in learning.

The essence of personalisation is that learning systems conform to the learner, and not the learner having to conform to the system of teaching. The *Personalisation and digital technologies* report (Green *et al.*, 2005) moves the personalisation debate forward by focusing specifically on the potential of digital technologies in four key areas:

1. enabling learners to make informed educational choices;
2. diversifying and acknowledging different forms of skills and knowledge;
3. creating diverse learning environments;
4. developing learner-focused forms of assessment and feedback.

The report also contains a Learner's Charter, which sets out a series of entitlements that young people should expect from their learning if it were personalised. Available online at: **www.futurelab.org.uk/research/personalisation/report_01.htm**

In a study of student empowerment, Kelvin Tan asks whether student self-assessment empowers or disciplines students (Tan, 2004). He concludes that student empowerment can only be realised if the ways in which we use self-assessment practices are first understood and it is realised that they do not necessarily become independent learners if the constraints and expectations are prescriptive or even mandatory. He explains that even though student self-assessment is a popular practice for enhancing student empowerment in the assessment process, some writers have warned that students' participation in the assessment process may discipline, rather than empower, students. His paper examines the issues of power that underlie student self-assessment practices.

Workstation remote control software

Imagine: you have taken your class to the ICT suite for the first time. They have entered the room with confidence or enthusiasm or excitement or bravado. You stand at the front, hoping to see eyes indicating that they are listening to you. What you see is the backs of heads and the backs of monitors. After several attempts at trying to get the attention of all the students, you resort to:

- **making every student turn around away from their screens;**
- **switching off all the monitors;**
- **moving the students away from their computers;**
- **talking over the tops of computers unable to see who is listening.**

There is another way...

Workstation remote control software enables you to control all of the computers from your computer. You can also watch the screen of individual students as they are working. In addition, you can project your computer screen image onto every other computer in the room. This is summarised as 'Watch, share or control'.

The facilities of most systems to enable teacher control of students' workstation include:

- interacting with your students either individually, as a predefined group or as an overall class;
- viewing real-time thumbnail images of each connected workstation;
- presenting your screen on all the monitors to demonstrate software, display your slide presentation or even watch video images;
- enabling you to prevent students loading distracting software application control;
- enabling you to prevent students accessing the internet on an individual or whole-class basis;
- building internet-permitted website lists to limit access and focus on relevant material;
- building internet-forbidden website lists to prevent access to inappropriate material;
- demonstrating a student's workstation screen in real time to the whole class;
- switching on and off all or individual computers (power management).

PRACTICAL TASK PRACTICAL TASK PRACTICAL TASK PRACTICAL TASK PRACTICAL TASK

Visit the ICT room and arrange for a demonstration of the workstation remote control system by a technician. Identify which of the facilities listed above are present and can be used easily. Practise making a slide presentation that you can view on your screen and the students can view on their screens, removing the need for a projector.

Recall observations of teaching and identify the strategies that are used in your placement school to gain the attention of the students for introductions, expositions, mini-plenaries and plenaries.

One teacher observed about their remote control system:

... is absolutely fantastic. I can power on/off the computers, monitor what they are doing, send/ collect the work (just pick up the resources that they need, select the destination and send). It creates any folders that are not there. Saved me 10 minutes on my lesson, use it all

the time now. I can also send them messages, log them off, blank their screens, reboot the computer, get them to register on the computer and print/save the register. I can zoom into a student's computer and then watch/control and work with them. In addition, I can use their screens as a whiteboard so that they can see what is on my screen, show them a movie and annotate the screen. I can also lock and unlock individual/all computers and also block all internet access. I can set the URLs that they can go to and block the ones that they are on. Their screen will only display the websites that I have authorised. I can also set the package that I want them to be working with, so prevents them trying to open the wrong package. You can also save your lesson plans, save your class groups and just select which one you want to use. This is a great facility and I am impressed with it. www.tes.co.uk/section/staffroom/thread.aspx?story_id=2208661&path=/ict/ &threadPage=1.

Today's modern classroom presents a very different set of challenges compared to only a few years ago. In providing your students with the latest IT infrastructure, a number of risks arise primarily relating to the misuse of that equipment and the lack of control over student activity. To combat this, our system has built on its existing student PC remote control functionality to include full application and internet control/restrictions, record and replay functionality and student PC Thumbnail view for real-time monitoring to ensure complete student attention and focus is encouraged at all times. As with any industry, time is precious so with this in mind, the latest version includes a range of time saving features, including automated lesson plans, automated student registration and file transfer distribution. (NetSupport School, 2006)
www.netsupportschool.com

Classroom performance system

The concept of a classroom performance system (CPS) is based upon 'Who wants to be a millionaire?', 'ask the audience'. It consists of sets of handheld interactive response pads. The simplest types have just four buttons. Your computer displays questions that can have multimedia content. It records the responses of all students to multiple-choice questions. CPS facilitates feedback from every student and therefore raises the sense of involvement in questioning sessions. They allow each student to participate simultaneously without embarrassing those who are uncertain or wrong. The anonymity can support deeper exploration of sensitive topics. The system helps you add interest to the lesson and creates interactive learning with instant feedback, whether you are using CPS for quizzes or formal examinations. Classroom performance systems can make a contribution to your assessment for learning strategies.

A SUMMARY OF **KEY POINTS**

> **During your induction period in a placement school; make sure that you become familiar with all the ICT facilities available to support your lessons.**

> **Tablet PCs, interactive whiteboards and classroom performance systems are expensive investments that are popular in secondary schools; ensure that you do not miss any opportunity to use them.**

> **Remote control of the computer and projector enables more flexible and effective presentations by teachers and students.**

FURTHER READING FURTHER READING **FURTHER READING** FURTHER READING

whiteboards.becta.org.uk is the 'catalogue' site. The catalogue enables you to look at IWB solutions, services, suppliers and pricing and is useful to see the range of costs from £600 to £1200 excluding the cost of the computer and projector.

Getting the most from your interactive whiteboard: A guide for secondary schools includes practical classroom examples and case studies (BECTa, 2004).

The BECTa site also gives advice when planning to purchase an IWB. That advice contains some practical and technical issues useful when considering the affordances and functionality of the IWB to which you have access. They include: access to and visibility of boards, the projector installation (is it fixed or is calibration required every lesson?), computer and additional hardware that is attached, cabling and health and safety issues, speakers. The document is available online:

BECTa Home > Procurement > Buying products & services > Whiteboards **schools.becta.org.uk/index.php?section=pr&catcode=ss_to_pr_cp_wh_04&rid=9680** (BECTa, 2006).

REFERENCES REFERENCES **REFERENCES** REFERENCES **REFERENCES** REFERENCES

BECTa (2004) *Getting the most from your interactive whiteboard: A guide for secondary schools.* Coventry: BECTa.

BECTa (2006) *Considerations when purchasing an interactive whiteboard.* Coventry: BECTa.

Green, H, Facer, K, Rudd, T, Dillon, P and Humphreys, P (2005) *Personalisation and digital technologies.* Bristol: Futurelab.

NetSupport School (2006) **www.netsupportschool.com**

Sheehy, K, Kukulska-Hulme, A, Twining, P, Evans, D, Cook, D and Jelfs, A (2005) *Tablet PCs in schools. A review of literature and selected projects.* Coventry: BECTa.

Tan, K (2004) Does student self-assessment empower or discipline students? *Assessment and Evaluation in Higher Education,* 29 (6): 651–662.

Twining, P, Evans, D, Cook, D, Ralston, J, Selwood, I, Jones, A, Underwood, J, Dillon, G and Scanlon, E (2005) *Tablet PCs in schools. Case study report.* Coventry: BECTa.

Wikipedia (2006) Interactive whiteboard. **en.wikipedia.org/wiki/interactive_whiteboard**

6
Health and safety when using ICT

By the end of this chapter you should:

- **have increased your awareness of health and safety issues;**
- **know your responsibilities towards yourself, your students and your co-workers;**
- **know your rights;**
- **understand your 'duty of care';**
- **be aware of the hazards associated with the ICT equipment you use;**
- **understand the issues associated with using students' data in ICT work.**

Professional Standards for QTS

Q3a, Q3b, Q21a, Q30

This chapter addresses the QTS standards relating to some of your professional duties and the statutory frameworks relating to health and safety within which you must work. It draws attention to practices and policies to which you must demonstrate a collective responsibility. It identifies strategies to safeguard and promote the well-being of your students and describes how to ensure a safe learning environment.

Introduction

The ever-increasing use of computer equipment in schools and training brings with it a greater potential for health and safety hazards. This chapter highlights those areas that you should consider when planning, teaching and evaluating your lessons. A pragmatic approach to health and safety is based on general premise that health and safety are fostered through ensuring that: there is a health and safety plan; hazards are assessed; and arrangements are made to avoid or reduce risks.

You need to know your responsibilities and encourage the integration of that knowledge and practice into the ICT curriculum and your actions when planning and teaching computer-based activities in your subject lessons.

Health and safety legislation

Employees who habitually use information technology for their work are covered by legislation; the Health and Safety Executive have published guidance. The legislation does not extend to students *per se* but much of the spirit of the legislation that applies to adults can apply to your students. In addition, students are protected by and you are controlled by legislation specifically designed to protect students, in particular, the Children Act 2004. For example, the legislation expects the provision of an adjustable chair for certain employees to assist proper posture. Adjustable chairs are not a legal requirement for students but posture issues should not be ignored and it would help to offer a range of different sized chairs.

PRACTICAL TASK PRACTICAL TASK PRACTICAL TASK PRACTICAL TASK PRACTICAL TASK

The overarching requirements of staff in schools include both the development of policy and the implementation of good practice. You need to be aware of the policies and practice of your placement schools. In your current school, consider who is responsible for the following and what role you should be taking:

- **generate a plan for health and safety;**

- **make an assessment of hazards;**

- **make arrangements to avoid risks or reduce risks;**

- **ensure that staff and students are aware of their responsibilities;**

- **ensure that staff and students are aware of the arrangements made for their safety;**

- **include within the scheme of work aspects of best practice in health and safety.**

Consider – how safe is your classroom?

Rights and responsibilities of adults in the classroom

When you are considering health and safety you must keep in mind both your rights and your responsibilities. It is important that your work with students also reflects these values. Your right to work in a safe and secure environment is only established by meeting your responsibility towards yourself and others you work with. The same understanding and attitude need to be communicated to students. The sheet below is used with younger students; it highlights those areas where they can make decisions and judgements and then can take action to change their behaviour or to advise their friends. The sheet can be used as the teacher notes for a class discussion or projected onto the screen to focus discussions and direct students' responses.

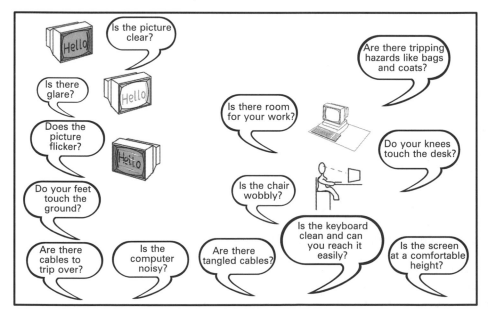

Fig. 20. Activity sheet for younger students

PRACTICAL TASK PRACTICAL TASK **PRACTICAL TASK** PRACTICAL TASK **PRACTICAL TASK**

For older students, issues that relate to vocational training are important. Their rights and responsibilities in the workplace need to be understood. Design another activity or information sheet suitable for the students you teach that will highlight the health and safety issues associated with their use of computers and other equipment in your lessons. If you teach science, PE, design and technology, art and drama, you may already have classroom rules that relate to safety. Modify a copy of those rules or displays to reflect the implications of using ICT.

Health and safety in the National Curriculum

Health and safety
1. This statement applies to science, design and technology, information and communication technology, art and design, and physical education.
2. When working with tools, equipment and materials, in practical activities and in different environments, including those that are unfamiliar, students should be taught:
a) about hazards, risks and risk control
b) to recognise hazards, assess consequent risks and take steps to control the risks to themselves and others
c) to use information to assess the immediate and cumulative risks
d) to manage their environment to ensure the health and safety of themselves and others
e) to explain the steps they take to control risks. (QCA, 1999, p42)

The checklist you devised for your students may have included some of the following questions. The list is taken directly from advice given to adult users. Consider what can be done in your situation to compensate for not having the recommended facilities.

- Is the picture clear?
- Are the characters readable?
- Does the screen need cleaning?
- Is the image free of flicker?
- Are the brightness and/or contrast adjustable?
- Does the screen swivel and tilt?
- Is the screen free from glare?
- Is reflection likely to cause discomfort?
- Is the keyboard separate from the screen?
- Can you alter the keyboard angle?
- Has the keyboard a matt finish to avoid glare?
- Are the keys on the keyboard clean and readable?
- Can you rest your wrists in front of the keyboard?
- Can you find a comfortable keying layout position?
- Is the desk large enough for the computer and documents?
- Is the surface free of glare and reflections?
- Is the chair stable?
- Does the seat height adjust?
- Does it swivel?
- Does the seat back adjust in height/tilt?
- Do your knees touch the desk?

- Can your feet touch the floor or footrest?
- Is there enough room to change your sitting position?
- Are levels of heat and noise from the equipment tolerable?
- Is the lighting generally acceptable?
- Does the air feel reasonably comfortable?
- Can you comfortably use the software?
- Have tripping hazards from trailing cables been avoided?
- Is the general condition of plugs and leads OK?

School placement guidance

If there is a difficulty regarding any health and safety matter, your school/curriculum mentor should be consulted. This is part of your rights and responsibilities for your own and your colleagues' health and safety. You also have a duty of care: this is a legal obligation imposed on an individual requiring that they exercise a reasonable standard of care while performing any acts that could foreseeably harm others. This duty of care does not derive from legislation, but it is has been upheld in the English courts as a duty which has derived from laws established through common use and case law precedents (TeacherNet, **www.teacher-net.gov.uk/management/atoz/h/healthandsafety**).

You should be sure that you know what action to take in an emergency. Because of the wide variety of work that is carried out and the possible complex layout of the various classrooms and buildings, it is not possible to produce a set of valid and detailed emergency instructions to cover every situation that you might meet. For this reason, each school has its own emergency instructions relating to particular locations. There should be, in every building, a notice setting out the procedure to be adopted in case of fire.

There are certain points that apply to all emergency situations.

- **You should commit to memory the instructions for emergency action.**
  (You will not have time to read them in an emergency.)
- **Remember that you are expected to act in the spirit of the instruction.**
  (There is no substitute for common sense.)
- **The most important consideration at all times is human safety.**
- **Remember that if you become a casualty someone must rescue you, possibly at personal risk to themselves.**
- **You should act quietly and methodically.**
- **You should not rush or attempt to pass others when leaving the scene of an emergency.**
- **The most senior person present should assume control of the situation, ensuring the safe evacuation from the premises of all persons, be prepared to warn the emergency services, etc., of known hazards. (When in control of a class of students, this could be you. Your first duty is the safe evacuation of the students; it is not to fight the fire.)**

If you have to telephone for assistance in an emergency, the following information must always be given:

- **who you are;**
- **where you are, including the location and telephone extension from which you are telephoning;**
- **the nature of the emergency and what services are required;**
- **the exact location where the assistance is required.**

You should ensure that the message has been correctly received by asking for it to be repeated back to you. It is essential that the message is clearly defined. Local terminology should not be used because for instance 'the chemistry block' means very little to the emergency services. It is important always to give the correct name for a building and the street where it is located. If the postcode is known, that should also be provided.

A difficult situation

You may find yourself in a difficult situation if you consider that your placement school is ignoring a health and safety issue. In the first instance, you should discuss the matter with your school mentor. If that does not resolve the issue then you should contact your tutor and explain the situation. You must not carry out any activity that would put a student's welfare at risk even if it means refusing to carry out a mentor's instructions. You should take careful notes in that situation and keep your tutor fully informed.

It is always possible that you find yourself in a dispute between a parent, a teacher and/or the school. It is very reassuring if you can call upon free and independent legal advice and for that reason it is strongly recommended that you become a member of a teachers' association:

www.teachernet.gov.uk/professionaldevelopment/professionalassociations/unions
ATL **www.askatl.org.uk** NAS-UWT **www.nasuwt.org.uk** NUT **www.teachers.org.uk**

When visiting a school

It is now common practice in schools that visitors sign in on arrival. You should be expected to do this on your preliminary placement visits and any other visits to schools. You may even have to sign in when you are on full-time placement.

If you have signed in, it is an absolute necessity to sign out on leaving the school. Consider the scenario: you and your colleagues arrive at the school at 10.00 a.m. and sign in; you have a meeting with a senior teacher before being sent to your different departments; at 11.45 your subject mentor says you are free to go to miss the student lunchtime rush; in your haste you leave without signing out; at 12.00 a fire drill occurs but today instead of it taking the customary five minutes to evacuate the building and to account for everyone – they are still looking for you after ten minutes and consequently you and your subject mentor suffer a little embarrassment. In the event of a real fire, a fire officer may be seriously injured searching a burning building for someone who is not there.

You must always sign out when leaving the school premises.

The hazards of ICT equipment

The ever-increasing use of information technology equipment in schools and training brings with it a greater potential for health and safety hazards. It is your responsibility as a teacher to take care of your students. It is also your responsibility to take care of your fellow workers. You should therefore, through your actions and attitude, encourage your students to be aware of the health and safety issues.

It is important that the screen of the monitor is kept clean and free from dust and smears. This is particularly important when:

- **there is the possibility of bright sunshine falling on the screen;**
- **the user will be spending a long period at the computer;**
- **the computer is being used in a high-resolution mode for detailed work such as desktop publishing or computer-aided design;**
- **there are flashing images (that may trigger seizures in people with photosensitive epilepsy).**

There are many sources of fatigue and stress and it would be difficult to attribute individual symptoms to working with computer screens. Some problems may be experienced because of:

- **unfamiliarity with the work, particularly new software or software that does not function properly;**
- **intense concentration;**
- **lack of time to fulfil commitments and sense of overload;**
- **poor operating conditions.**

During most on-screen curriculum activities, natural breaks or pauses will occur. These lessen the necessity for planned rest breaks but where spells of intensive on-screen work is unavoidable, it is good practice to ensure rest breaks are taken before the onset of fatigue and not in order to recuperate. Short, frequent breaks are more satisfactory than occasional longer breaks; for example, a ten-minute break after 50 minutes is better than a 20-minute break every two hours. It is important to change your posture as often as practicable and to report poor working conditions, for example, lack of ventilation, inadequate lighting and unreasonable noise.

This advice needs to be considered when students indulge in long periods of games playing, both at home and at school. You know that some students become engrossed in other activities such as exploring the internet or programming. Personal experience suggests that the students become so involved that they do not realise the passage of time. They are susceptible to poor posture, eyestrain and mental fatigue.

> *Observe health and safety regulations and common-sense rules, such as not eating or drinking at the computer. You would be astonished at the risks of passing on germs via the keyboard. Do the research, and you'll discover that toilet seats tend to be cleaner, i.e. less bacteria-ridden, than computer keyboards. This isn't surprising when you consider that toilet seats are more likely to be wiped with a disinfectant cloth than keyboards are. If you eat at the computer, or let keyboards remain filthy, you are giving completely the wrong message to students – as well as putting their health at risk. (Freedman, 2005)*

Sensing and control equipment

Control technology involves the use of programmable toys and devices, such as the Valient Roamer, computer-controlled floor and screen turtles, sensing equipment and the control interfaces. These are used in design and technology, PE, science, and geography areas.

Roamers are generally used on the floor. Consideration needs to be given to the physical state of the floor – in particular, cleanliness and surface texture. Students will inevitably be crawling round on the floor so it needs to be clean – no mud, school dinner debris, etc. Most school floors are either wood block, composite tile or carpeted. Before starting the lesson, you need to be take note of splintered wood, cracked tiles and frayed carpets, carpet edges and metal thresholds, and warn the students of the hazards. Students should always wash their hands after crawling around on the floor. Other students need to be aware so they do not fall over or tread on the fingers of those on the floor.

Ian Galloway Science Learning Centre

Fig. 21. Sensing equipment with temperature probe

Temperature probes should NOT to be put into mouths to take body temperatures. (Under the armpit may be acceptable; probes should be cleaned before being used by other students.)

Hot or iced water should be transported carefully and put in stable containers before being tested by students.

Eyes should be shielded from bright light sources.

Limit control equipment to 6V output only; that is unlikely to cause shocks.

Glass items are hazards – in common use are light bulbs and pH/oxygen sensors.

Mercury tilt switches must not be used – ball-bearing equivalents are available.

Do not use rechargeable batteries in circuits – even a 1.5V rechargeable battery will cause a burn if short-circuited.

PRACTICAL TASK PRACTICAL TASK PRACTICAL TASK PRACTICAL TASK PRACTICAL TASK

Consider the last lesson that you have observed where extra equipment was used to support teaching and learning.

- **Make a list of the potential hazards that exist.**
- **Make a list of the steps taken by the teacher to reduce the risks.**

Human guinea pigs

When using computers in the classroom you should consider physical harm that could occur. However, you must also consider any psychological harm that can occur. Data-handling activities are frequently based upon the analysis of personal details of students; those activities may relate to physical features, physical abilities and experiments involving students as subjects. When undertaking any practical work where students are subjects, the teacher must consider the risks of both physical and psychological harm.

Any risk of physical harm must be minimised. This could include such risks as cross-infection or hyperventilation. You must ensure appropriate hygiene. You must also be sensitive to the possibilities of psychological harm. This could include causing anxiety over health matters, for example, blood pressure or pulse rate, and lowering of self-image by drawing attention to height and weight differences or performance levels. You must make yourself aware of medical information available to the school before undertaking physiological experiments involving students. Students unfit for the proposed work must be excluded.

TEACHING TIP

Students must be fully informed of all risks and precautions, and experiments must be done using genuine volunteers only. A genuine volunteer gives informed consent. You must consider students' feelings before deciding to share data traceable to individuals within a class.

When using students' details as the source of raw data, consider the following:

- consider the risks of both physical and psychological harm;
- ensure appropriate hygiene, particularly if taking temperatures and pulse;
- be aware of medical information known about the students;
- inform students of all risks and precautions;
- only use genuine volunteers.

A SUMMARY OF **KEY POINTS**

> Health and safety focus upon rights and responsibilities; ensure you are knowledgeable on both.

> All actions should reflect the 'duty of care' we have towards each other.

> Consider all of the equipment you use in teaching and note the potential hazards; use the information in lesson plans.

> Some subjects have specific health and safety requirements under the National Curriculum; teaching unions and associations and subject bodies provide health and safety information. Your use of ICT in administration should also comply with health and safety guidance, especially with regard to posture, eyesight, strains and tensions associated with using over long periods unknown, faulty, inappropriate software and hardware.

REFERENCES REFERENCES **REFERENCES** REFERENCES **REFERENCES** REFERENCES

Freedman, T (2005) *Presentational dissonance and the teacher as role model.* **terry-free-dman.org.uk/artman/publish/article_291.php**

QCA (1999) *The National Curriculum programmes of study and attainment targets.* London: HMSO.

schools.becta.org.uk/index.php?section=is BECTa e-Safety resources.

www.opsi.gov.uk/acts/acts2004/20040031.htm Children Act 2004.

www.hse.gov.uk Health and Safety Executive (main site).

www.hse.gov.uk/services/education Health and Safety at school.

www.pc.ibm.com/ww/healthycomputing/vdt9-armhand.html IBM ergonomics.

www.teachernet.gov.uk/wholeschool/healthandsafety TeacherNet.

7
Inclusion and meeting individual needs

By the end of this chapter, you should be aware of:

- the physical aspects of your teaching environment, particularly when using computers, and how they relate to inclusion;
- resource design and the implications for inclusion, differentiation and accessibility;
- the gender divide and issues relating to girls and ICT;
- facilities to make the computer interface more accessible through user profiles and accessibility functions;
- the role of ICT in supporting students with special educational needs.

Professional Standards for QTS

Q3a, Q10, Q17, Q19, Q20

This chapter addresses the QTS standards relating to some of your professional duties and the statutory frameworks relating to inclusion, diversity, special needs and equal opportunities. It draws attention to a number of teaching, learning and behaviour management strategies. It identifies ways in which you can make personalised provision and how you can develop the literacy and ICT skills of your students. By meeting and discussing the issues with colleagues, you will know and understand their roles.

Introduction

The principles of Every Child Matters (**www.everychildmatters.gov.uk**) are underpinned by the government's aim for every child, whatever their background or their circumstances, to have the support they need to:

- be healthy;
- stay safe;
- enjoy and achieve;
- make a positive contribution;
- achieve economic well-being.

Also, you are charged with ensuring the support for students with special educational needs. 'Pupils with SEN should have the same opportunities as others to progress and demonstrate achievement' (DfEE, 1997, p24).

With these two motives in mind, this chapter considers the issues of inclusion and integration.

Through reading this chapter you will become more aware of the opportunities that ICT provides to support students with special educational needs (SEN). You will also be aware of the challenges presented by those same computers.

The inclusive ICT room

The inclusive ICT room has facilities, resources and systems in place that ensure that students can:

- **access the classroom;**
- **use suitable furniture;**
- **access the physical resources;**
- **see and hear the teacher's presentations;**
- **access a computer workstation and space to carry out other activities;**
- **read and understand the teaching materials/software;**
- **experience an appropriate ICT curriculum.**

The first step is perhaps not a step at all – but the turn of a wheel. It is considering whether the room is accessible by a wheelchair user.

PRACTICAL TASK PRACTICAL TASK **PRACTICAL TASK** PRACTICAL TASK **PRACTICAL TASK**

There is a need for a clear route from outside the building to the computer room door and then an easy route to a workstation. For a visually impaired student the same route would need to be free from hazards such as coat hooks or work surfaces jutting out into the walkway. Students using walking aids and crutches will need clear passageways – there needs to be rules about where coats and bags are placed and tidy habits such as always pushing chairs under surfaces when they are not in use. Students should feel that they are in a safe environment. You should be confident that you could evacuate the room quickly and safely if there is an emergency.

Walk from the main entrance of the school to the ICT workbase or your own classroom and identify the issues that the paragraph above raises. Is the provision suitable for a wheelchair user? What measures should be taken to accommodate a student (or teacher) with a physical disability? What hazards are present that might affect a visually impaired student?

In the ICT room

The furniture available in the computer room can have a bearing upon successful teaching and learning. For sustained work where study at the computer can be in excess of an hour, adjustable-height chairs would be preferred. In rooms where fixed-height chairs are in use, larger chairs should be available for the larger or shorter child. Students will be happy to use booster seats or cushions if it makes their time at the computer more comfortable. Remember, every child matters. The availability of a good working surface adjacent to the computer is also important, especially when working with students who are particularly disruptive when moving about the room, those who are clumsy and those who need extra support paperwork. It is your responsibility to encourage students to behave responsibly.

The location of the physical resources around the classroom is an important consideration. They have to be easily accessible by students with mobility difficulties. Also, our mobility as teachers should not be impaired. If you regularly have to service the printer, scanner or other specialist hardware you need easy access. If you have students who require immediate attention then you need to be able to navigate around the room quickly and easily. The inclusive classroom has clear pathways free of obstructions.

An inclusive computer room will have equipment and systems that ensure that no students are disadvantaged because of the provision. A ceiling-mounted projector is essential to ensure maximum visibility by the students watching your expositions. There should not be competition for good seats and there should not be an opportunity for the less engaged student to take up a position where they cannot see. You need to be aware of those students with hearing or visual impairment. Students with attention problems will be easily distracted by the presence of keyboards, mice and screens. There should be procedures in place to remove such distractions when there is a teacher presentation. For example, placing keyboards on the tops of monitors, invoking a black screensaver or switching off monitors at a central power point reduce distractions. There should be sufficient space so students can take a position to both see the screen clearly and be able to see the teacher speaking. Students with emotional or behavioural difficulties will be better behaved if there is space between them and the next student. Hearing-impaired children are disadvantaged if you turn to the board or screen when you are giving instructions or making explanations. They need to be able to see your lips when you are talking.

Issues of inclusion relating to the computer system itself include the following:

- **The screen** – is it bright enough, is there sufficient contrast, is there glare, and is it set at the best height? Having white writing on a black background by changing characteristics in the word processor or inverting the screen colours best accommodates the condition of photophobia. Screen guards need to be available for some students. The screen should be free from flicker and buzzing noises. (On a personal note, I have tinnitus and I hear a continuous buzzing sound. If a monitor buzzes, I cannot hear it but I know that it results in my tinnitus getting worse and me getting more irritable.)
- **The screen resolution** – is the basic text large enough to be read; have menus been reduced to avoid unnecessary complication; are icons clear enough? Screen settings can be chosen that make the desktop large enough or small enough for effective use by the students.
- **The computer** – is it easy enough to access ports and drives for using CDs, memory sticks and other peripherals?
- **The keyboard** – is an appropriate guard provided for those making involuntary movements; is it labelled with lower-case letters; is there a wrist or arm support? Using Sticky Keys avoids the need for two or three simultaneous key presses like 'Shift Control =' to get superscript characters.
- **The mouse** – is it clean and efficient; is there access to a tracker ball or graphic tablet as an alternative; is the lead long enough for use by a student in a wheelchair?

TEACHING TIP

Do not allow students to queue at the printer. While they are waiting, they are not cognitively engaged in the lesson. They may use the opportunity to misbehave.

PRACTICAL TASK PRACTICAL TASK PRACTICAL TASK PRACTICAL TASK PRACTICAL TASK

Modern computer networks enable individuals to be allocated a 'user profile' so at log-on the computer is changed to meet the individual's settings. The mouse accessibility options include the speed the pointer moves on the screen, the button positions and the speed of double-click or an alternative to double-clicking. An alternative to the mouse can be keyboard keys. The size and shape of the pointer can be changed to make it more visible. It can be made to leave a trail.

Sound systems can be implemented to give talking menus and keystrokes. The talking word processor can be set to play back each letter as it is typed to support the visually impaired user. It can be set to play back each word as it is written to support dyslexic students or poor spellers. It can be set to play back each sentence as it is completed; this helps less able readers and writers.

Investigate the user configuration options on the computer you use. Identify how to change the pointer size and shape, the resolution of the screen, facilities for the visually impaired and how to use Sticky Keys and a magnifier. The screen shot below may give you clues but also use the help facilities on the desktop.

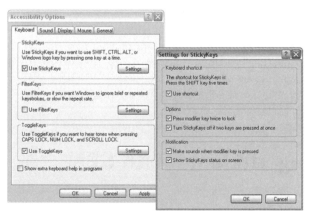

Fig. 22. Accessibility options (Apple and Windows)

The gender divide and inclusion

(a commentary by Reena Pau)

The teaching of ICT has often been cited as a reason for females' lack of interest in pursuing ICT or computing in further education (Lovegrove and Hall, 1987) or as a career. There are two possible reasons: the way that computers were introduced into schools and the way that it is currently taught in secondary schools.

Negative attitudes of females to computing began as early as 1985. A survey of 1,500 16–17 year-old students in Northern Ireland looking at the attitudes of computing and computers (Gardner, 1983) found that more boys than girls saw computing skills as essential for future prospects. Similarly, a survey of the attitudes of 1,600 16-year-old students (Wilder *et al.*, 1985) found that both boys and girls perceived the computer to be more appropriate for boys than for girls. Even today, we can see that females are less likely to choose ICT as a full-course GCSE option and carry this to A-level.

When computers were introduced into classrooms, there was little on the computer that was seen as 'fun' and they were often used to demonstrate mathematical concepts or to learn how to type. Games could be played. However, these were violent or sport-related. An implication of this was that girls were turned off computers for fun. They were associated with mathematics and learning how to type. A consequence of this was that boys were given more rights to the computer and a lot more attention in computer lessons; girls were often made to share a computer. This reinforced that it was not a career for girls, which was then reinforced in the classroom (Woodfield, 2000).

It is important that females have a positive experience of computers, as girls are more likely to lose interest in ICT between the ages of 11 and 14 (Gartner, 2004, p12). According to a study into decision-making by Jane Helmsley-Brown and Nick Foskett (2001), it is at this stage that students have rejected most jobs based on their perceptions.

Today, although we see an overall rise in GCSE ICT applicants, it is prudent to note that the number of girls choosing to take a short course in GCSE ICT has increased and they now outnumber the boys taking such courses. This is a reverse of the situation with the full GCSE option (QCA, 2005). This is an indication that females take ICT as a short course because they find it important. However, they do not want the commitment to carry it on as a full course. A survey found that among Key Stage 3 female students, they were more likely to find ICT uninteresting, the subject boring or technical and also difficult to judge if they got a good mark in it (Round, 2005). Teachers have a responsibility to convey enthusiasm and encouragement in ICT to ensure inclusion. Teachers along with family members are the most influential in helping girls to make career decisions. Teachers are seen as role models and are admired for their knowledge in ICT (Turner *et al.* 2002).

(Reena Pau is a researcher at the University of Southampton.)

Supporting students with SEN

There are four aspects to the way in which ICT influences upon your work with students with SEN:

1. how you teach ICT to students with SEN;
2. how ICT supports your teaching of students with SEN;
3. how ICT supports SEN students' learning;
4. how ICT supports your professional development with regard to SEN

The first area, how you teach ICT to students with SEN, is the principal domain of specialist ICT teachers and trainees. As in all subjects, you have to consider the values and motivations in your subject area. In ICT, the key word is 'capability' – it is ensuring that students become independent users of ICT, able to apply what they have learned to other situations. As in all subject areas, it is then important to understand the skills and needs of the learner. It is important to consider learning styles including the visual–auditory–kinaesthetic and deep/surface models of learning styles. A recommended read is *Meeting SEN in the Curriculum – ICT* by Mike North and Sally McKeown. Their book identifies the sorts of ICT activity that are associated with each style of learning. The book is a useful reminder that we might be neglecting some learners when we use one method of teaching all the time (North and McKeown, 2005, pp72–74).

Visual	Auditory	Kinaesthetic
screen images flow diagrams, timelines spider graphs and mind mapping video clips vodcasts (video podcasts) animated images, Flash files web and video conferencing emoticons (symbol based upon letters and punctuation) picons (icon based on a realistic picture)	spoken instructions talking word processor sound effects earcons (buttons that emit a sound when pressed) podcasts 'listen again' web features MP3 audio player (including iPods) MP3 audio recorder presentations with audio	games (based upon joystick or key presses or mouse) control technology (programmable devices) virtual reality authoring: animations, presentations, websites copying instructions and demonstrations skills development notetaking during your expositions

(Based on North and McKeown, 2005, p73)

Fig. 23. ICT for different types of learner

A further principle associated with teaching the ICT curriculum to students with SEN is that it is not 'watering it down' or 'taking it slowly'. These are simply inappropriate and misguided approaches. The alternative curriculum, whether in ICT or your own subject area, must ensure that the students gain a sense of achievement in what they do. They should be presented with the same number of achievable goals per lesson reflecting those set for the whole class.

The provision for students with SEN is determined by the way that your local authority and your school interprets the Special Educational Needs and Disability Act 2001; see **www.op-si.gov.uk/acts/acts2001/20010010.htm**.

ICT supporting your teaching of students with SEN

Students with severe hearing loss are being integrated into secondary schools because of the availability of wireless hearing aids. You wear a microphone-transmitter device around your neck and the student has a receiver connected to their hearing aid. They are able to hear your voice without much of the distractions of noise from the rest of the class. *Warning* – they can hear what you are saying even when you go out of the classroom.

Students with milder hearing loss must also be catered for. The ICT room is a noisy place, with computer and printer fans. There are many auditory distractions. The interactive white-board has returned the teacher to facing the wall when talking. All of these have a negative impact upon the student with a hearing loss. Make sure that you face the class when giving instructions or explaining concepts. It is important that students can see your lips when you are talking to them.

The readability of teaching materials is an important issue of inclusion. The materials used in the computer room are frequently created using a word processor and it is possible that several versions can be produced. However, to reduce the workload burden of resource differentiation, the resources for all students should be clearly presented using a sans serif font such as Comic Sans at 12 point and with plenty of white space. You should always use a level of language that is accessible to all students. There are strategies like bullet points, lists, graphics and sequences of instructions, which will help the less able reader or those that find organising their own work difficult, yet they do not impede the more able student.

The curriculum should be appropriate for all the students. At a simple but important level, are all the lessons conducted as if students will use contextual menus (right click) and the drop-down menus, or are keyboard shortcuts the way new techniques are introduced? The visually impaired user may prefer the latter, while a student with a physical disability may prefer the former. Some students would benefit from being able to make notes as the teacher describes the activities, while others would benefit from annotating a screen print-out. Some learn through listening and questioning. Is the way the curriculum is taught inclusive? The National Strategy for ICT Capability has been particularly challenging for the teacher trying to meets the needs of all students. Many of the lessons are doable by more able students but the necessary pace is inappropriate for less able students. You have to find alternative curriculum material and activities that enable students to succeed at an appropriate level. In some cases it is necessary to return to the National Curriculum and then devise new materials to enable students to achieve at their level of understanding.

ICT provides opportunities for you to differentiate activity, work and information sheets. The main methods are:

- **changing font size and text colour for the visually impaired;**
- **breaking down the tasks into smaller steps for those with concentration and behaviour issues;**
- **presenting them in electronic form for students using screen readers;**
- **converting an information sheet into a worksheet by making blank key words (cloze procedure).**

ICT supporting SEN students' learning

There is a wide range of devices that are used by students with SEN to support their learning. The following items are those most commonly found in secondary schools.

Some students need support organising their studies and their learning. ICT provides a range of software packages that enable the students to plan and organise their studies.

Concept mapping software, such as Inspiration, provides the means by which students can show what they understand and prepare the content of their studies for later revision.

There are different SEN where the student can benefit from having a recording of a lesson. Contemporary MP3 audio recorders are discreet, do not require tapes and have no moving parts. The recording can be easily transferred to a computer and copied to a CD for later use and archiving.

Spelling and grammar checkers enable students with writing difficulties (especially those with dyslexia) to check their work and be more confident in its public presentation. Some students find that handwriting is slow and the resulting text impossible to use for revision and review. They can use a range of text-recording devices including tablet PCs, dedicated word processors and XDAs. In most cases, students have to copy their typing into a PC for further processing and archiving.

ICT supports your professional development with regard to SEN

In your training and in the early stages of your teaching career you will continue to meet students with very specific educational needs. By establishing a good routine for obtaining information you will be aware of different special educational needs and the strategies used to best support the students.

PRACTICAL TASK PRACTICAL TASK **PRACTICAL TASK** PRACTICAL TASK **PRACTICAL TASK**

During school placements discuss with the special needs co-ordinator the provision for supporting students with learning difficulties and the gifted and talented. Identify the areas of their work where ICT makes a significant contribution, including the use of computers to support their administrative work and continuing professional development.

A SUMMARY OF **KEY POINTS**

> It is necessary to establish an inclusive teaching environment; when planning lessons it is impor-
tant to ensure that not only are the curriculum and chronology issues inclusive but so also are the
context, environment and resources.

> The design of supporting resources, in particular worksheets, activity sheets and information
sheets, can be enabled and enhanced through the use of ICT.

> Your use of ICT provides many opportunities to enable inclusion but there are also challenges that
must be met to ensure all students can participate in computer-based activities.

> ICT provides opportunities for your continuing professional development and in particular in the
context of diversity, inclusion, 'Every Child Matters', special educational needs and differentiation.

FURTHER READING FURTHER READING **FURTHER READING** FURTHER READING

www.direct.gov.uk/EducationAndLearning/Schools/SpecialEducationalNeeds The Direct
Government portal for special educational needs
www.everychildmatters.gov.uk/ete/sen/ Every Child Matters and special educational needs
www.nasen.org.uk National Association for Special Educational Needs

inclusion.ngfl.gov.uk National Grid for Learning inclusion and special educational needs

www.opsi.gov.uk/acts/acts2001/20010010.htm Special Educational Needs and Disability Act 2001

www.teachernet.gov.uk/wholeschool/sen TeacherNet support

REFERENCES REFERENCES **REFERENCES** REFERENCES **REFERENCES** REFERENCES

DfEE (1997) *Excellence for all children: Meeting special educational needs*. London: HMSO.

Gardner, H (1983) *Frames of mind: The theory of multiple intelligences.* New York: BasicBooks.

Gartner (2004) *IT insights: Trends and UK skills implications.* E-Skills and Gartner Consulting.

Helmsley-Brown, J, and Foskett, NH (2001) *Choosing futures: Young people's decision-making in education, training and careers markets.* London: RoutledgeFalmer.

Lovegrove, G. and Hall, W (1987) Where have all the girls gone? *University Computing,* 9 (4): 207–210.

North, M and McKeown, S (2005) *Meeting SEN in the curriculum – ICT.* Abingdon: David Fulton.

Round, A (2005) *Attitudes to computing courses and careers among secondary school pupils.* London: British Computer Society.

Turner, S, Bernt, PB *et al.* (2002) Why women choose information technology careers: Educational, social and familial influences. *Annual Meeting of the American Educational Research Association,* New Orleans.

Wilder, G, Mackie, D and Cooper, J (1985) Gender and computers: Two surveys of computer-related attitudes. *Sex Roles,* 13 (3/4): 215–228.

Woodfield, R (2000) *Women, work and computing.* Cambridge: Cambridge University Press.

Part 3

Supporting learning
and student development

8
Pedagogical content knowledge

By the end of this chapter you should:

- **have gained an increased awareness of teaching and learning theories;**
- **see how theory underpins and rationalises the strategies you will use to help students learn;**
- **understand the concept of pedagogical content knowledge;**
- **be better aware of the theory of constructivism;**
- **know concepts in ICT that relate closely to concepts in your subject.**

Professional Standards for QTS

Q10, Q14, Q25a

This chapter addresses the QTS standards relating to pedagogy. To meet the standards, you must show a secure knowledge and understanding of pedagogy within your subject area, and the theory is exemplified through examples drawn from the ICT curriculum. The chapter also describes a range of teaching and learning strategies and explains how you can adapt them to different ICT situations and your own subject area. There are examples of e-learning that you can include in your teaching.

Introduction

As a teacher, your challenge is to enable students to gain the skills, knowledge and understanding that you possess. In the field of ICT, the content of your subject knowledge will be ever-changing. You need to continually raise your own awareness of computer-based facilities and features. However, that is just part of the challenge of teaching in the computer world.

Not just knowing IT but also knowing how to teach IT

Through reading this chapter, you will see how the work of Lee Shulman clarifies the processes of teaching and, through reflections on the work of Piaget, we establish a rationale for using a range of representations of concepts (Shulman, 1987; Piaget, 1954).

There are many documents that define the content of the curriculum in general and ICT in particular. They include: the National Curriculum for ICT, The National Curriculum for all the other subjects, QCA Schemes of Work, the Key Stage 3 National Strategy for ICT, the Secondary National Strategy, and a plethora of QCA-based specifications for GCSE/GCE/GNVQ/AVCE examination courses. These tell you what the students have to know or be able to do. You then have to develop the means by which you teach subject content knowledge. This is called the 'pedagogical content knowledge'.

Lee Shulman, in the late 1980s, developed the construct of pedagogical content knowledge (PCK) in response to some of the problems encountered in teaching, especially science teaching. The principles he postulated have a bearing upon our work today. Shulman observed the sharp contrasts in the teaching paradigms through history – notably the change from the late nineteenth-century emphasis on content (knowledge) through phases until the current time of student-centred learning, meeting individual needs, cultural awareness, understanding youth, classroom management, behaviour modification, instructional materials and adherence to educational policies and procedures.

There is a growing body of thought that now turns the emphasis of good teaching from 'knowing the knowledge' into 'knowing how to teach the knowledge'. Lee Shulman breaks content knowledge (subject knowledge and understanding) into three parts:

Subject matter content knowledge	the curriculum	National Curriculum, examination specifications,
Pedagogical content knowledge	knowing how to teach	your teacher training, qualifying to teach
Curricular content knowledge	teaching units, lesson plans, text books	sample teaching units, QCA schemes of work

The National Curriculum, examination course specifications and pre-vocational success criteria provide the subject matter content knowledge. The third aspect is the structure of the teaching sessions. Interestingly, during the recent past teachers have been given a lot of the latter. The QCA schemes of work and the Key Stage 3 National Strategy training materials with the accompanying sample teaching units (STUs) provide us with a curricular content knowledge. They tell us how to organise the learning experiences.

Take a commonly taught example from Key Stage 3 ICT curriculum – Finding things out (1b). The subject matter is that students should be taught how to obtain information well matched to purpose by selecting appropriate sources, using and refining search methods and questioning the plausibility and value of the information found. This is a very useful area in the students' education and has a place in most subjects.

In English, students could be creating a newspaper report of a local event based on a search of several newspaper and news service websites. The students develop their reading strategies, planning for composition, language structure, punctuation and spelling skills.

In mathematics, students are continually challenged to check the plausibility of their answer by doing approximate calculations. When using ICT, such as a graphical calculator, to achieve the result, most of the processes will be invisible to the learner. It is even more important that the students check the plausibility of the result.

In music, history, RE, science and geography, students must consider the source of the information and the motivation of the author when gathering facts about a topic. Then they will be able to make better judgements about the plausibility of the results.

Applying the Shulman analysis

One of the items of subject matter in Key Stage 3 National Strategy is: 'AND, OR, NOT can be used to combine search conditions and make comparisons with words, short phrases or numbers. Refining search conditions is one of the best ways to narrow down the search'.

This subject matter does suggest order for the teaching but you have to turn to the supporting exemplar lesson plans produced by the QCA or the DfES to obtain curricular content knowledge. This suggests a classroom management/timeline of a lesson. However, as Shulman describes, we need to develop the middle ground of pedagogical content knowledge – how students 'learn' the rules of AND OR and NOT through your activities in the classroom.

Shulman's contention is that you have to consider the pedagogical content knowledge – how will you enable the students to learn? According to Shulman, pedagogical content knowledge is the 'particular form of content knowledge that embodies the aspects of content most germane to its teachability the ways of representing and formulating the subject that make it comprehensible to others'.

Anthropomorphism is a way in which you try to help students understand. The following example, from a trainee teacher, explains the meaning of the logical units of: AND, OR and NOT. Anthropomorphism is giving human characteristics to inanimate objects. In this example, the literal meaning is presented simultaneously with the metaphoric. The NOT logic is Notty, whose personality is ill-tempered and impossible to please. It is NOT what you specify that he gives you. Andrea is demanding and inflexible. She requires both items or in some cases three, four or five conditions to be met before she is happy. She doesn't give much back because she wants this AND that. Oreo is very easy-going and very flexible. He will accept this OR that and does not mind, providing that one condition is met. Oreo is easily satisfied and gives many returns.

Fig. 24. AND, OR and NOT by James Rudge

Another example of the personification of virtual objects is in the video *Warriors of the Net* (Elam *et al.*, 2002). Stars of the video include TCP Packet and the Router. At one point the Router is heard to mutter 'pick this up ... put this here ... whoops, sorry ... here it is ...'. Each of the devices on the internet behaves as if human. Entertain yourself for 15 minutes watching this short video on how the internet works (**www.warriorsofthe.net**).

PRACTICAL TASK PRACTICAL TASK PRACTICAL TASK PRACTICAL TASK PRACTICAL TASK

This task is to ensure that you have appropriate research skills activities to identify, locate and retrieve and use research-focused resources to support your continuing professional development. The first three references relate to PCK require you to locate the resources and after reading the papers make three or four salient points about each.

- Jegede, O, Taplin, M and Chan, S (2000) Trainee teachers' perception of their knowledge about expert teaching. *Teachers and Teaching: theory and practice*, 42 (3): 287–308

- McCaughtry, N (2005) Elaborating pedagogical content knowledge: what it means to know students and think about teaching. *Teachers and Teaching: Theory and Practice*, 11 (4): 379–395

- Shulman, L and Shulman, JH (2004) How and what teachers learn: a shifting perspective. *Journal of Curriculum Studies*, 36 (2): 257–271

(*Hint*: all are accessible through the original publishers websites with an Athens login.)

The next two topics require you to search the e-journals that are available to you and identify four articles that focus on pedagogy either in your own subject or in ICT teaching. Write out the reference using an appropriate format.

Finally, find these two papers based upon this information:

- Paper 1. Lesley McGuire is a lecturer at Ultraversity and has recently written about the role of patchwork and e-portfolios to support students providing evidence of their competencies.

- Paper 2. John Woollard is a teacher trainer and has written about different ways in which teachers teach difficult subjects using metaphors.

There are further hints about searching the internet and electronic journals in Chapter 15.

Constructivism

One theory of learning, called personal constructivism and based upon the work of Jean Piaget, is distinctive in that its core consideration is the dynamics of knowledge growth (Piaget, 1954). Piaget does not emphasise the social and linguistic context but the emphasis is placed upon the personal construction of knowledge. The social context for learning is described by Lev Vygotsky and described as social constructivism (Vygotsky, 1978).

The role of the teacher is to continually bridge the gap between the learners' current understanding and knowledge and the new information being introduced. It is like building a house: the students are half-built, all at different points but generally at the same stage. Let's say that you trying to build the first room. First goes up the scaffold and then you teach about laying the bricks. Teaching is all about putting up scaffolds and introducing small skills that enable bigger things to happen.

So, when you are teaching the students about ICT strategies you need to consider what they already know and can do. You have to enclose the new ideas in a framework of current understanding. For example, if you are introducing a modern languages simulation then you need to remind them of prior experience of simulations and issues regarding accuracy of grammar and specific vocabulary used in the simulation.

As part of that scaffolding you need to use various devices to represent what you are trying to get the students to learn. These include: prose, instructions, pseudo-code, code, tables, flowcharts, symbols, icons, pictures, diagrams, simulations, applications, artefacts, models, scenarios and role play (Woollard, 2005, p201). When the representation is by a diagram and labels it is pictorial; it is visual. An example of a simple diagram used in computing is that of the inside of the computer. It represents the truth but looks nothing like the real thing.

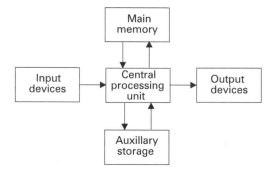

Fig. 25. Central processing unit

From the diagram we can see that the central processing unit (CPU) is at the heart of the computer and it has connections with the other four main devices There is an interchange of information between the main memory and auxiliary storage but the information flow is one-way in the case of the input and output devices. Those are the fundament or basic truths represented by the diagram. It is important that the diagram is accurate and precise. Making one line slightly thicker would imply (incorrectly) that it is more important or larger. If a line fell short of the destination then it might (incorrectly) imply discontinuity.

When teaching students about databases, you use the visual image or physical device of a library card drawer. The image gives the idea that the database is made of lots of cards with information on them lined up in a row. The concepts of find, search and sort can be described in the physical situation and better understood than through a description of the electronic process. The drawer acts as an analogy for the database file.

Fig. 26. Filing cabinet analogy

Metaphor and analogy

One way to teach is to create an explanation that spans some mental distance to make a comparison with a different idea – one that the learner already possesses. We see students struggle to articulate an idea; they resort to analogy or simile: 'It's rather like'. In computing we use analogy a great deal: a spreadsheet is like an accounting system, a cell is like a matchbox, a floppy disc is like an exercise book, a CD is like a text book ...

An analogy is also the representation of an event, object or idea but through the language of comparison. The concept is represented by a perceived similarity between the 'real' device and some other event, object or idea that has greater understanding or physical representation.

In some cases we move from the word 'like' to the word 'is'. The analogies become metaphors for the computer device. The screen of the computer 'is' the desktop, the protected area on the internet 'is' the walled garden and the self-replicating program that infects your computer 'is' a virus.

Metaphors exist in many forms within the world of computing. They are the currency by which program developers can exchange their ideas. They then become the means by which the applications are then promoted to potential users. The metaphor continues into the working practice of the users of the applications. Within the world of teaching and training, the metaphor becomes the vehicle which describes new programs and by which their functionality is identified.

An example of a metaphor that has been used to promote software is the one underpinning the Macromedia suite. The interface and all the tools of the Director program are based upon the idea of a film set. The user is the director making a 'film'. There is a cast for the film. The user can place items onto the payroll of the cast and then use them whenever and wherever they like in the film. Members of the cast are moved about the stage under direct instruction of a script (based upon a timeline). The metaphor is used for two reasons. Firstly, it quickly and precisely describes the purpose of the program. Secondly, it helps the user predict the facilities that may be present and identify and remember the names of the features in the program. Macromedia have successfully used the same representation of that metaphor in their most recent products. Constructivists argue that the new learning (of how to use the program) is based upon the structures of old learning (the workings of a film studio and film making). The metaphor is therefore a cognitive tool supporting (scaffolding) learning.

PRACTICAL TASK PRACTICAL TASK **PRACTICAL TASK** PRACTICAL TASK **PRACTICAL TASK**

The intention of this activity is to help you better understand the meaning of pedagogical content knowledge by considering and then identifying the process in the context of your own subject and then within an element of ICT teaching within your subject.

The following table identifies for each subject an important ICT concept to be understood by the students. Consider how you could go about helping the students understand that concept.

	ICT concept related to your subject	Possible ICT activity
Art and design	perspective	investigating perspective; interpolation of graphic elements; modelling using graphics
Design and technology	cost efficiency	investigating cost efficiency versus durability by trial and improvement in costing a project; modelling with a spreadsheet
English	evaluation – needs of the audience	how information is presented on a web page
Geography	graphical representation of data	downloading a map and annotating in a word processor or using GIS
History	bias and provenance of source	present a selection of web pages on a topic from a range of sources
Mathematics	programming and algorithm	LOGO and programmable devices; instructions for a computer to generate and transform shapes and paths
MFL	cultural awareness	exploration of the internet within a given brief; social implications of ICT
Music	transposition and tempo	experimenting with music presented in standard notation; changing variables to investigate output
PE	evaluation (of performance)	using digital video recordings, editing and annotating
Science	analogue to digital	using data-logging equipment to measure change in translucency or temperature
Religious education	ethics	interactive juxtaposition of the rules and mores of different beliefs/faiths

Fig. 27. Using ICT to support teaching of concepts

A SUMMARY OF **KEY POINTS**

> **The planning, resourcing, teaching and evaluating of lessons is underpinned by knowledge of learning and instructional theories.**

> **Pedagogical concept knowledge is an important part of your subject knowledge and understanding.**

> **Concepts in the curriculum are the most challenging to teach.**

REFERENCES REFERENCES **REFERENCES** REFERENCES **REFERENCES** REFERENCES

Elam, G, Stephanson, T and Hanberger, N (2002) *Warriors of the Net*. TNG IP for Peace. Medialabs. **www.warriorsofthe.net**

Jegede, O, Taplin, M and Chan, S (2000) Trainee teachers' perception of their knowledge about expert teaching. *Teachers and Teaching: theory and practice*, 42 (3): 287–308.

McCaughtry, N (2005) Elaborating pedagogical content knowledge: what it means to know students and think about teaching. *Teachers and Teaching: Theory and Practice*, 11 (4): 379–395.

McGuire, L (2005) Assessment using new technology. *Innovations in Education and Teaching International*, 42 (3): 265–276.

Piaget, J (1954) *The construction of reality in the child.* New York: Ballantine Books.

Shulman, LS (1986) Those who understand: knowledge growth in teaching. *Educational Researcher*, 15 (2): 4–14.

Shulman, LS (1987) Knowledge and teaching: foundations of the new reform *Harvard Educational Review*, 57 (1): 1–22.

Shulman, LS and Shulman, JH (2004) How and what teachers learn: a shifting perspective. *Journal of Curriculum Studies*, 36 (2): 257–271.

Shulman, LS and Sparks, D (1992) Merging content knowledge and pedagogy: an interview with Lee Shulman. *Journal of Staff Development*, 13 (1): 14–16.

Vygotsky, L (1978) *Mind in society.* Cambridge, Mass.: Harvard University Press.

Woollard, J (2004) Pedagogic content knowledge – not just knowing it but knowing how to teach it... *InteracTive* March/April 50. Birmingham: Questions Publishing.

Woollard, J (2005) The implications of the pedagogic metaphor for teacher education in computing. *Technology, Pedagogy and Education*, 14 (2): 189–204.

9
Assessment for learning through ICT

By the end of this chapter you should:

- have a good understanding of assessment for learning (AfL);
- be aware of AfL activities in your subject;
- be aware of ICT-based AfL activities;
- be aware of the personalising learning agenda;
- know the issues relating to writing multiple-choice questions;
- know the value of e-portfolios, patchwork and stitching.

Professional Standards for QTS

Q5, Q6, Q10, Q12, Q17, Q26a, Q26b, Q27

This chapter addresses the QTS standards relating to assessment and the requirement placed upon you to know and implement a range of approaches. Using ICT to support teaching and learning strategies, you will be able to assess the learning needs of those you teach. There is also a discussion of the contribution that can be made by others, especially parents, to the development and well-being of your students. The way in which you can ensure collaboration and co-operation is enabled by ICT is also identified.

Introduction

The key aim of all your teaching is to ensure learning takes place. Therefore, an important activity is **assessment of learning** to ensure that your teaching is being effective. However, assessment of learning is less effective than **assessment for learning**. This chapter will examine the principles of assessment for learning and assessment of learning; it will describe ICT-based strategies such as: questionnaire, quiz and examination design, e-portfolio structures as well as conventional classroom strategies.

> *Assessment for learning is the process of seeking and interpreting evidence for use by learners and their teachers to decide where the learners are in their learning, where they need to go and how best to get there.* (Assessment Reform Group, 2002)

The first classroom example will focus on a non-computer activity that effectively supports and assesses ICT learning. Role-play is an important teaching approach that enables students a high degree of self-expression, collaboration and exploration of a topic. It is particularly suited to the social, ethical, moral and political aspects of the ICT National Curriculum (QCA, 1999, p27).

Classroom example

Students read and discuss a variety of texts on the issue of whether people should be told when their personal details are being held in a computer. The texts should be presented as a folder of files of different types (word-processed documents, presentations, images, diagrams and charts, spreadsheets of data) on the intranet or learning platform. If you use a projector, the whole class can share and discuss the information. Alternatively, the material can be explored individually or in small groups. The students identify and analyse the range of points of view held by the stakeholders. In this example, police, health services, child welfare services, the commercial sector, parents, and pressure groups all have viewpoints. The students then participate in a simulated television programme in which they represent the range of views that it is possible to hold on the issue. The assessment of the activity is in terms of the students' capacity to argue a point of view based upon knowledge and information provided, their use of persuasive language and techniques appropriate to audience and context and their use of both verbal and non-verbal language.

In this example the **assessment for learning** is carried out through the students reflecting upon their own performance. One approach is to give them clear guidance to what a satisfactory, good and very good contribution would be like.

Activity	Very good	Good	Satisfactory
Making statements	Made several clear points using examples from the information	Made several clear points taken from the information	Made several points
Listening to others	I've used examples of other students to support my ideas	What other students have said have changed my ideas	I've listened to the others without interrupting
Responding to others	Acknowledging the value of others' arguments through word and gesture	Using word and gesture to show your support without interrupting	Using gesture to show your support.
Being persuasive	Changing the opinion of others through discussion of their points	Changing the opinion of others through your points	Making your points clear

Fig. 28. Self-assessment of an interpersonal skill

This self-assessment grid could be used to assess the contributions being made to a blog, wiki, forum or e-mail interchanges.

Key requirements in developing effective peer and self-assessment skills of ICT activities:
- *Expected learning outcomes must be explicit and transparent to students.*
- *Students need to be able to identify when they have met some or all of the success criteria.*
- *Students need to be taught the skills of collaboration in peer assessment.*
- *Students need to be able to assess their own progress to become learners that are more independent.*

Assessment for learning – Whole-school and subject specific training materials Unit 5 Peer and self-assessment **www.standards.dfes.gov.uk/keystage3/respub/afl_ws**

The self-assessment grid is introduced before the activity and can be part of you saying 'what I'm looking for' (WILF) in this activity. The self-assessment can be made more formal by asking the students to write down under the four activity headings what they did: this is **assessment for learning**. Alternatively, you can use the grid to guide your grading of the students' performance: this is **assessment of learning**.

This activity is then continued by the students creating a script and computer presentation similar to those used on news programmes to introduce and describe an issue in a succinct and balanced way. Students with more advanced skills could produce a segment of a news programme with the visuals from a presentation package and a voice-over audio track.

The principles are:
- *Assessment for learning should be part of effective planning of teaching and learning.*
- *Assessment for learning should focus on how students learn.*
- *Assessment for learning should be recognised as central to classroom practice.*
- *Assessment for learning should be regarded as a key professional skill for teachers.*
- *Assessment for learning should be sensitive and constructive because any assessment has an emotional impact.*
- *Assessment for learning should take account of the importance of learner motivation.*
- *Assessment for learning should promote commitment to learning goals and a shared understanding of the criteria by which they are assessed.*
- *Learners should receive constructive guidance about how to improve.*
- *Learners need information and guidance in order to plan the next steps in their learning.*
- *Assessment for learning develops learners' capacity for self-assessment so that they can become reflective and self-managing.*
- *Assessment for learning should recognise the full range of achievements of all learners.*

Based on **www.qca.org.uk/downloads/4031_afl_principles.pdf** poster
www.qca.org.uk/907.html

Fig. 29. The principles of assessment for learning

Cross-curricular applications

The ICT curriculum provides English teachers with a range of topics that can be the focus of role-play, debate and discussion (adopting an avatar in a bulletin board activity or an e-mail interchange), persuasive writing (a formally formatted letter to the Chair of Governors of the school), analysis of ideas (using mind-mapping software) and structured writing. There are some topics stemming from the social, economic, ethical, moral, political and legal implications of ICT that can be the focus of teaching in other subject areas.

- **Geography: discussion of employment trends with service industries and finance being developed in countries where computers are part of the schooling, whereas the 'tiger economy' countries are developing through the manufacture of electronic and computer-based devices.**
- **Religious education: consider the underpinning principle of different religions and how that affects both the ethical rules and moral attitudes towards copying of software and music, distribution of**

materials and the propagation of strong religious beliefs. An ICT artefact could be the description of the religious background causing a current outbreak of political unrest or hostility. The presentation would be in the style of the contemporary news programme.

- History: the study of Ned Ludd and anti-industrialisation movement of the early eighteenth century could be presented in the current news programme style. Students could be encouraged to draw parallels between the English social movement that saw the destruction of early textile machines and the current anti-globalisation movement. Try the Google search 'Ned Ludd industrialisation'.

Consider an ICT-based activity that would support assessment for learning in your curriculum area.

Quizzes and forms

In teaching, we have to motivate and interest the students. Contemporary television programmes can be used to gain the interests of the students and then to act as the vehicle for the teaching activity. 'Who wants to be a millionaire?' is one such programme. Because of its quiz-like nature, it can be used as part of an assessment process. The quiz can be replicated in presentation software and you can modify the content (questions and alternative answers). When used with the whole class, you can assess the general level of performance and understanding. That judgement can form the basis of lesson planning for the next lesson. By introducing elements of competition and ensuring that the students are given time to prepare for the quiz, the activity can be a motivator for learning as well as a tool of assessment. However, as with all forms of assessment we must have a clear understanding of what we are trying to assess.

Consider

A traditional way of thinking about teaching is to divide the outcomes into skills, knowledge, understanding and attitudes. We create learning activities and opportunities to develop all four areas. When teaching with ICT it is often necessary to teach the skills of using the equipment or specific software. We need to give students the underpinning knowledge to enable those skills to be rehearsed. The more challenging and interesting aspects of teaching are developing the students' understanding of concepts and the development of their affective domain (Bloom and Krathwohl, 1956). These two areas are also more challenging when considering assessment. Consider the last test, examination or questioning session you taught or witnessed. Which areas of learning are being assessed: skills, knowledge, understanding or attitudes?

skills	repeat as an observable performance
knowledge	recall of factual truths
understanding	explain in other contexts
attitudes	describe in terms of self and others

Fig. 30. SKUA – skills, knowledge, understanding and attitudes

The SKUA analysis is adapted from the seminal work *Curriculum 11-16: towards a statement of entitlement: curriculum reappraisal in action* (DES, 1983), which has since been developed and presented as:

- **know that ... (knowledge: factual information, for example names, places, symbols, formulae, events);**
- **develop/be able to ... (skills: using knowledge, applying techniques, analysing information, etc.);**
- **understand how/why ... (understanding: concepts, reasons, effects, principles, processes, etc.);**
- **develop/be aware of ... (attitudes and values: empathy, caring, sensitivity towards social issues, feelings, moral issues, etc.)**

in the Key Stage 3 training materials for the foundation subjects (DfES, 2002).

PRACTICAL TASK PRACTICAL TASK PRACTICAL TASK PRACTICAL TASK PRACTICAL TASK

For the next lesson you are planning, devise a short formative but formal assessment activity. You must have some questions that will evidence in turn skill, knowledge, understanding and attitude. The order is important because skill and knowledge questions are frequently 'closed', with single answers right or wrong. The understanding and attitude responses are likely to be explanations or descriptions. More questions that are 'open' will be used.

This exercise highlights a major issue associated with computer-assisted assessments. The 'closed' questions can be easily replicated on the computer – the computer can determine if the answer is correct or not. A computer does not easily assess the questions that require the students to respond with description and explanation.

The assessment activity could be presented in one of the following formats:

- **a word-processor document where the student completes the answers in text boxes;**
- **a spreadsheet with clearly identified cells for the answers;**
- **an e-mail sent to all the individuals of the class – they insert their responses and send a reply;**
- **a request to the students to send an e-mail to your school e-mail address with their responses;**
- **a web-page form in which they enter their responses and when they submit it, it sends the answers as an e-mail to you;**
- **a presentation package sequence of pages in which the students enter their answers and then re-save the file.**

The example above is using the computer to assist with the assessment process. The students complete the activities online or on-screen and the marking reporting of assessment can be carried out on-screen or with printouts.

TECHNICAL TIP

On-screen marking of word-processed documents can be very effective if a 'track changes' function is used. The teacher's changes are automatically highlighted and comments can be inserted. The grammar and spelling checkers are useful. The 'find' function quickens the search for keywords or parts of the document. However, computer-assisted assessment can be most efficient when the computer also marks the work.

Single-answer questions

Unfortunately, the computers we use in the classroom cannot understand and they cannot make judgements; they simply compare the student's answer with the teacher's answer and say 'match' or 'not match'. There are degrees of sophistication of the matching process using wildcards and alternatives but the systems we have to use are very primitive compared with human marking. It is the sophistication of the use of the techniques that gives value and credence to computer-marked work.

A wildcard is a character that may be used in an answer term to represent one or more other characters. The two most commonly used wildcards are the following.

The question mark '?' may be used to represent a single alphanumeric character in an answer expression. For example, '?' allows flexibility with the case of characters; so ?esktop would allow Desktop or desktop.

The more useful wildcard is the asterisk '*', which may be used to specify zero or more alphanumeric characters. For example, the '*' allows the quiz to determine the root of a word and allow any aspect of that root; so program* would allow program, programme, programming, programmed, programmer.

An answer consisting of a lone asterisk and no other alphanumeric characters will permit every response given by a student!

Wildcards are used in internet search engines and database searching.

Fig. 31. Examples of wildcard and alternative answers

Multiple-choice questions

The most popular form of computer-assessed assessment is the multiple-choice question (MCQ). Such questions are extremely easy to implement on a computer but the writing of MCQs is fraught with hazards. There is a useful guide in the book *Integr@ting technology in learning and teaching* (Maier and Warren, 2000, p141). It highlights the precautions and potential of MCQs, giving examples of how questions can be devised to assess at different levels and it uses Bloom's cognitive domain taxonomy (Bloom and Krathwohl, 1956) to illustrate the point.

Which is the most correct statement? A multiple-choice question is a:

- **computer-based assessment procedure;**
- **poor way to assess attitude;**
- **choice of one correct answer;**
- **way to present simple questions.**

That question was particularly difficult because there is not one clearly correct answer and it illustrates the challenge of writing sophisticated questions. When you are working on any quiz or multiple-choice test, you should ask a colleague to check the questions and answers for:

- ambiguity;
- double questions;
- leading questions that imply the correct answer;
- negatives and double negatives.

The multiple-choice question provides a challenge to the learners with the introduction of negative marking. Students gain marks for correct answers but lose marks for incorrect answers. Students have to be much more strategic about whether or not to make guesses when they know one or two answers are incorrect but they are still not sure which is the correct option.

PRACTICAL TASK PRACTICAL TASK PRACTICAL TASK PRACTICAL TASK PRACTICAL TASK

For your subject area investigate the examinations that students enter at the end of Key Stage 4 and in post-16 schools and colleges. In addition to the conventional essay-type questions, what other summative assessment methods are used? Do any of the examinations in your subject area use MCQs? Do they use negative marking?

Now investigate opportunities for students to practise those techniques. Visit websites such as Bytesize, ProjectGCSE and Revision Notes:

www.bbc.co.uk/schools/gcsebitesize

www.gcse.com

www.projectgcse.co.uk

www.revision-notes.co.uk

E-portfolios for coursework and assessment

A developing strategy for assessing students and evidencing their experience and attainment is the use of portfolios. These are collections of items that provide the evidence for claims. According to Richardson and Ward (2005), 'The term portfolio as used in the UK generally describes a collection (or archive) of reflective writing and associated evidence, which documents learning and which a learner may draw upon to present her/his learning and achievements.' With the growing expertise of students to use information technology to produce evidence and the increasing focus upon the ICT curriculum, there is a growing requirement that work is assessed in the electronic form.

PRACTICAL TASK PRACTICAL TASK PRACTICAL TASK PRACTICAL TASK PRACTICAL TASK

There are a number of challenges associated with assessment of work presented electronically, including:

- How do we ensure that students have the skills of analysis and synthesis required if they are both researching and presenting within the electronic medium?
- How do we secure the work once it has been submitted?
- How do we 'mark' the work?
- How do the criteria associated with presentation change when work is created using software rather than traditional 'paper and pencil'?

- **How do we give feedback?**
- **How do we determine the true author of the work?**

With a group of two or three colleagues discuss the questions and suggest three or four actions that can be taken to meet the challenges. When you have written down your suggestions, read on to see the responses made by a group of experienced teachers.

E-portfolios – the students' work on the intranet

There are three aspects of e-portfolios in school use of ICT: e-portfolio items, e-portfolio systems and e-portfolio presentations (see Grant, 2005, for a detailed discussion). E-portfolio items are anything that might be stored or referenced in an e-portfolio system such as:

- **word-processed, image and web-page files;**
- **spreadsheet, database and files;**
- **animation, sound, video files and multimedia presentations.**

Emerging standards in the commercial and academic world recognise certain key types of e-portfolio items and their labelling with metadata that enables the items to be searched for, selected and ordered. e-Portfolio systems consist of a collection of tools that support the creation, modification, archiving, accessing and assessment of e-portfolio items. Operations such as uploading products to a file store, entering reflective statements, making presentations can be carried out over the internet. For a comprehensive review of e-portfolio systems, see Richardson and Ward (2005).

Important developments in learning platforms (also called VLEs or MLEs) have been documented by BECTa.

The Association for Learning Technology (Roberts *et al.*, 2005, p5) reports that e-portfolios are one means by which governments are seeking to build knowledge economies. The Department for Education and Skills asserts that they seek to 'Provide integrated e-portfolios [for Schools] by 2007' and to provide, 'A personalised learning space, with the potential to support e-portfolios available within every college by 2007–08' (DfES, 2005). It has been suggested that the European Commission should develop a portfolio system as a method for lifelong learners to demonstrate their formal and informal qualifications and competence. Reasons given for the interest in these developments include:

- **reducing contact time while also increasing the quality of contact time;**
- **increasing learner autonomy and self-direction;**
- **stimulating reflection and deep learning;**
- **helping lifelong learning;**
- **facilitating progression of learners within and between institutions and between national education systems.**

David Miliband (Minister of State for School Standards), in January 2004, stated:

> *Decisive progress in educational standards occurs where every child matters; careful attention is paid to their individual learning styles, motivations, and needs;*

there is rigorous use of student target setting linked to high quality assessment; lessons are well paced and enjoyable; and students are supported by partnership with others well beyond the classroom.

Personalised learning also means making the school student-centred above all else. Effective learning must inform classroom layout, school organisation and the overall ethos. **www.teachernet.gov.uk/management/newrelationship/personalisedlearning**.

An e-portfolio is an important way in which students can take control of the evidence gathering; e-portfolios are facilitated in learning platforms, VLEs and MLEs.

One aspect of the Every Child Matters agenda is 'engaging and helping parents in actively supporting their children's learning and development'. The home-accessible learning platform is one way in which you can provide access for the parents of your students to your teaching materials and assessments. 'For secondary schools, the core offer is similar [including study support, family learning and parental support opportunities], encouraging schools to open up facilities such as sports, arts and ICT' (DfES, 2004, p3).

Patchwork and stitching

An interesting development in e-portfolios is 'patchwork', based upon the work of Richard Winter from Anglia Ruskin University. Patchwork is a metaphor for the process where students first gather a number of resources to evidence their experience and understanding. These pieces of evidence are 'stitched together' with a narrative or overarching document. In its original form the essence of patchwork is:

that it consists of a variety of small sections, each of which is complete in itself, and that the overall unity of these component sections, although planned in advance, is finalized retrospectively, then they are 'stitched together'. Thus, a 'patchwork text' assignment is one that is gradually assembled during the course of a phase of teaching and consists of a sequence of fairly short pieces of writing, which are designed to be as varied as possible and to cover the educational objectives of the teaching. Each of these short pieces of writing is shared within a small group of students as part of the teaching–learning process. At the end of the course, students add a reflexive commentary to the short pieces they have already written, which they may also, if they wish, revise and edit. (Winter, 2003, p112)

There are a number of benefits arising from the use of this approach. Because the work is constructed of several independent pieces of writing, the process can be extended over time. The assessment is of sustained progress and not a snapshot approach of a test or examination. The small-scale writing tasks can be varied in format, style and genre. They are not limited to written items but may be electronic in nature. They may include, for example, a slide presentation, a set of notes on a topic, accounts of personal experience like a school visit or an interview, a poster or a photograph of a wall display, creative or fictional writing, metaphoric representations, diagrams, charts and even physical artefacts represented by images or descriptions.

Each individual item is shared with other students, encouraging collaboration and co-operation. The discussions stimulate ideas and promote a greater self-awareness of the value of the work. Peer appraisal techniques and social-constructivist learning practice can be accommodated. It also gives the students a greater sense of control over their learning.

Finally, students submit an overall piece of writing which draws together the various items. This activity accommodates higher-order writing skills of analysis and synthesis. Students are able to review and modify their work. They can draw together the disparate parts and identify the relationships and connections within the topic of work. It promotes a more holistic approach to learning and in this way they 'stitch the patches together'.

Meeting the challenges of electronically submitted work

The following responses were given by experienced teachers when discussing issues relating to marking computer-based work and plagiarism.

How do we ensure that students have the skills of analysis and synthesis required if they are both researching and presenting within the electronic medium?

'*We can use planning sheets to make sure that they identify bullet points for and against, that they list the sources of the evidence*' (from a geography teacher).

'*Yes, in science we use a writing frame: introduction, question, method, results etc. – it helps them break down the writing into separate tasks.*'

'*I make my students write down the important points on paper as they are researching, then they can only use those points when they are writing*' (RE teacher).

'*I don't like them copying and pasting.*'

'*I give them a detailed list of questions to answer in whole sentences; they then have to put them together and change them a bit to make is make sense as a whole paragraph*' (English teacher).

How do we secure the work once it has been submitted?

'*Near the end of the lesson I pass round a memory stick and they save onto that. Sometimes one person saves over the top of another piece of work. I do tell them to name the work with their own name!*'

'*I get them to e-mail it to me on my school address – that works well because I can read it at home.*'

'*My technician copies the class's folder onto a CD for me to check near the end of the unit.*'

'*They give me floppy discs and memory sticks and I copy onto my computer – it is OK with my GCE group.*'

How do we 'mark' the work?

'*Track changes in Word is good. All my comments are in green and if I don't like something I just delete it.*'

'*I can't work off the screen but we've got a fast laser printer – I have to keep reminding them to make sure that there are no blank areas in the middle or the end.*'

'*I just scan on the screen and jot down comments – most of the time I just grade it and then jot down some improvements.*'

'*Walking round the classroom I notice the work I must look at in detail but most of them seem to succeed.*'

How do the criteria associated with presentation change when work is created using software rather than traditional 'paper and pencil'?

'It's really easy to check their spelling and grammar now – you would think they would correct their own.'

'I think it makes them spell better' (science teacher).

'We have got pages set up so the margins and borders and the fonts are fixed.'

'Some are much slower at typing so they print off and take it home to correct before handing in.'

'We've had to use scanners so that they draw with a pencil and then insert the image into their word processing.'

'It is the content not the look that is important.'

How do we give feedback?

'Just like before, I give them back a comment slip which I write when going through their work.'

'Track changes does it all – I just save it back in their folder.'

'I always show the whole class on the screen some examples of good work, I sometimes show some poor bits. I just keep the comments in my mark [traditional] book.'

'I've got an electronic mark book.'

How do we determine the true author of the work?

'Because they have to write from their notes I ask to see them if there is a problem.'

'If you look in properties of the word processor file you can see who started the work.'

'You know how good they are so it shows up if they copy.'

Fig. 32. Marking computer-based work

TECHNICAL TIP

If you have asked the whole class to submit a piece of work, then you need to have some organisation to avoid the mess of a folder of files of work with little indication of who they are from, what they contain and whether you have marked it. A useful strategy is to require your students to name the file with a specific convention. Using a computer convention on specification could be:

{surname}{initial}_Ass1b_{Form} for example, SmithJ_Ass1b_7

You may have students with double-barrelled names, and Mary O'Hara would cause difficulties. You need to be sure that they understand the limitations placed on file naming and which characters are illegal. When you have assessed the work, you use the File > Save As option and add a suffix to the file name. I conventionally use the grade awarded as the suffix, for example SmithJ_Ass1b_7 becomes SmithJ_Ass1b_7_A. Avoid having problems when you collect the final piece of work by getting the students to practise the process of e-mailing or uploading with a partially finished piece of work.

Student self-assessment

The ninth principle of the AfL initiative is 'Assessment for learning develops learners' capacity for self-assessment so that they can become reflective and self-managing' (QCA, 2005). The successful implementation of e-portfolios is dependent on the students making good judgements of what to include and what not to include. The challenge presented by ICT is that it is too easy for students to submit vast quantities of information trawled from the internet and CD-ROMs. In traditional approaches to portfolio work they would, at least, to have written out all the material that was to be submitted. It is imperative that there are both rules relating to the submittability of work and guidance on submittability.

Self-evaluation is one stage in the self-directed learning cycle. The theoretical model is of self-evaluation, leading to goal-setting, leading to action planning, leading to action, leading back to self-evaluation (Petty, 2004, p352).

The use of ICT has an important role to play in the development of students' independent learning. You therefore need to be aware of the facilities offered to accommodate, support and stimulate independent learning as well as being fully aware of the challenges that ICT can bring.

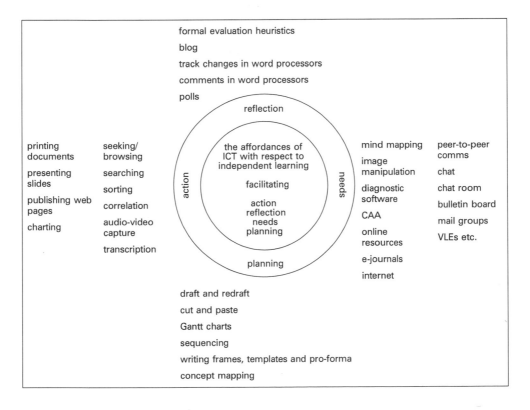

Fig. 33. The affordances of ICT with respect to independent learning

The developing areas of computer-assisted assessment within schools are:

- **the promotion of learning platforms by the DfES through BECTa and the Joint Information Systems Committee (JISC);**
- **the subsequent opportunity to use online quizzes using MCQs and other question types;**
- **the introduction of computer-based end-of-key stage assessment (beginning in 2006 with ICT);**
- **the use of classroom performance systems;**
- **the integration of school information management systems with curriculum assessments and report writing.**

You should be aware of the developments in your own school. Using the areas above as prompts, discover the ways in which your school is planning to utilise ICT in the near future to support monitoring, assessment, recording and reporting of students' attainment and progress.

A SUMMARY OF **KEY POINTS**

> **The personalised learning agenda is current and highly valued.**

> **The AfL initiative is important and should be represented in every lesson plan.**

> **ICT offers many opportunities to enable AfL.**

> **Implementing e-portfolios is a developing area of the curriculum.**

> **Plagiarism presents challenges to teachers.**

FURTHER READING   FURTHER READING   FURTHER READING   FURTHER READING

ALT, the Association for Learning Technology (**www.alt.ac.uk**), is a professional and scholarly association that seeks to bring together all those with an interest in the use of learning technology. With over 200 organisations and over 500 individuals in membership, it promotes good practice in the use of learning technology in education and industry and facilitates collaboration between practitioners, researchers, and policy-makers.

OFSTED (2003) *Good assessment practice in information and communication technology* is an examination of good assessment practice focusing on marking and feedback to students, using assessment to inform teaching and learning and using assessment to set targets. It describes the key characteristics of assessment for learning, including marking and feedback strategies, formative use of summative assessment and target-setting. It is available from OFSTED Publications Centre, e-mail: **freepublications@ofsted.gov.uk**

OFSTED (2003) *Information and communication technology: the transfer of pupils between key stages 2 and 3* is a report of the ICT subject conference held in February 2003. Available at: **www.qca.org.uk/293_3238.html**

Recommended reading is 'Assessment and classroom learning' by Paul Black and Dylan Wiliam (1998), which is an extensive review of research on formative assessment.

The Personalised Learning website describes what has been learnt about personalised learning in practice and policy to date. Its intention is to provide you with support for the development of personalised learning and to celebrate the initiatives in the leading schools. **www.standards.dfes.gov.uk/personalisedlearning**

REFERENCES REFERENCES **REFERENCES** REFERENCES **REFERENCES** REFERENCES

Assessment Reform Group (2002) cited in QCA (2005) *Assessment for learning.*

Black, P and Wiliam, D (1998) Assessment and classroom learning. *Assessment in Education*, 5 (1): 7–75.

Bloom, BS and Krathwohl, DR (1956) *Taxonomy of educational objectives. Handbook 1: Cognitive domain.* New York: Longman.

DES (1983) *Curriculum 11-16: Towards a statement of entitlement.* London: HMSO.

DfES (2002) *Training materials for the foundation subjects.* London: Department for Education and Skills.

DfES (2004) *Every Child Matters: Change for children in schools.* London: Department for Education and Skills.

DfES (2005) *e-Strategy harnessing technology: Transforming learning and children's services.* **www.dfes.gov.uk/publications/e-strategy**

Grant, S (2005) *Clear e-portfolio definitions: A prerequisite for effective interoperability.* **www.simongrant.org/pubs/ep2005**

Maier, P and Warren, A (2000) *Integr@ting technology in teaching and learning.* London: Kogan Page.

Miliband, D (2004) *Personalised learning. Putting the learner at the heart of the education system.* **www.teachernet.gov.uk/management/newrelationship/personalisedlearning**

Petty, G (2004) *Teaching today.* Cheltenham: Nelson Thornes.

QCA (1999) *The National Curriculum programmes of study and attainment targets.* London: HMSO.

QCA (2005) *Assessment for learning.* London: Qualifications and Curriculum Authority. **www.qca.org.uk/afl**

Richardson, H and Ward, R (2005) *Developing and implementing a methodology for reviewing e-portfolio products.* JISC Centre for Recording Achievement. **www.jisc.ac.uk/uploaded_documents/05%20epfr%20REPORT%20version%201.0%20final.doc**

Roberts, G, Aalderink, W, Windesheim, H, Cook, J, Feijen, M, Harvey, J, Lee, S and Wade, VP (2005) *Effective learning, future thinking: Digital repositories, e-portfolios, informal learning and ubiquitous computing.* Spring Conference Research Seminar Dublin, Eire: ALT/SURF/ILTA1. **www.alt.ac.uk/docs/ALT_SURF_ILTA_white_paper_2005.pdf**

Winter, R (2003) Contextualising the patchwork text: Addressing problems of coursework assessment in higher education. *Innovations in Education and Teaching International*, 40: 2.

10
Communicating, manipulating and using images

By the end of this chapter you should:

- be aware of the role of ICT to support teaching and learning through graphs, charts, mind-maps, flowcharts, timelines, maps and photographs;
- understand the contribution ICT can make to the teaching of your subject through visual stimuli;
- understand the value of visual imagery in classroom teaching and how it supports learning;
- be aware of the copyright issues relating to images and resources taken from the internet.

Professional Standards for QTS

Q4, Q10, Q17

This chapter addresses the QTS standards concerning your skills in numeracy and ICT to support your teaching and wider professional development. It will develop your knowledge and understanding of a range of teaching and learning strategies and enhance your ability to communicate effectively.

Introduction

This chapter is about visual literacy. For some, 'visual literacy' can be the interpretation of meaning drawn from classical pictures and the fine arts; some relate visual literacy to the skills of drawing; while others see it as the appropriate selection of icons to represent tools in a software application. An all-embracing definition provided by the International Visual Literacy Association is:

> a group of vision competencies a human being can develop by seeing and at the same time having and integrating other sensory experiences. The development of these competencies is fundamental to normal human learning. When developed, they enable a visually literate person to discriminate and interpret the visual actions, objects, and/or symbols, natural or man-made, that are [encountered] in [the] environment. Through the creative use of these competencies, [we are] able to communicate with others. Through the appreciative use of these competencies, [we are] able to comprehend and enjoy the masterworks of visual communications. (Fransecky and Debes, 1972, p7)

This definition covers important aspects of teaching. The area of 'communication' is emphasised in every subject of the National Curriculum. Visual literacy is also a life skill that enhances enjoyment and appreciation of the visual imagery we encounter.

My own definition stems directly from classroom practice: 'Visual literacy is the application of the skills, knowledge and understanding associated with diagrams, pictures, icons and symbols that enable teachers and learners to communicate, manipulate and use to support learning.' The emphasis is placed upon pedagogy with an acknowledgement of the need to consider learning theory.

The role of the visual in your classroom

There are three powerful reasons for using diagrams, pictures, icons and symbols in the classrooms: visual literacy, visual learners and visual stimulation.

Firstly, the familiarity with a varying and growing range of images will make your students more able to interpret new images that they come across. Diagrams, pictures, icons and symbols are important because it is through this visual imagery that you can effectively communicate the ideas and concepts in your teaching. ICT offers important facilities to enable students to create, modify and share those images as part of the learning process. This is a development of their visual literacy.

Secondly, we are becoming more aware of learning styles and that students have different preferred or effective learning approaches. They are frequently described as VAK (visual, auditory and kinaesthetic) although it is argued that there are many other styles of learning that utilise different cognitive strengths or intelligences (Gardner, 2000). The auditory learners are frequently accommodated through 'the spoken teacher exposition'. Many teachers explain the difficult concepts. Good teachers then use kinaesthetic and visual methods to enrich that explanation and the supporting presentation. The visual learners are accommodated by the use of images.

The third reason for promoting visual aspects of teaching is visual stimulation. The simple observation that some readers will skip from picture to picture in a textbook suggests that diagrams are more interesting and perhaps more informative than the text. Diagrams and images can be motivating and perhaps, at the most simplistic level, attract the attention of the student.

PRACTICAL TASK PRACTICAL TASK PRACTICAL TASK PRACTICAL TASK PRACTICAL TASK

Iconic representation of the National Curriculum.

National Curriculum subjects are often represented by icons.

Identify a group of icons within your own area of study and consider how you can use them to help students understand the concepts within your subject. For example, science can be represented by icons for chemistry, biology and physics, and in turn these could be represented by, e.g. for physics, icons indicating light, sound, energy, forces and motion, radioactivity, etc. Identify the areas of your curriculum and then locate icons to identify those areas.

Hint: use Google Image Search to locate on the internet appropriate images.

Learning and understanding through mind-mapping

We will now consider different areas of ICT practice that either enable or enhance aspects of visual literacy, visual learning and visual stimulation:

- **the use of mind-mapping techniques to produce diagrammatic representations of the learnt work;**
- **the use of flowcharts to represent the algorithm of actions;**
- **the use of satellite images, maps and photographs to support knowledge and understanding of issues related to locality;**
- **using graphs and charts to represent data and derive information.**

Making spider diagrams supports learning in several ways. The activity:

- **structures the concepts being learnt;**
- **organises the learning for the student;**
- **communicates the content (back to the teacher);**
- **structures the teaching for the teacher.**

Asking students to generate spider diagrams as a group activity links in with the principles of social constructivism and collaborative learning (Vygotsky, 1978). It can be a useful way for you to identify the errors and misconceptions that are persistent with a number of students and as such can be a useful form of assessment for learning.

Key software for mind-mapping includes the popular Inspiration and Kidspiration, available through TAG Developments, but there are a number of free or open-source titles. More structured approaches include the use of presentation software wizards or previously prepared slides that structure the students' construction in the same way that writing frames do in traditional teaching.

A spider diagram is a useful starting activity for design and technology, ICT and art projects. By creating it on the computer (using mind-mapping software or drawing packages), it will have the quality of presentation that is required for summatively assessed (project or course) work. It can be used as an organising device for students' writing and creative work. The example below is from Teacher-ICT.com and shows the functionality of web browsers. 'Spider diagrams are an excellent way to condense a lot of information onto one page, and can be an invaluable aid to revision. Students could use their knowledge, the internet and their textbooks to help them create their own' (Jones, 2006).

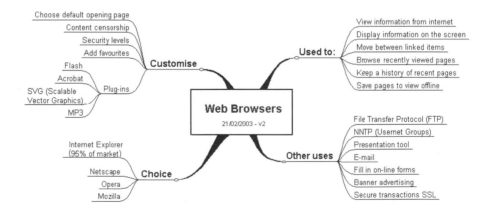

Fig. 34. Spider diagram from Teach-ICT.com

Mind-mapping software can be used in geography or science lessons to enable the students to show that they understand the connections between different aspects of the subject.

Communicating through flowcharts

The use of flowcharts and other charts has increased as a direct consequence of the National Strategy for ICT Capability. The sample teaching units make direct reference to the activity of mapping processes. Gantt charts can be a little daunting for some students but there are useful alternatives, which are also suitable for younger students. For example, ask your students to try making a cup of tea at: **www.primaryresources.co.uk/online/making-tea.swf** in a Flash or introduce a simple timeline program like TimeLiner from TAG Developments.

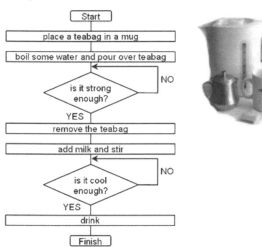

```
procedure maketea
objects: mug, teabag, water, milk;
actions: pour, put, boil, stir, drink;
conditions: strong, cool;
begin
boil water;
put (teabag, mug);
pour (water, mug);
repeat [ ] until strong = TRUE
put (teabag, NOT mug);
pour (milk, mug);
stir (mug);
repeat [ ] until cool = TRUE
end
end procedure
```

Fig. 35. Making a cup of tea

This mapping process is an important metacognitive skill. Looking at a complex situation and being able to analyse it in terms of simple operations in a linear, looped and conditional sequence is important in many areas of study. For example, in biology the ATP-driven sodium balance across cell walls, enabling active transmission of metabolites, is a looped and conditional sequence of events that could be expressed in this way.

PRACTICAL TASK PRACTICAL TASK PRACTICAL TASK PRACTICAL TASK **PRACTICAL TASK**

An alternative program for creating flowcharts is SmartDraw. SmartDraw can be used in a wide variety of contexts to represent processes, for example, those involved in maturity of sand dunes (geography), steps undertaken to resolve a polynomial (mathematics) or using a burette and indicator to measure molarities (science). Flowcharts can be simple linear sequences but they are also useful in representing processes where decisions must be made or conditions met. For example, a piece of music or a song is made of a structure that contains loops (repeats). This is represented in standard form (musical staves) but your students might learn more quickly through a flowchart representation. Think of an example from your subject area where a process takes place that has conditions or choices to be made. Another popular program for creating and representing flowcharts in a way that will motivate your students is Flowol. Used with the mimics that illustrate the processes like funfair rides and lighthouses, the software emulates multitasking programming, subroutines, feedback and computer control of external devices. Control technology activities are an important part of the design and technology curriculum.

Accessing information: satellite images, maps and photos

The new generation of map software enables you to provide students with experience of exploring their own area with high degrees of fidelity. Representations using the regular 1:50,000 and 1:25,000 Ordnance Survey notation can now be overlaid with aerial photographs and historical maps. This gives students a sense of their place in history and a better understanding of the overall environment. Measuring tools and the facility to change the colour tone, scale and orientation of maps enables students to use the maps in presentations. For example, they could exemplify environmental factors by labelling a map local to their school. The personal nature of this contextualised learning adds motivation for most students.

Using an aerial photograph of the school, a local area that the students are familiar with or an area under study, you can:

- **raise awareness of environmental issues;**
- **stimulate for some interpretative artwork; and**
- **promote your students' deeper questioning, greater spatial awareness and increased cognitive development.** (Woollard, 2003a, pp14–15)

Mapping software supports teaching and learning in geography and history. A citizenship activity of planning and implementing a community event can be supported by the use of local maps. In modern foreign languages, maps can support studying the country and culture or using local maps and satellite images for annotation in the target language.

Representing concepts: graphs and charts

Graphs and charts are two different forms of representation. Graphs are 'continuous'. They are usually represented as a line that reflects an analogue value that changes over time, whereas charts represent discrete values. Graphs can be brought into your teaching in many ways.

In science work, the computer is used to monitor values over time, such as the temperature of a cooling container of water. In geography, we could measure the outside temperature over a period of time, showing the daily cycles and perhaps more short term, the effect on wind and temperature of the sun going behind a cloud. In PE or PSHE, students might use monitoring equipment to measure pulse rate before, during and after exercise and display the recovery rates.

A popular pedagogic strategy is the 'living graph' or 'fortune line' (DfES, 2005), where students represent values, events or changes on a graph, with time usually going along the lower axis. The computer can enable these to be drawn more easily and then presented or printed in an attractive form. Ideas for living graphs include:

- **in design and technology or ICT, drawing the sequence of activities related to the cycles of a washing machine, or the programming of a video recorder;**
- **in PE, describing areas of greatest effort requirement and powers of endurance on a modern triathlon of swimming, cycling and running (the graph visualisation can be used to illustrate the**

techniques of mental rehearsal for an event);

- in history, plotting events over time such as those leading to the outbreak of a war;
- in mathematics, using graphs to describe the speeds and distances of different students' journeys to school.

> The Leading in Learning series of documents produced by the DfES includes a number of thinking-skills strategies, including 'living graphs and fortune lines'.

TECHNICAL TIP

To draw a living graph of a situation:

1. *imagine the events as a series of values;*
2. *in a spreadsheet, type the numbers across the top and highlight them using click and drag;*
3. *select the charting tool, select 'scatter graph with a curved line', click 'Finish'.*

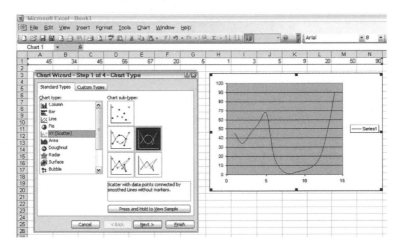

Fig. 36. A living graph created using a scatter graph in a spreadsheet

The graph here represents 'we started off OK and improved but after 5 we went to pot, it took us a long time to recover but in the end we were doing well'.

Making sense of charts

There are many sorts of charts and even professionals are criticised for using the wrong representations of data or using them in a misleading way. As part of our responsibilities in citizenship, we should be helping students understand and interpret the data being presented to the public through charts and graphs. The power of ICT is in 'provisionality'. When demonstrating to the students, you can quickly switch from one form of chart to another and back again. You can demonstrate different charts very quickly using a single computer and a projector. The technology encourages methods of 'trial and improvement', exploration and prediction (Woollard, 2006).

PRACTICAL TASK PRACTICAL TASK **PRACTICAL TASK** PRACTICAL TASK **PRACTICAL TASK**

Consider in which areas of your curriculum the students can describe the data as charts.

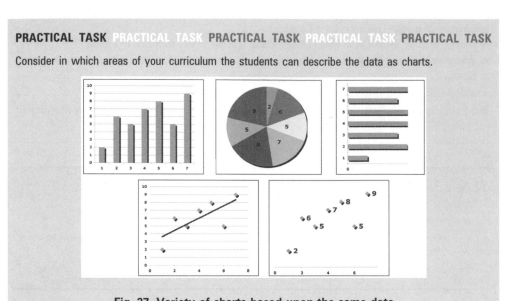

Fig. 37. Variety of charts based upon the same data

Bar charts represent quantities like the amounts of rainfall in each month (geography); the number of times 'estranged love' is referred to in each chapter of a novel (English); or the number of seeds growing in each pot (science). Graphs represent values that change over time or distance like the speed of a buggy (DT); temperature in an incubator (science); or value of a quadratic (mathematics). Pie diagrams are used when a single amount is divided into a number of items. For example, how students spend their pocket money or divide their study time (PSHE); the balance of political parties in a government, council or ward (citizenship). A scatter graph is used when there is a relationship between two values like the amount of light and the height of the plant (science) or the population of a country and the area of land (geography). This type of graph is good for identifying correlation.

ICT is effective in this area because:

- students can easily change the type of chart to make it the most appropriate;
- you have the freedom to say 'try drawing the chart without the gridlines (etc.)';
- the students can easily change the input data and format after the chart has been constructed – this feature of provisionality of ICT enables learners to explore and discover.

TEACHING TIP
You should be aware of various discussions and theories relating to learning styles. Many of your students will learn through the visual domain and it is important to produce a rich programme of visual activities.
Here are seven ICT-related activities that will enhance your use of images in your teaching.
1. Use an internet search engine image option to collect pictures and diagrams to illustrate concepts – try searching for 'ICT' or 'motherhood' or 'space travel' in Google's image search engine.
2. In your next lesson use simple diagrams to represent complex activities – do not just talk about it! Tip – use Microsoft Word drawing facilities to create 'organisational charts'.

3. Create a simple diagram for the students to make their own notes on – 'writing frames' are popular in English and science lessons – 'image frames' can be popular everywhere.

4. On your next information sheet use emoticons or smilies to annotate presentations :-) is a good point, :-(is a bad point, and :-o is a surprising point.

5. Get the students in small groups to create a mind map on the computer of the topic near the end of the unit of work – these can be used to identify errors and misconceptions.

6. Use a mind-map from a previous group to help present the topic to a new group. Using an interactive whiteboard, students can enter new links in front of the class.

7. Consider using simple timeline software to show the structure of a unit of work.

RESEARCH SUMMARY RESEARCH SUMMARY RESEARCH SUMMARY RESEARCH SUMMARY

A survey of the literature reveals the association of many concepts with visual literacy: describing visual and structural patterns, employing accurate vocabulary; visual overload; visual understanding; comprehending visual media; alert to visual manipulation; training in visualisation; effective visual materials;

science of spatial complexity; visual conventions; kinds of visual communication (Bruner, 1966; Fuller, 1979; Messaris, 1994; Zimmer and Zimmer, 1978).

There is a recognised shift in modern society, as a direct influence of modern technologies such as television, digital video and computers, from the dominance of verbal communication to ever-increasing visual communication. The impact upon pedagogy is an important area of research. Gunther Kress, Steve Long, Ilana Snyder and Jay Bolter focus much of their research upon the role of the visual in pedagogy and learning (Bolter and Grusin, 1999; Kress and van Leeuwen, 1996; Kress, 1998; Long, 2001; Snyder, 1998, 2001). This area of research will be of particular interest to English and language trainees. It also has implications for technology trainees using principles of design and communication in their work.

The role of ICT through the manipulation of images is having an impact on the art and design curriculum. Work by John Lansdown, Pam Meecham and D Allen cast light upon the value and drawbacks to the effective but sometimes trivial manipulation of the visual form (Lansdown, 1995; Meecham, 1999; Allen, 1994). Art and design teachers should visit the Computers in Art and Design Education website for current work in the areas of computer-aided art and design work.

Epistemological studies by Bo Heffler and Francesco Cano-Garcia draw our attention to the need to support different learning styles that, in addition to auditory and kinaesthetic, include the visual learner. Work by Howard Gardner in the area of multiple intelligences also considers the visual skills and affordances described as spatial intelligence or the development of mental images to solve problems. The potential role of the visual metaphor is an interesting area of development described by Robert St Clair (Cano-Garcia and Hughes, 2000; Gardner, 1983; Heffler, 2001; St Clair, 2001). This area is of particular interest to trainees who have difficult concepts to teach, such as those found in the sciences and mathematics.

Useful web pages

cmap.coginst.uwf.edu/info is a definitive description by Joseph Novak of concept maps and how they can be used – the theory underlying concept maps and how to construct them. Joseph Novak has also written about work in science and mathematics education that will also be of interest to ICT teachers (Novak, 1990).

www.digitalworlds.co.uk The Digital Worlds software comes with digital data covering an area of 40 square miles around your school. The CD comes with high-quality aerial photographs, historic maps, height data and the current Ordnance Survey maps. There is also a set of 2001 census data for your area and a satellite image.

www.google.co.uk/imghp is a direct link to the Google image search engine.

www.ordnancesurvey.co.uk/education *Mapping news* is a paper-based magazine that shows how map resources can be used in the curriculum.

www.smartdraw.com SmartDraw software is used to create flowcharts.

freemind.sourceforge.net is one of many sources of mind-mapping software free-of-charge.

www.standards.dfes.gov.uk/keystage3/respub/ws_lil_ts DfES site containing the Leading in Learning materials including living graphs and fortune lines.

www.taglearning.com Tag Learning has many useful software titles including Kidspiration and Inspiration, that are used to generate spider diagrams quickly and with a high level quality of presentation.

Further considerations

We have focused these discussions on the generic pedagogic aspects of visual literacy. However, there are also aspects of visual literacy that apply to specific curriculum areas. If you are teaching English, art or history you can further your understanding through looking at references to the interpretation of art, art history, iconography and symbolism in ancient and classical art works. Scientists, mathematicians, geographers and musicians can consider the role of symbols and signs to represent concepts. RE teachers may be interested in the comparative iconography of religions. Teachers of language could consider the role of the visual image in spelling, writing and reading. PE, drama and art teachers can consider the visual forms created in performance. Technology teachers can consider the visual form when creating advertising and display materials to promote products and the design of information in terms of fitness for purpose or needs of the audience.

Read the programme of study for your subject at Key Stage 3 and identify specific references to visual elements within the subject and then identify ways in which ICT can enable you to introduce them more easily to the students through electronic or hard-copy presentation.

TEACHING TIP

As you train to be a teacher, you must be aware of the different learning styles that need to be accommodated in classrooms. The visual learner can be supported by careful use of the visual image. Images are stimulating and are likely to be motivating and retain the attention of your students. Images can be evocative (cartoons or popular characters representing concepts). Images can be memorable – for example, associating a simple image of a skull with Hamlet's soliloquy may ensure that the

---

students recall the text in an examination.

ICT can support you in your preparation. It can be used to find or create and then manipulate images. Even the simplest diagrams look better and are more likely to be accepted if they are professionally produced rather than hand-drawn.

ICT can support you in your classroom expositions providing animation, interactivity, colour and immediacy to your explanations.

There are significant copyright issues when you are using images from other sources; these are discussed in Chapter 15.

A SUMMARY OF **KEY POINTS**

> **Graphs, charts, mind-maps, flowcharts, timelines, maps and photographs support teaching and learning.**

> **The unique contribution that ICT makes is provisionality: students can experiment, explore and manipulate and so engage more fully in the concepts and data the images represent.**

> **Using ICT enables you to prepare high-quality and stimulating teaching materials.**

> **Visual imagery is a powerful teaching aid.**

FURTHER READING   FURTHER READING   **FURTHER READING**   FURTHER READING

Teaching and using ICT in secondary schools by Terry Russell. For ICT teachers, chapter 7 deals with how to teach design issues to Key Stage 4 students regarding icon and logo evaluation. There is a section describing a case study of ICT support for art (Russell, 2001, pp160–164).

'Living graphs and fortune lines' is one of eight different strategies that develop thinking skills and is presented in the Leading in Learning series. They are available on the web with separate posters for each subject of the National Curriculum at: **www.standards.dfes.-gov.uk/keystage3/respub/ws_lil_ts**

Thinking through geography by David Leat (1998) is a useful book for all teachers as it describes a series of powerful pedagogic strategies including 'living graphs' (pages 23 to 38) and another visual strategy, 'reading photographs' (pages 135 to 155).

The mind map book by Tony Buzan (2000) shows how the use of mind-maps can help students learn and remember information through a range of techniques.

'Learning through diagrams' is an article in InteracTive that describes some other applications of using graphics to support teaching (Woollard, 2005). InteracTive is a useful source of practical and teacher-focused uses of ICT.

'Beyond map skills' describes further uses of maps to support learning in a range of curriculum areas (Woollard, 2003a).

Despite the rather negative sounding title, Larry Cuban's book, *Oversold and underused: Computers in the classroom*, identifies clear reasons for using ICT to support teaching and learning. One example cited relates to the strength of ICT to motivate students by supporting communication through the visual medium. He describes the work of Alison Piro, who rationalises that there are 'three ways that information technology can be beneficial' to her students:

- **by granting them direct access to facts, ideas and primary sources;**
- **by linking images and concepts to sound and film allowing students to produce creative and professional presentations rather than collages on poster boards;**
- **by motivating students.** (Cuban, 2003, p69).

REFERENCES REFERENCES **REFERENCES** REFERENCES **REFERENCES** REFERENCES

Allen, D (1994) Teaching visual literacy – some reflections on the term. *Journal of Art and Design Education*, 13 (2): 133–143.

Bolter, JD and Grusin, R (1999) *Remediation: Understanding new media*. Cambridge, Mass.: MIT Press.

Bruner, J (1966) *Toward a theory of instruction.* Cambridge, Mass.: Belknap Press.

Buzan, T (2000) *The mind map book.* London: BBC Publications.

Cano-Garcia, F and Hughes, EH (2000) Learning and thinking styles: an analysis of their interrelationship and influence on academic achievement. *Educational Psychology*, 20 (4): 413–430.

Cuban, L (2003) *Oversold and underused: Computers in the classroom.* New York: Harvard University Press.

DfES (2005) *Leading in learning: developing thinking skills at Key Stage 3. Handbook for teachers.* London: Department for Education and Skills.

Fransecky, R and Debes, J (1972) Toward a visually literate student, in *Visual literacy: a way to learn – a way to teach.* **www.ivla.org/organization/whatis.htm**

Fuller, RB (1979) *R. Buckminster Fuller on education.* Amherst: University of Massachusetts Press.

Gardner, H (1983) *Frames of mind: The theory of multiple intelligences.* New York: Basic.

Gardner, H (2000) *Intelligence reframed: Multiple intelligences for the 21st century.* New York: Basic.

Heffler, B (2001) Individual learning style and the learning style inventory, in *Educational Studies*, 27 (3): 309–316.

Jones, D (2006) *Spider diagrams – web browsers.* Warwick: Teacher-ICT.com. **www.teach-ict.com/as_a2/topics/software/software.htm**

Kennewell, S (2006) *A practical guide to teaching ICT in the secondary school.* Oxford: Routledge.

Kress, G (1998) Visual and verbal modes of representation in electronically mediated communication: the new forms of text, in Snyder, I (ed), *Page to screen: Taking literacy into the electronic era*. London: Routledge.

Kress, G and van Leeuwen, T (1996) *Reading images: The grammar of visual design.* London: Routledge.

Lansdown, J (1995) cited in Long, S (2001).

Leat, D (1998) *Thinking through geography.* Cambridge: Chris Kington Publishing.

Long, S (2001) What effect will digital technologies have on visual education in schools? in Loveless and Ellis (eds) *ICT, pedagogy and the curriculum.* London: RoutledgeFalmer.

Loveless, A and Ellis, V (2001) *ICT, pedagogy and the curriculum.* London: RoutledgeFalmer.

Meecham, P (1999) Of webs and nets and lily pads. *Journal of Art and Design Education*, 18 (1): 77–83.

Messaris, P (1994) *Visual 'literacy': Image, mind, and reality.* Boulder: Westview.

Novak, JD (1990) Concept maps and Vee diagrams: Two metacognitive tools for science and mathematics education. *Instructional Science,* 19: 29–52.

Reyhner, J, Martin, J, Lockard, L and Sakiestewa Gilbert, W (2000) *Learn in beauty: Indigenous education for a new century.* Flagstaff: Northern Arizona University. **jan.ucc.nau.edu/~jar/LIB**

Russell, T (2001) *Teaching and using ICT in secondary schools.* London: David Fulton.

Snyder, I (1998) *Page to screen: Taking literacy into the electronic era.* London: Routledge.

Snyder, I (2001) Hybrid vigour: Reconciling the verbal and the visual in electronic communication, in Loveless and Ellis (eds) *ICT, pedagogy and the curriculum.* London: RoutledgeFalmer.

St Clair, R (2000) Visual metaphor, cultural knowledge, and the new rhetoric, in Reyhner *et al.* (2000) *Learn in beauty: Indigenous education for a new century.* **jan.ucc.nau.edu/~jar/LIB**

Vygotsky, LS (1978) *Mind and society: The development of higher mental processes.* Cambridge, Mass.: Harvard University Press.

Woollard, J (2003a) Beyond map skills. *Mapping News.* Southampton: Ordnance Survey. **www.ordnancesurvey.co.uk/education**

Woollard, J (2003b) Questions, questions. *Interactive*, 14–15. Birmingham: Questions Publishing.

Woollard, J (2005) Learning through diagrams. *Interactive*, 59: 20–21. Birmingham: Questions Publishing.

Woollard, J (2006) Prediction, in Kennewell, S (ed) *A practical guide to teaching ICT in the secondary school.* Oxford: Routledge.

Zimmer, A and Zimmer, F (1978) *Visual literacy in communication: designing for development.* Amersham: Hulton Education.

11
Thinking skills and social learning through ICT

By the end of this chapter, you should be able to:

- **identify ICT-enabled opportunities in your curriculum to promote thinking skills;**
- **understand the value of thinking skills to support learning;**
- **conduct an ICT-based lesson without computers;**
- **facilitate discussion of ICT-related topics;**
- **enrich your curriculum through ICT-based activities.**

Professional Standards for QTS

Q10, Q14, Q17

This chapter addresses the QTS standards relating to pedagogy. To meet the standards, you must show a secure knowledge and understanding of pedagogy within your subject area, and in this chapter the theory is exemplified through examples drawn from the Secondary Strategy. The chapter also describes a range of teaching and learning strategies and explains how you can apply your ICT skills and adapt them to different ICT situations and your own subject area.

Introduction

At the front of The National Curriculum Key Stage 3 and Key Stage 4 is a section called 'Promoting skills across the National Curriculum'. At all key stages, students learn, practise, combine, develop and refine a wide range of skills in their work across the National Curriculum. Some of these skills are subject-specific (painting in art and design), some are common to several subjects (enquiry skills in science, history and geography). Some skills are universal, for example the skills of communication, improving own learning and performance, and creative thinking (QCA, 1999, p22).

Thinking skills are an important aspect of the National Curriculum. 'By using thinking skills students can focus on "knowing how" as well as "knowing what" – learning how to learn'. The following thinking skills are embedded in the National Curriculum: information-processing skills, reasoning skills, enquiry skills, creative thinking skills and evaluation skills (QCA, 1999, p23).

A third aspect of all students' education is co-operation and collaboration. 'The key skill of working with others includes the ability to contribute to small-group and whole-class discussion, and to work with others to meet a challenge' (QCA, 1999, p22). All subjects provide opportunities for students to hear, share and express views.

This chapter is concerned with thinking skills and a number of techniques that can be used to support students' 'how to learn' experiences. ICT plays a role in enabling you to create those learning opportunities and by providing the environment within which that learning can take place.

Thinking skills, using ICT and collective memory

One aspect of the National Secondary Strategy is the re-emphasis upon thinking skills activities. An aspect of ICT teaching is that you can find yourself with a class and no working computers. A further aspect of teaching is that you need to promote collaborative and co-operative skills in your students.

Collective memory exercises could perhaps provide a solution for all three. This section could be called 'getting kids out of their seats and talking'.

Here are some key phrases drawn from the thinking skills aspects of the National Curriculum.

Generating ideas	Predicting outcomes	Comparing/contrasting information
Developing ideas	Anticipating consequences	Identifying and analysing relationships
Hypothesising	Drawing conclusions	Giving reasons for opinions/ actions
Applying imagination	Developing evaluation criteria	Inferring
Seeking innovative alternatives	Applying evaluation criteria	Making deductions
Asking questions	Judging the value of information and ideas	Making informed judgements/ decisions
Defining questions for enquiry	Finding relevant information	Using precise language to reason
Planning research	Sorting/classifying/sequencing information	

Fig. 38. Thinking skills

Near the front of the raspberry-coloured National Curriculum for ICT is a section that does not get very much attention but is part of the statutory requirements.

> *Promoting other aspects of the curriculum*
> *For example, ICT provides opportunities to promote:*
> *• thinking skills, through helping students identify relevant sources of information, develop ideas and work collaboratively to solve problems.* (QCA, 1999, p9)

There is a range of activities that are recommended for developing thinking skills, and 'collective memory' is one of those. Your preparation is 'creating a diagram or map on an A4 sheet of paper'. The class is divided into groups of four to seven, with three to six groups in the room. Each group has to make a copy of your sheet as accurately as possible.

Collective memory exercises are visual. They are usually diagrammatic representations of topics, issues, concepts or skills. They can and should have text but that necessarily has to be minimal. The curriculum of ICT is predominantly visual or can be represented in a visual way.

There is an interesting book by Alan Gardner called *ICT through diagrams* in which he represents the GCE ICT specification in diagrammatic form (Gardner, 2002).

A major aspect of the ICT curriculum is the creation of complex charts, diagrams and reports. ICT offers the functionality to enable the creation of accurate representations of situations through tables of data or animations of an activity.

Quoted from the DfES exemplification of thinking skills in ICT:

> *The creation and development of control software requires the use of flowchart symbols and conventions, and in order to reconstruct the image in the allotted time the students must observe and be aware of the connection between the elements of the flowchart ... [collective memory] helps to promote better understanding within a particular context.* (DfES, 2005, p12)

As part of the pre-vocational aspects of ICT education, the collaborative nature of collective memory activities is a much-needed experience. Those working in the IT industry are not lone-working programmers toiling at the endless improvements to their programs. IT workers are collaborative; they work in teams; they sub-divide tasks; they relate to other people and they work to common aims. Collective memory exercises that promote collaborative discussion and activity develop important skills for all students.

Another important part of the collective memory exercise is the creative aspect of visual literacy. The students do not simply have to see, remember and understand a diagram but they also need to develop the skills of presentation, drawing and writing. The final product is their communication to an intended audience of what they can remember and deduce. The activity promotes recall that is more accurate. This makes collective memory activities an extremely useful revision exercise. These activities have important implications for reporting in mathematics, science, history and geography where accuracy of illustration is as important as accuracy of the written or spoken word.

PRACTICAL TASK PRACTICAL TASK **PRACTICAL TASK** PRACTICAL TASK **PRACTICAL TASK**

Follow these instructions to create your own 'collective memory' exercise.

The first step is to identify a suitable curriculum focus. It has to be visual or be able to be represented as a diagram. An example is this slide created by a trainee teacher, to represent the economic impact of the internet. Originally, small groups used the A3 printed sheet as the focus for a round-table discussion. Exactly the same resource can be used for a collective memory exercise.

Fig. 39. A3 presentation by trainee teacher Shahrzad Mossadeghi.

The following suggestions come from the DfES exemplification material:

- **shared folders or conferencing can offer exciting opportunities for students to try out and evaluate particular strategies for sharing information;**
- **the system life cycle is ideal as a 'collective memory' activity and students' thinking will evolve through establishing effective methods for accurate recall, leading to healthy debate about directional flow, areas of responsibility and an explanation of headings;**
- **a flowchart illustrating the controlling of a lighthouse showing the way in which individual sub-routines for the main beam, the foghorn and aircraft beacon are triggered and repeated in response to the low levels of light sensed by an input device;**
- **a hierarchical website schematic showing relationships, links and navigation bars;**
- **a template structure with embedded guidance for publishing a structured corporate newsletter;**
- **lines of textual and numerical information, which can draw a particular shape or cause an event in 'MSWlogo' (programming language);**
- **a branching database map showing how field headings and classifications have been evolved.**

The materials are available from the internet at: www.standards.dfes.gov.uk/keystage3/respub/ws_lil_ts

Your next stage is to plan the sequence of the activity.

As a trainee teacher, you are expected to plan lessons in great detail. This enables your tutors and mentors to be sure that you are considering all the important elements and issues. In your career, there will be times when the same degree of recorded planning is necessary. For example, during school inspection, peer observation, appraisal and when you are providing work for a cover or supply teacher.

Clear planning is particularly important if you are giving it to a colleague teacher to carry out. The following instructions are quoted directly from the DfES handbook.

In this strategy students work in small teams to recreate a map, picture, diagram, photograph, advertisement, poem, sheet of music or other item that has some obvious physical structure. Each team sends one member at a time to look at the image for 10 seconds. They return to their group and start to reproduce the original. After a short period of time, the next representative from the group looks at the map for 10 seconds. After each turn, groups reflect and plan the next visit. After a few turns each, students are asked to compare their versions with the original.

You should choose a topic for a collective memory activity and plan your sheet. Using word processing, drawing or desktop publishing software, create an A4 sheet of images and small blocks of text. Print it in colour and print a copy of the instructions. Laminate the two sheets together and you have the resources to support 30 minutes of collaborative and visual, auditory and kinaesthetic activity.

TEACHING TIP

Collective memory activities are useful classroom management techniques to keep students on task and focused. They encourage collaborative work and the foster a good working relationship between students and between the teacher and students. Collective memory exercises tackle the teaching of higher-order skills and thus enhance any lesson that is simply focusing on the content of the curriculum – this is particularly important in ICT where many lessons focus on skills and product.

These activities have a low resource/planning requirement. They can be the 'lesson in the back pocket' ready to use at any time – this is particularly important in ICT teaching when we may find ourselves with computers but no electricity or when the room has been double-booked.

The activities are very good for revision exercises in that they probe the understanding of the students, enable you to assess what they remember and enhance the students' memory and recall.

Engaging with the lesson – odd-one-out

Getting learners to think about and engage in the content of the lesson is frequently challenging. In particular, it is both important and difficult when there is a new body of knowledge to be gained and a new set of words to be learned. It is at these times that pedagogic strategies can be effectively deployed.

There is one book that I use most frequently to support the way I teach. For an ICT teacher it has perhaps a surprising title – it is *Thinking through geography* (Leat, 1998). David Leat wrote about a set of powerful pedagogic strategies that support the teaching of geography, which are based on the classroom experience of a number of teachers from the North East of England. Although they are illustrated with the use of geography concepts, they need not be specific to the subject content and they can be applied to ICT or any other subject.

The first strategy Leat describes is 'odd-one-out', where students are required to handle keywords. With any game-like activity, there is an element of fun and the opportunity to make the activity enjoyable.

The aim of this strategy is to support teachers who do not want their students to be bored and demotivated but want their students to become independent and questioning learners. Moreover, as David Leat puts it, 'we do want parents to come to parents' evenings asking about lessons that their offspring have actually talked about at home'.

The first step is to list the words and/or concepts that will be considered in a new topic. This topic is the manipulation of images. For the best results you need an A4 sheet of two columns of 20 words. 'You have been given a list of words which you might have come across when changing images on the computer. These are important to understand if you are going to make effective web page, desktop publishing or visual resources.' Working with a partner, students look up the words of each set and paste them into a line. They highlight the odd-one-out in each set.

Set A	1	2	29	1	resize	11	hue	21	contrast	31	save
Set B	39	16	37	2	rotate	12	copy	22	bitmap	32	scale
Set C	10	13	2	3	vector	13	blur	23	paste	33	delete
Set D	8	13	2	4	picture	14	reflect	24	WordArt	34	handle
Set E	6	22	3	5	animated	15	safe colours	25	sharpen	35	print
Set F	29	3	24	6	GIF	16	border	26	clipart	36	rgb
Set G	40	19	37	7	crop	17	skew	27	enlarge	37	canvas size
Set H	41	21	38	8	emboss	18	negative image	28	insert	38	grey scale
Set I	18	10	13	9	JPEG	19	palette	29	images	39	layer
Set J	15	19	20	10	mirror	20	brightness	30	aspect ratio	40	colour depth

Fig. 40. Odd-one-out activity

Then you ask the students to add one more word to the group but keep the same odd-one-out. At this stage the students may make mistakes. However, the important point is that they are thinking about the concepts, they are articulating their reasoning and that they are working together.

The ICT concepts identified by the image sets above are: reversible changes, features of image programs, properties of image files, actions carried out upon images and the product of actions.

The final task is to ask the students to sort all the words into four to six groups. If the words are presented as a vertical column in a word processor, then they can simply drag each word into a table of, say, seven columns. Afterwards they could put a label at the top of each column. The same exercise can be carried out using a spreadsheet. This gives students an experience of moving data around a sheet. The common headings might be 'changing' (actions), 'colour', 'types', and 'parts of images'. The debriefing after this activity is most important. It might form part of the plenary for the whole lesson as it conveniently reminds the students of the concepts that they have identified. It would also form a good starting point for the next lesson and a clear reminder of the keywords associated with the lessons.

PRACTICAL TASK PRACTICAL TASK PRACTICAL TASK PRACTICAL TASK PRACTICAL TASK

The activity of odd-one-out is a very powerful pedagogic strategy but it is time-consuming to generate the sets of keywords associated with a particular topic. You might ask more able or older students to create lists of words and even the sets for younger students. This activity would form a useful revision exercise near the end of a course or module.

Consider the next topic you have to teach in your subject area. Make a list of the vocabulary associated with the topic. Number the words and then create ten sets of three words with a clear odd-one-out. Present them all as a single word-processor or spreadsheet file.

TEACHING TIP

David Leat and his teachers speculated on the importance of this type of activity. Obviously, the students gain a better knowledge of the vocabulary – many ICT lessons 'talk about' and 'do' but do not necessarily write down or see the words associated with the work. The deeper thinking is that students will identify the relationships between different aspects – 'what can you do to a Paint image?' and then 'can you do the same to a clip art or WordArt image?'

Many of your students are visual learners and you will be accommodating their learning style by enabling them to see the words and manipulate them. Importantly, the game or competitive aspects of trying to find relationships with speed is stimulating and is more likely to be motivating and retain the attention of the students.

A SUMMARY OF **KEY POINTS**

> **The Thinking Skills initiative has important implications for efficient and effective teaching and learning in all areas of the curriculum.**

> **There are many ICT-enabled opportunities to promote thinking skills.**

> **Discussion is an important strategy for ensuring students understand the concepts and adopt appropriate attitudes.**

> **Your curriculum can be enriched through ICT-based activities.**

FURTHER READING   FURTHER READING   **FURTHER READING**   FURTHER READING

David Leat's book *Thinking through geography* (1998) contains a number of really useful strategies that can enhance your lessons and be enhanced through the use of ICT including:

* **'living graphs' created in a spreadsheet;**
* **using a word processor to prepare cards for 'mysteries' and story-boards for 'story-telling';**
* **using an interactive whiteboard for physically sorting 'classification' exercises;**

- **using the internet as the source and the projector for the presentation of 'reading photographs'.**

A follow-up book by Adam Nichols, *More thinking through geography*, introduces the ideas of 'maps from memory', the 'five Ws', 'concept maps' and 'predicting with video'. All of these activities can be enhanced by the use of ICT either in your preparation of resources or in the students' classroom activity (Nichols, 2001).

David Leat and Steve Higgins, in their paper 'The role of powerful pedagogical strategies in curriculum development', introduce the idea of powerful pedagogical strategies (Leat and Higgins, 2002, pp71–85).

The DfES has published a series of posters – one for each subject of the National Curriculum and RE. These are a useful starting point for thinking about 'thinking skills'. **www.standards.dfes.gov.uk/keystage3/respub/ws_lil_ts**

REFERENCES REFERENCES **REFERENCES** REFERENCES **REFERENCES** REFERENCES

DfES (2005) *Key Stage 3 National Strategy. Leading in learning exemplification in ICT.* London: Department for Education and Skills.

Gardner, A (2002) *AS and A Level ICT through diagrams (Oxford revision guides).* Oxford: Oxford University Press.

Leat, DJK (1998) *Thinking through geography.* Cambridge: Chris Kington Publishing.

Leat, DJK and Higgins, SE (2002) The role of powerful pedagogical strategies in curriculum development. *The Curriculum Journal*, 13 (1): 71–85.

Nichols, A (2001) *More thinking through geography.* Cambridge: Chris Kington Publishing.

QCA (1999) *The National Curriculum programmes of study and attainment targets.* London: HMSO.

Part 4

The future
and the wider world

12
Education for sustainable development

By the end of this chapter you should:

- **have a fuller understanding of the education for sustainable development (ESD) initiative and the underlying principles;**
- **be aware of the contribution that ICT can make to the students' awareness;**
- **know the implications of ESD for your use of computers and computer-related resources;**
- **have practised your small-group questioning skills;**

Professional Standards for QTS

Q15, Q17, Q23, Q25a, Q25c

This chapter addresses the QTS standards relating to your knowledge and understanding of relevant statutory and non-statutory curricula frameworks, namely education for sustainable development. It shows how the curriculum can be taught using ICT. By applying similar strategies in your own subject area, you will be contributing to the requirement to use ICT and e-learning. Using questioning techniques is also considered.

Introduction

The United Nations has declared 2005–2014 the Decade of Education for Sustainable Development, with a theme 'Environmental Conservation and Protection'. The UK response has included a sustainable development task force and a sustainable development commission as well as a range of government departments, including the Department for the Environment, Farming and Rural Affairs (DEFRA) and DfES, commissioning publications and projects. There is a big drive to make an impact upon schools and the curriculum. Education for sustainable development builds on environmental education and runs as a theme through a number of school subjects.

Sustainable development is about improving the quality of life for everyone – now and for future generations.

> *Education for sustainable development enables students to develop the knowledge, skills, understanding and values to participate in decisions about the way we do things individually and collectively, both locally and globally, that will improve the quality of life now without damaging the planet for the future. There are opportunities for students to develop their understanding of sustainable development within the school curriculum, in particular in their work in geography, science, PSHE and citizenship.* (QCA, 1999a, p25)

The underlying principles include:

- understanding the need to maintain and improve the quality of life now without damaging the planet for future generations;
- essential life skills crucial for children and young people to understand and appreciate the effect of their actions on their own lives, the lives of others, and on the environment.

> *Through the Extended Schools initiative, we are exploring ways in which schools can actively support sustainable development in their local communities, leading to practical improvements in local quality of life.* (DEFRA, 2005, p38)

The role of ICT in education for sustainable education

Education for sustainable development is a statutory requirement in science, geography, design and technology and citizenship. There are also opportunities to promote sustainable development in other subjects, and to use this as a stimulating context for learning across the curriculum. Therefore, teaching ICT capability has an ESD focus or ESD can be taught using ICT facilities.

The DfES is funding the Qualifications and Curriculum Authority to develop a website to guide and support schools and colleges. It offers examples of best practice for sustainable development across the full range of subjects, including finding out about ESD, teaching and management and continuing professional development.

Take for example the requirement that students review, modify and evaluate work as it progresses and that they reflect critically on the impact of ICT on their own and others' lives, considering the social, economic, political, legal ethical and moral issues (QCA, 1999b, p41). Your students might consider the use of internet shopping, video conferencing or e-mail and decide how ICT could contribute to sustainable development. We can give opportunities for students to consider how ICT can exaggerate the effects of actions; for example, spamming and viruses, the effects on small and remote communities or the tendency towards globalisation.

Classroom activity

Agree with your mentor in school an issue of interest and collect resources. Design and print an A3 poster to reflect that aspect of ESD. In your school, use the poster as the focus of a discussion with a small group of students. Try to ascertain the students' understanding. If they appear to have a good understanding, try to pose questions that allow them to apply their understanding. If they appear to have less understanding or knowledge than you expect, then try to take their ideas further with discussion and questioning. Think about the questions you asked and the discussion you had.

- How closed or open were the questions?
- Did the students seem to understand the questions?
- Did you reinforce good ideas?
- Did you give positive or negative feedback?
- Did the students have opportunities to ask questions?
- Was the level of understanding what you expected?
- Did the discussion appear to help the students' understanding?

Sustainable development and ICT

It was not that long ago when there was a vision of the 'paperless office'. It really did not come to fruition and, coupled with the impact of the chemicals used in everyday computing and the use of electricity, ICT is not necessarily an environmentally friendly activity. There are many ways in which ICT areas in school can contribute to a more sustainable future and, importantly, contribute to the school's efforts in providing an education for sustainable development.

It is important to be seen to be doing, as well as saying, what to do. You lead by example and, as a teacher, you have both the responsibility and the opportunity to influence the next generation. There are a number of things you can do to develop the ICT curriculum and the use of ICT in other curriculum areas to better reflect the values of sustainable development. For example, you should ensure power-saving features are used – especially on screens and printers. However, there is a caution. Do not impose conditions that have a negative impact upon the students' learning – when you say 'now turn to your computer and', you do not want to wait for computers to come out of hibernation. You should use power-saving facilities and the vocabulary in a positive and correct way. You should make recycling, reusing and reducing consumption a virtuous act and not a chore to be carried out. By providing recycling and reusing banks you can encourage participation through example and knowledge through action.

On 27 January 2003, the EEC advised of a new directive called WEEE (Waste from Electrical and Electronic Equipment). This directive became effective on 13 August 2005. It makes manufacturers and importers of electrical equipment responsible for the cost of recycling the products. All printer cartridges are now supplied with a free postage envelope for the return of the used cartridge (**www.netregs.gov.uk**).

PRACTICAL TASK PRACTICAL TASK **PRACTICAL TASK** PRACTICAL TASK **PRACTICAL TASK**

With two or three trainees carry out an 'ideas shower' around the theme of sustainable development. Take responsibility for recording the different ideas as text boxes in presentation or word-processing software. Consider the design of a checklist for students of action they should be taking in the classroom to support sustainable development. Use your record of the ideas shower and, by click and dragging, divide the points into different areas that might be the focus of a topic in the checklist. Publish the checklist as a presentation slide or an A4 poster. Finally, consider the value and affordances of asking students to record ideas showers directly onto the computer and using the software to rearrange and group them in a virtual environment before publishing them to a wider audience.

The three Rs – Reduce, Reuse, Recycle – is a common way of representing strategies that support sustainable development.

Classroom practice

When students are drafting and redrafting work, you should be encouraging on-screen editing and redrafting with less dependence upon making the correction on paper. You can reduce waste, but this must be with a positive attitude – not just because paper costs money but rather the fact that reducing consumption is better for the environment and the skills of on-screen editing and manipulation of material are a useful step towards ICT capability.

You can promote and celebrate the activities in ICT that contribute to sustainable actions in different ways: a notice in assembly when the first 100 cartridges are recycled; display of environmental logos taken from the products used; liaising with the school's ESD co-ordinator; and putting ESD in the curriculum development plans.

There is a particular role for ICT teachers. Most GCSE syllabuses require teaching of the social and economic impact of ICT as part of understanding in the subject, and deeper study of sustainability issues is possible. For example, instead of basing the projects (A4 leaflet, poster and PowerPoint presentation) on the disco or local garden centre, you can move the focus towards sustainable development. Small groups of students can work together on a focus – promoting a particular aspect like World Food Day, United Nations Day, World Children's Day. Through these activities students can be valuing human rights, considering rights and responsibilities, celebrating human diversity.

It is important to realise that you are required to consider the social, ethical, economic and moral implications of ICT. The Dearing Review of the National Curriculum in 1999 also included the legal and political dimension (QCA, 1999b, p41). ICT promotes education for sustainable development through developing students' understanding of the implications of ICT for working life, society and the environment. The National Curriculum for ICT requires Key Stage 3 students to extend the breadth of their study of ICT, including talking about the significance of ICT to individuals, communities and society. This provides an opportunity to discuss sustainability issues. The National Curriculum in a wide range of subjects has elements where sustainability and the impacts of human activity need to be understood, including geography, history, science, PSHE, citizenship and religious education.

TEACHING TIP

The ICT curriculum prepares students to participate in a rapidly changing world in which work and other activities are increasingly transformed by access to varied and developing technology. Increased capability in the use of ICT promotes initiative and independent learning, with students being able to make informed judgements and to consider the implications of ICT for home and work both now and in the future. The curriculum offers opportunities to use sustainable development as a context for learning. Social, economic and environmental issues can provide motivating contexts for developing a wide range of ICT skills. You should see education for sustainable development as a positive opportunity to place your ICT capability teaching in a real-world context.

A SUMMARY OF **KEY POINTS**

> Education for sustainable development is an important initiative and our effective teaching in this area may be rewarded in very dramatic ways.

> ICT has a significant contribution in raising the students' awareness.

> Computers and the associated technologies have significant implications for sustainable development.

FURTHER READING   FURTHER READING   **FURTHER READING**   FURTHER READING
The government's approach – delivering UK sustainable development together.
www.sustainable-development.gov.uk/publications/uk-strategy99

The National Curriculum approach to ESD. Education for sustainable development is an approach to the whole curriculum and management of a school, not a new subject. It has its roots in environmental education and development education. As a result, many of the building blocks of education for sustainable development are already present in every school. This website has been designed to help teachers, curriculum co-ordinators, school managers and governors to develop approaches to education for sustainable development. **www.nc.uk.net/esd**

The QCA Education for Sustainable Development website has four clearly identified strands describing ESD and its role in teaching, school management and professional development. There is a section (found through the link 'ESD by subject' within the 'Teaching' strand) that gives information on opportunities for ESD within modern foreign languages, including references to specific units in the QCA/DfES schemes of work for French, German and Spanish. **www.qca.org.uk/13510.html#ESD**

'Say it Loud' is an annual sustainable development festival celebrating the sustainable development work of school students through drama, music and displays. It is supported by the Royal Geographical Society. Their work on education for sustainable development consists of an Ecological and Carbon Footprints website, which introduces to teachers the concepts behind web-based footprint calculators. Teaching advice and guidance are provided via classroom exemplars and the advantages of using such tools are also discussed. **www.rgs.org**

The TeacherNet information is linked from **www.teachernet.gov.uk/sustainable-schools** and Friends of the Earth from **www.foe.co.uk/learning/educators**

Finally, there are two web pages that link to subject-specific examples of ESD in action in classrooms. **www.nc.uk.net/esd/teaching/case_studies/case_study_q.htm www. nc.uk.net/esd/teaching/esd_by_subject.htm**

REFERENCES REFERENCES **REFERENCES** REFERENCES **REFERENCES** REFERENCES

Department for Environment Food and Rural Affairs (2005) *HM Government Securing the future – delivering UK sustainable development strategy.* London: The Stationery Office.

QCA (1999a) *The National Curriculum programmes of study and attainment targets.* London: HMSO.

QCA (1999b) *Information and communication technology.* London: HMSO.

13

The social, economic, ethical and moral implications of ICT

By the end of this chapter you should:

- understand the implications for the pervasive use of ICT in teaching;
- be able to explain the difference between morals and ethics;
- recognise appropriate opportunities to teach aspects of PSHE through the use of ICT;
- understand the implications of the 'digital divide' and how that is changing.

Professional Standards for QTS

Q18, Q23, Q24

This chapter addresses the QTS standards relating to the influences upon your students' progress and well-being relating to social, ethnic and cultural influences, the pervasive use of computers in society and the digital divide. The application of ICT skills to support teaching is exemplified. The use of ICT in homework and out-of-class activities is identified.

Introduction

An important strand running through the ICT National Curriculum and the attainment level descriptions is social, economic, ethical and moral implications of the use of ICT. The widespread and invasive use of technology can be examined in many subject areas. Each new development in information technology raises new social, economic, ethical and moral issues.

Studying historical events can help us understand the changes we are living through. The earlier introduction of technology should be considered to help our understanding of the implications of change. For example, the availability, the acceptance and the eventual introduction of calculators into the school curriculum illustrate the social changes that occur. At one stage, there were teachers of mathematics refusing to accept the use of calculators yet now it is an essential and expected part of the curriculum. With the introduction of new technologies there are economic and moral issues relating to equality of opportunity, disenfranchisement and the 'digital divide'. The use of information may pose a threat to the welfare of a group within society or the same technology may be used differently or more extensively to create different social, economic, ethical or moral issues.

PRACTICAL TASK PRACTICAL TASK PRACTICAL TASK PRACTICAL TASK PRACTICAL TASK

The following examples of the implementation illustrate the pervasive nature of information technology. The scenarios can be described and the students asked to analyse them by considering the general questions relating to the social, economic, ethical and moral issues.

- What are the social advantages and the social disadvantages to the general public, the authorities, employees and employers, the commercial world and minority groups?
- The interests of the elderly, ethnic minorities, single families, the unemployed, vegetarians, those with serious or long-term illness, those with learning difficulties, etc., may be considered.
- The economic advantages and disadvantages should also be considered.
- The ethical issues are identified by considering the law, codes of conduct, rules and regulations that may be affected by the introduction of a particular information technology facility.
- The moral issues may be teased out by asking: is it right, or what is wrong about it? This area is the most prone to personal interest and bias. You need to enable students to express an informed opinion based upon their own values and not to prescribe a particular point of view.

The pervasive nature of ICT in society

The point of sale terminal (PoS) is an example. The success of the supermarket culture in part relates to our use of motor vehicles, which contributes to the success of out-of-town shopping. However, the use of computers in many areas of operation, including the point of sale, has added to supermarket efficiency and therefore success. The students could compare the use of ICT by the supermarket with that of the corner shop. Even in the local village shop there is computerisation of the till and sending stock orders. Stock control (handling information) ensures that shops do not run out of products, being more able to see trends in sales and use the data to predict future sales (modelling). By linking the data with the advertising strategies, supermarkets are able to both predict and manipulate sales levels of a range of products. Supermarkets use an ever-widening range of communicating information software to advertise their messages including desktop publishing printed material, multimedia on television and the internet.

The automatic telling machine (ATM) is another example of how computers have influenced our lives. Banking services are aimed at those members in society that have a regular disposable income. Over the past 30 years they have become more customer-friendly and have widened their scope to a range of payments and other money services. These services are not available to people who do not have access to town centres. The services do not involve contact with people – some customers are less happy about dealing solely with a machine. What are the implications of tele-banking and internet banking?

The smart card is a credit-card-sized device with a microchip that can contain a large amount of information. The information on the card can be read or changed by a computer. A smart card can be used in a variety of ways: as a credit card that keeps a record of the amount of money the owner has remaining, an identity card containing much more information than could be printed on the face of the card, or perhaps a medical warning card. The current debate about identity cards can be considered.

Hypothetical scenarios for student discussion

The following scenarios can be used as the basis of discussion or investigation; they are hypothetical but lead the students into a range of topic areas that have social, economical, ethical and moral implications.

DIFD (Detection, Identification, Fining and Debiting) is an automatic detection of road speed, identification of the car registration, fining the car owner and debiting the bank account of the owner. DIFDsystems could eliminate much of the time-wasting and money-consuming bureaucracy surrounding magistrates courts. The system would be simple to implement and would be effective because the punishment would be immediate and targeted on the owner of the miscreant vehicle.

AutoTubeDriver is the totally automatic tube train system with no drivers present. The trains would run to predetermined timetables. Track control would ensure that safety margins between rolling stock were maintained. Doors would automatically open and close, with sensors detecting the presence of passengers. Fire protection services would be controlled by a range of sensors with automatic alarms, fire extinguishers and section isolation. The use of CCTV which would be automatically triggered if the emergency bar, which passes along the platform and all subways, was pressed, would ensure passenger safety from muggers.

Written assessment tasks for students

- Compare the use of a word processor with traditional writing and drawing.
- Compare the use of a desktop publisher with paper cut-and-paste methods.
- Compare the facilities of a calculator, a spreadsheet and a charting program with traditional methods.
- Describe their own use of a word processor and assess its effectiveness.
- Describe their use of a database program, indicating how they question the plausibility of the information and the possible implications of incorrect information being entered into their system.
- Describe their use of a control package and an application in industry context.
- Select a job position and describe the current and possible future impact of new technologies on methods of working.
- Participate in a debate about a moral issue or ethical issue associated with the development and use of new technologies.
- Present the ethical or moral issues associated with one aspect of the use of information technology.
- Present the social or economic issues associated with one aspect of the use of information technology.
- Focused on one piece of familiar software, suggest a range of uses in commercial, manufacturing and/or a leisure setting.

A context for discussion

The following scenario is an example of how to focus a student discussion or activity to draw in a range of everyday applications of ICT. When creating and then describing scenarios to students, you need to reflect their past experiences and motivations.

A park ranger (David) has recently retired from work at an English Nature SSI in the Beacon Hills at the age of 58. Now at home all day, hobbies and interests are important. His elderly mother (Catherine), who suffers from a heart condition, lives 10 miles away in a small village. His grandchildren (Mattie and Becky) attend Roxborough School and have access to a range of computers; they also have a computer at home.

- Describe a medical technique that uses an electronic device that will make Catherine's health more secure.

- Describe a device that Catherine could have in her home that would mean she could call for help most easily – describe a device that would automatically call for help if Catherine did not get up on a particular morning.
- There is not a bank or post office in the village where David lives. Describe an information service and a banking service that he could use from his home.
- Describe how David and his grandchildren could use the internet to keep in touch with each other and describe how Mattie and Becky use information technology in their work at school.

These notes are useful starting points for discussions and factual lessons. Students need to be able to discuss the social, economic, ethical and moral aspects of information technology. That discussion should be based upon a wide experience and knowledge of information and communication systems. These discussions can be placed in core ICT lessons but many are better placed in the context of subject teaching.

PRACTICAL TASK PRACTICAL TASK PRACTICAL TASK PRACTICAL TASK PRACTICAL TASK

Identify a PSHE area that fits within your subject teaching and then devise, plan and perhaps teach an ICT-focused activity.

The National Curriculum for PSHE can be downloaded by going to **www.nc.uk.net**, taking the PSHE option from the subject dropdown menu and then selecting Key Stage 3 or 4 as appropriate.

In PSHE:

during key stage 3 pupils learn about themselves as growing and changing individuals and as members of their communities with more maturity, independence and power. They become more self-aware, and are capable of more sophisticated moral reasoning. They take more responsibility for themselves and become more aware of the views, needs and rights of people of all ages. They build on the experience, confidence and competence they developed in key stage 2, learning new skills to help them make decisions and play an active part in their personal and social life. They learn how to plan and manage choices for their courses and career. They continue to develop and maintain a healthy lifestyle, coping well with their changing bodies and feelings. They also learn to cope with changing relationships and understand how these can affect their health and well-being. They make the most of new opportunities to take part in the life of the school and its communities. **(QCA, 1999, p189)**

Subject area	NC for PSHE statement	Application of ICT
Art and design	feel positive about themselves by taking part in a public performance	presenting their work as a series of photographs on an internet site
Design and Technology	meet and work with people	use an MP3 recorder to interview potential users of a product being designed and made
English	participate, for example, improve personal safety in their neighbourhood	design a personal safety information web page for pensioners (specific audience)
ICT	prepare for change, for example, by preparing for new styles of learning at Key Stage 4	exploring the school Key Stage 4 VLE and viewing current project work
Mathematics	what influences how we spend or save money and how to become competent at managing personal money	creating spreadsheet models of pocket money or wage expenditure
MFL	to communicate confidently with their peers and adults	sustain an e-mail conversation with another student in the target language
Music	feel positive about themselves by taking part in a public performance	using MIDI or pre-recorded sound tracks

PE	to recognise the physical and emotional changes that take place at puberty and how to manage these changes in a positive way	advise the students on good websites to obtain reliable and relevant information
Science	how to keep healthy and what influences health, including the media	using the internet to access healthy eating sites
RE	empathise with people different from themselves	gaining experience of people from other cultures and religions through online communication
Careers education	students should be taught how to make real choices based on their own research	using online careers databases

Fig. 41. Integrating citizenship into curriculum activities using ICT

The digital divide

During the past five years we have become aware of an equal-opportunities issue relating to accessibility to computer technology. The growing use of word-processor-generated coursework, electronic presentations by groups and individual students and the reliance upon the internet to provide the source of information and revision material like Bitesize (BBC, 2006) and SamLearning (2006) revision means that some students, because of their home background, may be disadvantaged.

Disenfranchisement is the most severe form of disadvantage. It occurs when a student has no opportunities to access learning resources when away from the classroom. This may result from a disadvantaged background, religious belief or personal disposition towards computers. It is important that you are aware of students that do not have an appropriate level of access to computers outside of your classroom. During the next five years, we are likely to see a different form of digital divide forming. With the ever-increasing availability of hardware, in the form of computers, mobile telephones with GPRS, games machines with internet and a windows environment and PDAs with generic software, students are more likely to have access to a computer to support their homework, revision and project work. You need to plan homework and other out-of-class activities that will sustain students' progress. Their use of ICT in those activities can enhance, extend and consolidate their learning.

The new digital divide will occur when there is a disparity between different students because of their abilities to handle information through sort and analysis; search and browse the internet; efficiently and effectively make presentations and printouts; as well as the disparity that occurs because of their intellectual and educational abilities. With the increased dependence on the computer to support teaching, learning and assessment may doubly disadvantage some students.

The Luddite response might be to reduce the level of use of computers. However, history tells us that progress is relentless. We must use the affordances of ICT to meet the challenges presented by ICT.

Howard Besser has written an interesting paper called 'The next digital divides', in which he contends that 'you must begin focusing public attention on a whole range of other digital disparity gaps [not just access to hardware], including: effective use of information, the ability for an information user to be more than a passive consumer, and the availability of relevant, useful, appropriate, and affordable content' (Besser, 2001). There are implications for how we present the issues relating to the pervasive use of ICT in schools and society in general.

A SUMMARY OF **KEY POINTS**

> **The pervasive use of ICT in teaching has important implications.**

> **Moral and ethical teaching is important but challenging.**

> **There are good opportunities to teach aspects of PSHE through the use of ICT.**

> **The digital divide continues to exist and changes are making the divide more significant for the disenfranchised members of society.**

REFERENCES REFERENCES **REFERENCES** REFERENCES **REFERENCES** REFERENCES

BBC (2006) *Bitesize.* London: BBC. **www.bbc.co.uk/schools/gcsebitesize**

Besser, H (2001) The next digital divides. *Teaching to Change LA*, 1: 2. **www.newliteracies. gseis.ucla.edu/publications/Digital%20Divide%20article.doc**

QCA (1999) *The National Curriculum programmes of study and attainment targets.* London: HMSO.

SamLearning (2006) **www.samlearning.com**

14
ICT and citizenship

By the end of this chapter you should:

- **have identified the connections between citizenship and your subject;**
- **understand how ICT can support your knowledge of citizenship;**
- **know how ICT can be used to support your teaching of citizenship in your subject;**
- **appreciate the contribution the ICT curriculum makes to citizenship.**

Professional Standards for QTS

Q4, Q7b, Q15, Q17, Q23

This chapter addresses the QTS standards relating to your knowledge and understanding of relevant statutory and non-statutory curricular frameworks, namely the teaching of citizenship. It shows how the curriculum can be taught using ICT. There is an emphasis on communicating effectively through a number of web-based technologies and other technologies such as vox-pop recordings. By applying similar strategies in your own subject area, you will be contributing to the requirement to use ICT and e-learning in your teaching. You will also be using ICT in your wider professional activities.

Introduction

Citizenship education has been part of the National Curriculum in the UK since 2002. The citizenship curriculum is designed to ensure that students learn self-confidence and socially and morally responsible behaviour extending beyond the classroom, towards those in authority and towards each other. Students should also learn about becoming helpfully involved in the life and concerns of their neighbourhood and communities. Schools encourage citizenship through community involvement and service to the community. Citizenship is also concerned with students learning about the institutions, problems and practices of our democracy. It is about how students can become effective in the life of the nation, locally, regionally and nationally. These intentions form three interrelated strands that run through education for citizenship:

1. knowledge and understanding about becoming an informed citizen;
2. developing skills of enquiry and communication;
3. developing skills of participation and responsible action (QCA, 1999a, p184).

There are direct parallels with aspects of the ICT curriculum reflected in the following statements drawn from the programmes of study.

'Information and communication technology (ICT) prepares students to participate in a rapidly changing world in which work and other activities are increasingly transformed by access to varied and developing technology'. Students are also expected to use ICT to 'access ideas and experiences from a wide range of people, communities and cultures'.

They should also consider 'its implications for home and work both now and in the future' (QCA, 1999b, p14).

The challenge to modern society is to motivate citizens, particularly the young, to be active and engaged in society and in the political process. People have to face rapid changes in society, produced by commercial activities and technological developments. To enable democratic societies to survive, citizens need to participate in political and common processes. The aim of citizenship education is to encourage students to be active and engaged citizens. Citizenship exposes students to a range of materials from government sources, quangos, commercial organisations and pressure groups. Students need to establish informed and balanced judgements. ICT facilitates the breadth of material necessary. 'ICT has revolutionised the way we see the world. The use of electronic communication has simplified tasks and expanded boundaries, but the accompanying responsibilities must be understood and implemented' (DfES, 2004).

PRACTICAL TASK PRACTICAL TASK PRACTICAL TASK PRACTICAL TASK PRACTICAL TASK

Consider the strands of citizenship outlined above and identify areas of your own curriculum area that reflect similar aspects of learning. Visit the DfES citizenship curriculum website (www.dfes.gov.uk/citizenship) and explore the information designed to brief teachers.

Explore the resources and download relevant pages of the Citizenship CPD handbook (DfES, 2005). Annotate some pages with your own reflections and opinions and use this as part of your evidence for meeting the standards. You will also be evidencing your use of ICT to support your own continuing professional development.

Hint: To find this document you may have to carry out a Google search for DfES 'Making sense of citizenship'.

Citizenship across the curriculum

Citizenship is more than a subject of the National Curriculum. It is an experience and a body of knowledge that draws from all other areas. The statutory teaching requirements for citizenship include many references to other National Curriculum subjects. The table below outlines additional activities that support the teaching of subjects using ICT.

Identify a citizenship element to a lesson you will be teaching in the near future. Amend your planning sheet to add the extra learning outcome and any necessary resources. Include the keywords you will use and some points to aid your plenary session. Here are some examples from across the curriculum.

English	use leaflets and the associated websites of local places of interest as the resource for some persuasive writing: 'come to . . . it's the place to be'
Mathematics	download the national and local statistics for council spending upon different services and use them as the focus of discussion and presentation in the form of charts
Science	identify a local environmental issue and use the internet for research – present the findings as a collage of printouts
ICT	initiate a discussion of the local facilities for using the internet, including libraries, cafes and pubs, local WiFi hot-spots and local suppliers of computer hardware and services
Design and Technology	through the internet identify a small number of local engineering/production plants that use techniques related to the students' current skills development or topic area
Geography	by enabling the students to use a mapping website, they locate and identify parish, local council, parliamentary constituency, county and national boundaries within, say, a 10-mile radius of the school
History	using an MP3 player/recorder to capture the voices of older members of the community – saving them to a CD or the student's e-portfolio or the school's learning platform
MFL	raise awareness of village, town and city twinning and the opportunities to use e-mail to correspond with people in the target language
Music	raise awareness of local bands and organisations supporting musical events – use the internet to research and produce a community 'local events' noticeboard for display in the music department
Art	raise awareness of local board artists (contemporary or historic), artists in residence and local employment for artist by showing the class a small collection of websites you have discovered through a search engine
PE	raise awareness and encourage participation in local activities or competitive sport by asking students to search the internet and report back the following week
RE	support the students in their use of a web search engine and a mapping website to research the number and location of local religious groups and buildings, for example, **maps.google.co.uk** and **www.streetmap.co.uk**
PSHE	using a web search engine and a mapping website, research the number and location of local health-related organisations and buildings and present them to the students as a map

Fig. 42. Enabling citizenship across the curriculum using ICT

The e-word and the pervasive nature of ICT

The ever-pervasive developments in computer-based technologies have touched upon all aspects of life. Many traditional activities have been profoundly changed or alternative structures and activities have developed. The language has changed too. Traditional activities such as learning, mail, commerce, banking, shopping, etc., have developed a parallel set of activities: e-learning, e-mail, e-commerce, e-banking, e-shopping, etc. Two new words in the citizenship vocabulary are 'e-democracy' and 'e-government'. E-democracy is the two-way process between the citizen and another citizen, politician or council; and e-government is a one-way process of government services being offered and accessed online.

Citizenship has its e-citizenship parallels influenced by developments in ICT. In the same way that ICT can have influence in other areas, it can both support the way that citizenship is taught and it can change the way citizenship is taught. Importantly, it has changed the citizenship curriculum because citizenship is also about the online participation in an online society. Your students need to be ICT competent to prevent them from being disenfranchised from some aspects of government.

ICT supporting the teaching of citizenship

The programmes of study for citizenship require students to access a large amount of information. ICT can help increase knowledge and understanding of being informed citizens by providing access through the internet to a vast body of otherwise inaccessible information.

Citizenship and good social relationships are underpinned by communication. ICT provides support for the traditional means of communicating through speech and writing. Tape recorders and voice recorders have advantages over open and informal discussion. The students become more precise in what they are saying if it is recorded and if they are aware that others will listen to it. Using a word processor can enhance the presentation of the written form and, for some, it makes it easier to produce the work. The use of cloze procedure and writing frames helps direct, structure and encourage students' writing.

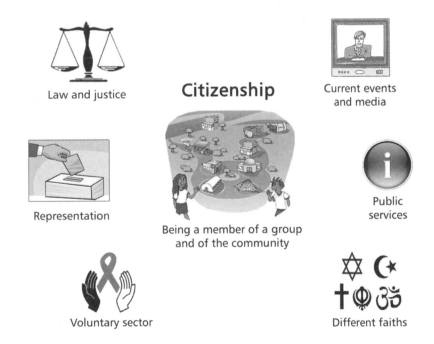

Law and justice

Citizenship

Current events and media

Representation

Being a member of a group and of the community

Public services

Voluntary sector

Different faiths

Fig. 44. Citizenship picture map

The use of computer simulations and other interactive materials encourages students to ask 'what if...?' questions and examine consequences. Simulations permit safe explorations and rehearsals of scenarios that might be hazardous or unavailable to students in real life.

Multimedia, the combination of different forms of presentation, can encourage learning processes by visual and auditory stimulation and not just the written word. The use of an interactive whiteboard, software and the internet can create dynamic, enjoyable and imaginative lessons. Images can be powerful in learning and the internet is a prolific source of photographs; for example, drug users, the effects of alcohol, anti-social behaviour, etc.

The use of the internet in teaching can enable a better focus on the learning topic. This subject-orientation or contextualisation encourages active and explorative learning with the teacher acting as a guide rather than the font of all knowledge. This approach encourages independent learning. The classroom use of a projector and screen can make clearer learning objectives and outcomes and a clearer focus for discussions. The use of a picturemap display to represent and remind you and your students of the different aspects of the topic.

ICT changing the teaching of citizenship

There are a number of recent technology developments that have changed the way in which we teach. The communication aspects of citizenship have changed from simply writing text to many different forms, including text messaging, e-mail, blogs, chat rooms, wikis and bulletin boards let students discuss ideas. Recent research has highlighted the value of these media even when the discussions remain limited to the audience of the immediate class. The following table highlights some of the advantages and challenges of the new forms of communication within the classroom environment.

The main advantage and challenge of all of these forms of computer-based communication (CMC) is that it opens up the potential of communicating beyond the classroom. Students can seek advice from and present their ideas to both other students and adults beyond the classroom and outside your control or influence. You must be aware of internet safety issues discussed earlier. An important aspect of online communication is that the anonymity of ICT lets students experiment with roles, personae and opinions. Students adopting different avatars can enable them to see other people's points of view better.

Ground rules for talk

One teaching programme that has been successful in improving the quality of learning was based around how to understand and apply the following ground rules for talk:

- **all relevant information is shared;**
- **the group seeks to reach agreement;**
- **the group takes responsibility for decisions;**
- **reasons are expected;**
- **challenges are accepted;**
- **alternatives are discussed before a decision is taken;**
- **all in the group are encouraged to speak by other group members.**

This approach has been found to encourage students' use of 'exploratory talk', an educationally effective way of discussing and negotiating ideas with one another. A full description of this approach to teaching, including many of the lesson plans, is now available from **www.thinkingtogether.org.uk** (Dawes et al., 2004).

English and ICT – the National Curriculum for Key Stage 3 makes direct reference to students experiencing group discussions and interaction including exploring, hypothesising, debating

ICT facilities	Common examples	Strengths	Challenges
bulletin boards, hypermail, forum	**www.tes.co.uk** **www.talkingteaching.co.uk**	responded to by interest groups and so relevant information; it is an open and shared experience supporting social constructivism; asynchronous so students do not have to be online at the same time	difficult to encourage student participation; monitoring and moderation procedures have to be in place
chat (IRC)	MSN Messenger Yahoo Messenger	closed; users need only ever meet 'friends'	exposure to inappropriate content and language, off-task behaviour
chat rooms	UK.Teachers.Net **uk.teachers.net**	School-based chat rooms are secure from outsider intrusion and when moderated provide a safer environment for collaborative work than e-mail	little control over who you might meet in open rooms; exposure to inappropriate language
e-mail	Hotmail, school-based mail services,	One-to-one and one-to-many; efficient use of time; well-known technology	spam; viruses
text (SMS)	RU up 4 IT	in vogue; web-based texting is free	secret from the teacher
blogs		reflective, archived, open	public accessibility unless restricted to a learning platform
wiki	Wikipedia	reading for purpose, current	is it authoritative?
web cams	Traffic **www.romanse.org.uk** Countryside **www.wasdaleweb.co.uk** Cityscape **www.camvista.com/ england/london** and many more **www.bbc.co.uk/england/ webcams**	motivating and add context to the teaching	perhaps encourages exploration of inappropriate web cams
web presence	intranet, VLE or e-portfolio presentations	the student has total control of the material; not exposed to inappropriate comment	can be technically challenging
RSS	BBC services	current and up to date	new, unfamiliar technology

Fig. 43. ICT and CMC strengths and challenges

and analysing as well as the students taking different roles in organising or leading discussions. 'Interaction may be face-to-face or by electronic means' (QCA, 1999a, p48).

Teaching ICT capability through citizenship

Through citizenship lessons students can be taught to be systematic in considering the information they need and to discuss how it will be used and how to obtain information well matched to purpose by selecting appropriate sources, using and refining search methods and questioning the plausibility and value of the information found.

There are models available that enable students to use ICT to test predictions and discover patterns and relationships, by exploring, evaluating and developing those models and changing their rules and values.

An example drawn from mathematics is modelling the effects on screen by asking the students to draw shapes using a LOGO program.

Unit 8.4 of the Key Stage 3 Strategy for ICT capability is 'Models and presenting numeric data'. It builds on Unit 7.4, which introduces students to using spreadsheets for modelling, and for presenting numeric data. **www.standards.dfes.gov.uk/keystage3/respub/ ictsampley8**

When presenting their views and reflections upon their responsibilities, students can be taught how to interpret information and to reorganise and present it in a variety of forms that are fit for purpose. They should be using a range of ICT tools efficiently to draft, bring together and refine information and create good-quality presentations in a form that is sensitive to the needs of particular audiences and suits the information content.

Citizenship lessons provide opportunities for students to be taught to use a wide range of ICT facilities, including e-mail, to share and exchange information effectively, for example, web publishing, video conferencing. The curriculum encourages students to use current events as project topics, including: human rights, animal welfare, environmental issues, criminal justice system, religious issues, nuclear armament, etc. Current global economic and political data can be used to contextualise spreadsheet and data-handling activities.

The citizenship curriculum has a special focus on enabling students to reflect critically on their own and others' behaviour and attitudes. This can include sharing their views and experiences of ICT, considering the range of its uses and talking about its significance to individuals, communities and society. The discussions should consider how they might use ICT in future work and how they would judge its effectiveness, using relevant technical terms. This would lead to our students being more independent and discriminating when using ICT.

> 'During Key Stage 3 pupils become increasingly independent users of ICT tools and information sources.'
>
> 'They think about the quality and reliability of information, and access and combine increasing amounts of information.'

Students should be taught 'to be systematic in considering the information they need and to discuss how it will be used'.

Students should be taught 'how to obtain information well matched to purpose by selecting appropriate sources, using and refining search methods and questioning the plausibility and value of the information found'.

Students should be taught 'how to collect, enter, analyse and evaluate quantitative and qualitative information, checking its accuracy'.

'During the key stage, pupils should be taught the knowledge, skills and understanding through working with others to explore a variety of information sources and ICT tools in a variety of contexts.'

Extracts drawn from the National Curriculum for information and communication technology (QCA, 1999b).

ICT changing the citizenship curriculum

The impact of ICT on the role of the citizen and therefore upon citizenship education is immense. It impacts upon the way in which democratic processes occur, the way in which government informs and controls and the way in which we communicate with the organisations in authority.

Democracy is a three-phase process. The first phase is information transfer; we seek and are given information about prospective representatives. Those representatives also canvas our vote by sending out and proclaiming their views and opinions. The second phase is the election where we make our choice. The third phase is the communication between elected representative and their constituents.

E-democracy is about participating in a government or democratic activity online, or using the internet and e-mail to further a cause or express an opinion. Developments that are more recent include podcasting and RSS whereby we automatically receive updates and changes to information from our selected websites. In the first phase of the democratic process the traditional procedure has been for the candidates to influence the voters by the use of argument. The power of the internet to unite disparate people with common causes is now enabling the voters to influence the messages of the candidates. In the third phase of the democratic process, the ability to connect people from all over the world who share the same beliefs and principles through a website or e-mail discussion group could be a factor in changing government policies. E-mail and text messaging have made it much easier to contact representatives, such as councillors, MEPs and MPs. This may enable a better partnership between the elected and their constituents.

School links

As schools develop their citizenship, social, language and geographical educational opportunities, the forming of links with schools in other parts of the country and in other countries is becoming more popular. Linking is not simply making the occasional or regular exchange visits but it is the sustained communication between two or more institutions at all levels of the school structure. The use of e-mail, web cams, web conferencing, chat and SMS can sustain those communications on a one-to-one basis. However, schools are exchanging information through their websites, bulletin boards (for sustained open/shared conversations), mail groups (for mass mailing) and chat rooms. These links provide interest and motivation in many areas of the curriculum including food technology, religious education, geography and modern foreign languages.

PRACTICAL TASK PRACTICAL TASK PRACTICAL TASK PRACTICAL TASK PRACTICAL TASK

Identify a controversial issue that relates to your curriculum area. Use a handheld camcorder and set up a 'vox pop' area for students to express their opinions. The area could be decorated with images drawn from the internet and keywords related to the issue.

---

vox populi, n.[Latin] the voice of the people; popular opinion. Abbr.:vox pop

Art and design	lottery money expenditure on fine art or supporting community activities
Design and Technology	use of hardwoods from virgin forest; sustainable forestry
English	understanding novels such as *The Crucible* in the light of current politics
Geography	global warming and the impact of travel, consumption and recycling
History	holocaust denials
ICT	open-source software; issues of piracy, copyright and plagiarism
Mathematics	use of statistics to prove, confuse or mislead
MFL	current socio/political/economic relationships with target language country
Music	attitudes to music piracy, copyright, sales and promotion through the internet
PE	drugs and sporting events
Science	understanding disease and risk: Creutzfeldt–Jakob disease, avian 'flu, foot-and-mouth, inoculation
RE	orthodox and militant religious activity

Fig. 44. Vox pop ideas

E-government

E-government includes the use of the internet and other ICT facilities to inform the population of laws and regulations and for individuals to seek information directly from government sources. The *Modernising government* White Paper sets out a target for all government services, local and national. The following sites can be used to illustrate the principles of e-government facilities or to locate information to support citizenship lessons and debates.

Direct government **www.direct.gov.uk**

Health and welfare services, for example, NHS Direct **www.nhsdirect.nhs.uk**

Revenue services, for example, online tax returns **www.hmrc.gov.uk/sa**

Education services, for example, National Grid for Learning (NGfL) **www.ngfl.gov.uk**

Licensing and enforcement services, for example, Driver and Vehicle Licensing Authority **www.dvla.gov.uk**

Government has recognised the value of online services and has passed a number of laws and established roles within ministries ensuring that e-government is viable.

E-literacy

Associated with the increasing ICT competencies of people within the community is the concept of e-literacy, digital literacy or media literacy. In 2001 the Department for Culture, Media and Sport issued a policy statement on media literacy and critical viewing skills. It states:

> With an increased awareness of the importance of media literacy, there is an environment developing that should be more receptive to a structured learning programme designed to inculcate critical viewing skills. Beyond these, broadcasters and other service providers need to start thinking about their own responsibility to foster well-informed and critical viewers...

Media literacy is defined by the UK Department for Culture, Media and Sport as the ability 'to appraise critically, and assess the relative value of, information from different sources, and gain competencies in understanding the construction, forms, strengths and limitations of screen based content'. Ofcom, the Office of Communications, is the regulator responsible for the UK communications sector, and the Communications Bill gives Ofcom the function of promoting media literacy. The communications White Paper, *A new future for communications*, elaborates on the Bill and with regard to media literacy states that 'Ofcom will promote systems to help people make informed choices about what they and their children see and hear; and have a duty to promote media literacy, working with DfES, the industries and educators' (MediaSmart, 2001).

A useful resource relating to e-literacy is Paul Gilster's **www.ibiblio.org/cisco/noc/ primer.html**

PRACTICAL TASK PRACTICAL TASK PRACTICAL TASK PRACTICAL TASK PRACTICAL TASK

As a citizen, go on to the internet and identify the latest proceedings of government relating to education. *Hint:* www.parliament.uk

www.explore.parliament.uk

Consider whether the internet access could mean that you would follow the issues more closely. Are you more likely to join in a debate with colleagues?

Visit the BECTa website and follow these links to the e-citizenship page:

BECTa > Learning & teaching > Citizenship & PSHE > What is e-citizenship?

schools.becta.org.uk/index.php?section=tl&catcode=as_cu_sec_sub_02&rid=1800

FURTHER READING FURTHER READING FURTHER READING FURTHER READING

Association for Citizenship Teaching (ACT) **www.teachingcitizenship.org.uk**

Citizenship Education: the global dimension **www.citizenship-global.org.uk**

Citizenship Foundation **www.citfou.org.uk**

Council for Education in World Citizenship (CEWC) **www.cewc.org.uk**

Department for Culture, Media and Sport (DCMS) **www.culture.gov.uk**. The DCMS is responsible for government policy on the arts, sport, the National Lottery, tourism, libraries, museums and galleries, broadcasting, creative industries including film and the music industry, press freedom and regulation, licensing, gambling and the historic environment. It sees media-literacy as being an important element in its strategy to ensure inclusion, sustainability and sustainable communities. **www.culture.gov.uk/PDF/media_lit_2001.pdf**

Department for Education and Skills citizenship website **www.dfes.gov.uk/citizenship**

MediaSmart **www.mediasmart.org.uk/media_literacy** Media Smart is a independent media literacy programme providing students with the tools to help them understand and interpret advertising.

National Institute of Adult Continuing Education **www.niace.org.uk** NIACE is a non-governmental organisation supporting adult learners. **www.niace.org.uk/information/Briefing_sheets/39_ICT.pdf** ICT in active citizenship.

TeacherNet **www.teachernet.gov.uk/supportpack** an excellent set of short video clips to develop your understanding of teaching citizenship through ICT.

Thinking Together **www.thinkingtogether.org.uk**

Virtual Teacher Centre **vtc.ngfl.gov.uk/docserver.php?temid=59** citizenship area

A SUMMARY OF **KEY POINTS**

> **The challenge to modern society is to motivate citizens, particularly the young, to be active and engaged in society and in the political process – you have a responsibility in that activity.**

> **There is a direct connection between your subject and the citizenship curriculum that you should exploit to reinforce citizenship education.**

> **ICT has an important role in developing your knowledge of citizenship.**

> **ICT has an important role in supporting your teaching of citizenship in your subject.**

USEFUL WEB LINKS USEFUL WEB LINKS USEFUL WEB LINKS USEFUL WEB LINKS

British Council: go to **www.britishcouncil.org** and enter 'school link' into their search engine.

The World Ecitizens Project on **www.worldecitizens.net** aims to encourage understanding between peoples and communities and to share the fascinating diversity within nations and across the world.

Link Community Development on **www.lcd.org.uk** – click the 'Link Schools Programme' button.

The School Leaders Zone of the GlobalGateway, **www.globalgateway.org.uk**, suggests that the international dimension is enriching for any subject and is essential for up-to-date citizenship/PSHE.

Internationalism is increasingly seen as a way to move schools into the future and makes a great focus for school development plans. You are most likely to meet the impact of these developments in your subject area because the school can attract funding, and you gain from increased interest from parents and the local community. The DfES released in 2005 the first of its Action Plans outlining how internationalism will be brought into schools:

www.globalgateway.org.uk/Default.aspx?page=2119

Times Educational Supplement 'make the link' page on **www.tes.co.uk/make_the_link**

REFERENCES   REFERENCES   **REFERENCES**   REFERENCES   **REFERENCES**
REFERENCES

Dawes, L, Mercer, N, and Wegerif, R (2004) *Thinking together: A programme of activities for developing speaking, listening and thinking skills.* Birmingham: Imaginative Minds.

DfES (2004) *ICT across the curriculum: Citizenship.* London: Department for Education and Skills.

DfES (2005) *Making sense of citizenship.* **www.dfes.gov.uk/citizenship/section.cfm?sectionID=1&hierachy=1&articleID=157**

MediaSmart (2001) *Media literacy.* **www.mediasmart.org.uk/media_literacy**

QCA (1999a) *The National Curriculum programmes of study and attainment targets.* London: HMSO.

QCA (1999b) *Information and communication technology.* London: HMSO.

15
Using ICT to support your research and studies

By the end of this chapter you should:

- be proficient in carrying out internet searches for teaching resources and academic references;
- be able to utilise Athens and other specialist services for accessing e-journals;
- be able to use synchronous and asynchronous techniques to solicit information through the internet;
- be able to handle inaccurate references to web pages;
- be able to cite and list references accurately and have a higher awareness of plagiarism;
- understand the ethical issues associated with classroom-based and online research.

Professional Standards for QTS

Q2, Q3, Q4, Q7b, Q13

This chapter addresses the QTS standards relating to your professional duties and your professional development. It also considers the requirements that ensure you communicate effectively, use research and statistical data to support your teaching and use ICT to support your wider professional activities; and through ethical research show the positive values, attitudes and behaviour expected of your students.

Introduction

During your training, you will be given opportunities and perhaps the requirement to present your understanding of the education processes in a formal way. Many routes to QTS, particularly those at postgraduate level, include searching the academic literature and presenting the results of your own research in the format of Masters level assignments. The first part of this chapter deals with exploring the web and gaining information that already exists. There are implications for classroom teaching and developing similar skills with your students in school. There is also advice on how citations/references should be structured and can be managed using software. The second part considers the issues and techniques when using the internet to solicit information. There is a discussion of research methods, data collection and the use of information-analysis software.

An important question to ask is 'why classroom research by teachers?' A strong response comes from David Hopkins, who considers that the issue influences professionalism, classroom practice, the social control of teachers and the usefulness of educational research. We need to justify our claim to be professional because 'systematic self-study is a hallmark of those occupations that enjoy the label professional' (Hopkins, 2004, p31). The importance of the role of research in the work of teachers is reflected in the resources and support for research provided by the government, its agencies and other public bodies:

www.dfes.gov.uk/research The Department for Education and Skills Research site provides details of all the research the Department has commissioned or published since 1997. It is also the gateway for those wishing to participate in DfES-sponsored and commissioned research.

www.becta.org.uk 'What the Research Says' papers, including:

- **What the Research Says about ICT and classroom organisation**
  www.becta.org.uk/page_documents/research/wtrs_classroom.pdf
- **What the Research Says about ICT and reducing teacher workloads**
  www.becta.org.uk/page_documents/research/wtrs_workloads.pdf
- **What the Research Says about portable ICT devices**
  www.becta.org.uk/page_documents/research/wtrs_porticts.pdf
- **What the Research Says about VLEs in teaching and learning**
  www.becta.org.uk/page_documents/research/wtrs_vles.pdf

ICT in Schools Research and Evaluation Series – No.18 is a most significant review of the research literature about ICT and pedagogy (Cox *et al.*, 2003). **www.becta.org.uk/page_-documents/research/ict_pedagogy_summary.pdf**

www.scre.ac.uk The Scottish Council for Research in Education Centre (SCRE) has been supporting Scottish education through research since 1928; it conducts educational research and supports the use of research outcomes through the dissemination of findings.

www.nerf-uk.org The remit of the National Education Research Forum (NERF) is to transform educational research in United Kingdom, communicate modern research practice and share ideas.

www.hero.ac.uk Higher Education and Research Opportunities (HERO) is the gateway to UK universities, further and higher education colleges providing support for research.

www.nfer.ac.uk The National Foundation for Educational Research (NFER) is the UK's leading independent research organisation carrying out research in the field of education.

Searching the web

The internet is an open system for publication – anyone may display information and opinion. Consequently, there is a wide range of material and great variation in the quality of that material. Information should be considered in terms of accuracy, validity, reliability, credibility and accessibility. Before making use of any material, you must consider its provenance and whether you consider it authoritative.

The authorship, credibility and authenticity of internet documents are relatively difficult to establish and special care must be taken when using such documents for social science research. 'Internet documents, therefore, needed to be subjected to the researcher's own quality audit along the lines recommended in relation to books and journals – but with even more vigour and rigour' (Denscombe, 1998, p160).

If you are given a website reference, the URL gives many clues to its source – those ending with, edu, edu.xx or ac.uk indicate educational and academic sources, whereas com, com.xx or co.uk indicate independent commercial or private sites. The ending gov relates to public government sites and org indicates independent organisations which includes charities, Quangos and NGOs. You must consider the degree of influence the owner of the site has over the content of the individual pages submitted and whether that influence is a positive and ethical one or not.

You would consider a site ending in ac.uk to be acceptable as it is a UK-based, further or higher education establishment controlled through and inspected by a range of government agencies. In general, the rule is that if the traditional, paper-based publications of an organisation are 'trusted' then the pages of their website can be trusted, with the proviso that some organisations allow the public to express views on their web pages or the organisation has published a disclaimer.

Search engines and searching techniques

Search engines indiscriminately list the pages containing the keywords of the search. The basic prioritisation is in the number or level of matches between the keywords of the page and the search criteria. However, the search engine determines the pages found. Consider the commercial motivation of the search engine and the techniques available to web page writers for ensuring that the search engine displays their pages.

What are the criteria for choosing a search engine? Speed, display design, advertising, sponsorship . . .

In research terms, search engines are not new. Historically, libraries have employed a range of techniques, based upon cataloguing, citation indexes and cross-referencing to help researchers find the information that is present in traditional material: books, journals, pamphlets and newspapers. What is different is the speed of searching and the confidence we have that if the computer says there are no references to our topic within a website, that in fact, there is no reference.

It is important to note that none of the search engines is better than the quality of the web pages it is searching. Further, the relevance of the material discovered is dependent upon the search techniques deployed.

Being competent in searching for information and images is a very useful teacher skill. The majority of search engines have 'Help' pages associated with them. You should scan the support pages associated with your most frequently used search engine. Different search engines have different rules with regard to entering complex search criteria. However, like database programs they are generally based on 'Boolean' principles of using AND, OR and NOT. For example:

- **'battle' AND 'horse' reveals only those pages containing both the keywords 'battle' and 'horse'**
- **'napoli' OR 'pompeii' reveals all the pages with either of the keywords 'napoli' or 'pompeii'**
- **'python' NOT 'monty' would reveal all the 'python' pages but not those with 'monty'**

Some criteria narrow down the search results while others broaden them.

The Google search engine is very popular. The particular advanced search strategies it employs enables you to search only for pages:

- **that contain all the search terms you type in;**
- **that contain the exact phrase you type in;**
- **that contain at least one of the words you type in;**
- **that do not contain any of the words you type in;**
- **written in a certain language;**
- **created in a certain file format;**
- **that have been updated within a certain period of time;**
- **that contain numbers within a certain range;**
- **within a certain domain, or website;**
- **that don't contain 'adult' material.**

The Google support page gives a lot more information about searching strategies: **www.google.co.uk/support**

PRACTICAL TASK PRACTICAL TASK PRACTICAL TASK PRACTICAL TASK PRACTICAL TASK

- **Investigate and evaluate the following three websites designed for exploring information. They have strong visual elements to the display of results.**
- **KartOO is a meta-search engine with visual display interfaces** – www.kartoo.com
- **Touch Graph** – www.touchgraph.com
- **Visual Thesaurus** – www.visualthesaurus.com
- **Consider the implications for students' learning about a particular topic.**
- **Attempt to capture the screen display and use it in supporting resources for a lesson.**

TECHNICAL TIP
On a Windows^{TM} PC press the PrtScr key – this makes a copy of the screen image on the clipboard. It can then be pasted into a word processor or edited with an art program. Using Alt + PrtScr captures just the current window.
On Linux and Apple computers use the Grab or KSnapshot programs and capture either part or all of the screen or a window. The image is copied to clipboard or saved and then used in word processing or edited with an art program.
en.wikipedia.org/wiki/print_screen
en.wikipedia.org/wiki/Grab_(software)
docs.kde.org/stable/en/kdegraphics/ksnapshot

The wrong URL

The error messages 'Not Found – the requested URL was not found on this server' or 'Can't find the server' are usually the result of:

- **writing down a URL incorrectly, carelessly or inaccurately;**
- **entering the URL incorrectly or carelessly;**
- **a web page having been renamed or deleted.**

It is a basic ICT skill that we teach our students precision in their ICT work. In Key Stage 2, students should be taught 'how to prepare information ... using ICT ... checking it for accuracy' (QCA, 1999, p18).

If a URL does not work, there are various steps to take:

1. Check that it has been entered correctly – letter by letter, upper/lower case is important, special characters sometimes 'move' on the keyboard, the underscore character _ is frequently missed.
2. Check the syntax – does it seem to be OK or has it been typed incorrectly in the source material?
3. Shorten the URL in an attempt to find a page that can be loaded. It may then be possible to see links to the referenced page. For example, the following reference to the PGCE course handbook will be unsuccessful but it is possible to discover it by shortening the URL: **www.pgce.soton.ac.uk/it/handbook/handbook.doc**.
4. Return to the source document and identify keywords that can be used in a search engine.
5. 'Not Found – the requested URL was not found on this server' usually means the error is after the first / symbol.
6. 'Can't find the server' usually means the error is before the first / symbol.

Modern web browsers have the facility to bookmark a web page. That is, it enters the reference (URL) into a list. In the future, clicking on the reference (bookmark) can retrieve that page. Some software allows the option to bookmark and save for reading offline – in this way a shorter period of time is spent on the internet and more time can be spent reading the pages identified while browsing.

PRACTICAL TASK PRACTICAL TASK PRACTICAL TASK PRACTICAL TASK PRACTICAL TASK

- **Write down (with neat handwriting) a URL so that another person can enter it correctly.**
- **Decide, by looking at them, which of the following URLs are correct and which would not work**
- **Before trying the URLs, write down a generic description for a URL:**
  it must have ...
  it must not have ...
  it might have ...
- **When you have tried the URLs, identify what simple error has prevented them working.**
- **If you expected them not to work and they did, what changes to your description of a URL must you make?**

http://www.bbc.co.uk	www.soton.ac.uk	www.sheffield,ac.uk	www.mit.edu
http://yahoo.com	http://www.tamworth.ac.uk	jason@soton.ac.uk	http://www.jason@soton.ac.uk
www.projectgcse.co.uk	WwW.sOtOn.Ac.Uk	BECTa.org.uk	http://www.ofsted.gov.uk/publications/
http://www.dfes.gov.uk/Aboutus	http://www.dfes.gov.uk/aboutus	http://www.nc.uk.net	'www.teachernet.gov.uk'

Fig. 45. URLs right or wrong

Make sure that you have a good internet connection, then see how quickly you can locate the following resources:

- a copy of *Treatise on parents and children* by George Bernard Shaw (or another book relevant to your subject area) from the Project Gutenberg Online Book Catalog www.gutenberg.org;
- this week's copy of the *Times Educational Supplement* www.tes.co.uk;
- a detailed map of your placement school using Digimap edina.ac.uk/digimap (Athens login required); and
- a location map identifying the main catchment area www.streetmap.co.uk.

Keeping up to date

There are many ways of staying up to date with the latest research and resources. Many of the databases mentioned above have alerting services. For example, the Zetoc is a database of the tables of contents of the British Library's current journals and conference proceedings. Zetoc Alert allows you to receive e-mail alerts as new issues of relevant journals are published: **zetoc.mimas.ac.uk**

Many e-journals also allow you to register for contents pages to be e-mailed to you as new issues appear. Both IngentaConnect **www.ingentaconnect.com** and SARA **www.tandf.co.uk/sara** provide alerting services, which forward contents pages of forthcoming journals from various publishers to you by e-mail.

TECHNICAL TIP
It can be very convenient to work from home but some resources that are available on the internet from a university computer cannot be accessed from other computers. The usual solution is to use a VPN (virtual private network) service. While using your computer and connected to the internet using your usual connection, you set up a VPN connection. Your college or university will have to provide the details in the form of server address, account name and password. Using VPN should enable you to access all of your library resources, e-journals and other locally based information services from your home.

Writing references in your work

Citing other people's work and using the correct referencing format are essential. From an academic standpoint, you are allowing the reader to trace your line of research. From an ethical standpoint, your acknowledgement of the work of others is ensuring you are not committing plagiarism. The style of referencing and citation varies across institutions and publications. Once you know which system you are using, it is important that you are consistent.

The 'Harvard system' is frequently recommended but even within the Harvard system you will see variations in approach. If you are in any doubt, then consult your tutor. Here is an example definition of citation and referencing which the publisher Learning Matters uses.

After a reference to a publication show author's surname and date of publication in brackets, separated by a comma – (Littleton, 2001).

If a direct quote has been given in the body of the text, also insert the page number – (Tatton, 1999, p23).

The presentation of references takes the format:

Books	Williams, C (2001) *Behaviour management in the primary school.* London: Routledge
Chapters in edited books	Durrant, P (1989) Assessment for ICT at Key Stage 1, in Hutton, L (ed) *Developing ICT in the primary school.* Exeter: Learning Matters
Articles in journals	Wigglesworth, D (2002) Talking and learning in young children. *Journal of Educational Psychology,* 52: 1–36

Note the use of italics to indicate the title of the publication. Some conventions allow the use of underscore as an alternative. I strongly recommend that the use of underscore is restricted to indicating URLs or hypertext links.

Checklist of skills

Spend time on the internet to ensure that you are competent and confident to:

- **carry out a general search of the internet;**
- **carry out a 'complex' search using Boolean operators;**
- **use several search engines;**
- **identify a search engine that you will use regularly;**
- **try using a meta- or site-based search engine;**
- **visit your library website, identify the availability of e-journals;**
- **visit an indexing website;**
- **organise your bookmarking system to support your professional writing;**
- **identify a strategy for obtaining material to support your next assignment.**

Bibliographic and referencing software

Bibliographic software, also known as reference-management software, enables you to manage references to journal articles or books of interest to you. It will automatically capture, store and then present the references to material that you have used in your study.

Reference Manager **www.refman.com**
EndNote **www.endnote.com**
ProCite **www.procite.com**
Biblioscape **www.biblioscape.com**

Each has connection files to a range of databases for automatic listing of papers you have read. Each can print or export the references in a range of types with customisable fields.

Plagiarism

Plagiarism is the unauthorised and undeclared copying of written materials with the intention to declare it to be your own. It particularly applies in academic and scientific circles and with the submission of assignments. There is mounting evidence to support the widely expressed concerns that student cheating including plagiarism is common and is on the increase (Park, 2003). Chris Park's paper reviews the literature on plagiarism by students and explores seven themes: 'the meaning and context of plagiarism, the nature of plagiarism by students, how do students perceive plagiarism, how big a problem is student plagiarism, why do students cheat, what challenges are posed by digital plagiarism and is there a need to promote academic integrity?' (Park, 2003, p471). It concludes that the increase in plagiarism is because of the increased accessibility to academic works through the internet and the students' rationalisations of their cheating behaviours. Many higher education institutions employ plagiarism-detection software. Assignments are entered into a growing database and an individual's work is compared with all the other assignments submitted and published work within the database.

As a consequence of the increase in plagiarism, all higher educational institutions are taking steps to deter and detect it. As part of that strategy, there is an increase in the amount of information and advice on how to avoid plagiarism.

Read carefully the advice given by your tutors with regard to plagiarism, quotation, citation and referencing of work.

TEACHING TIP

Plagiarism is an issue in your classroom. With the increased access to inappropriate as well as appropriate materials through the internet, the 'cut-and-paste' mentality of some students and the subsequent lack of engagement in the content of the material, learning is not taking place. The traditional approach was time-consuming and included going to the library, locating the right book and copying out the work by hand. There was a tendency to be minimalist and finding the short, easy passage that met the needs. There was certainly no real motivation to draft and redraft. Consequently, although there was an increased engagement with the words, the refinement process was not extensive.

Another issue is the existence of essay-writing websites. They are often justified on the grounds that they provide the students with useful revision material and they provide models upon which students can base their work. They can lead students into temptation and unless you deal with the situation firmly, may establish a work pattern that will lead the student into much grief in their future studies.

On the one hand, the use of material from the internet can be criticised and frowned upon as copying, stealing, illegal use and breach of copyright; but on the other hand, there are valued genre, creative work based upon satire, parody and caricature.

The steps you must take include:

- ensuring students acknowledge the source of their work;
- raising the awareness of the ethical issues and requirements;
- discussing the moral issues;
- developing paraphrase and précis skills;
- providing opportunities for students to present the ideas in other forms, such as spider diagrams and concept maps.

Ethical issues of ICT-based research

If you are undertaking research with human participants then you should consider the ethical issues. The following questions highlight potential ethical dilemmas. If you answer 'yes' to any of these questions then you need to outline the issue and discuss it with your tutor or mentor before proceeding; the ethical issues should be reported in your assignment or research report.

Are you obtaining informed consent? The word 'informed' is important. Simply saying to the class that you are doing research and 'is that OK?' is not receiving informed consent. If your study involves participants who are particularly vulnerable or unable to give informed consent, such as students with special educational needs, then particular care should be taken. An online questionnaire should have a link to a full explanation of why and how the data are being collected.

Will deception of participants be necessary during the study? For example, the covert observation of members of a chat room or the use of an avatar to conceal your status within a discussion group could be considered 'deception'. It is a principle that studies should be conducted based on obtaining informed consent from all interested parties. The UN Convention on the Rights of the Child article 12 requires you to assure 'the child who is capable of forming his or her own views the right to express those views freely in all matters affecting the child, the views of the child being given due weight in accordance with the age and maturity of the child'. This is also in the spirit of the Children Act (2004) and the Every Child Matters initiative, where choice and destiny are determined by the student and processes are not done to them. **www.everychildmatters.gov.uk**

You may be considering a study involving discussion of topics that the participants would find sensitive, such as sexual activity or drug use. Before carrying out any such activity you should receive the full guidance and permission of mentors and tutors.

If your study involves prolonged or repetitive testing or physical testing such as the use of electronic sports equipment for gathering data for analysis, you must ensure that the best interests of the students are your primary consideration. The UN Convention on the Rights of the Child article 3 reads: 'In all actions concerning children, whether undertaken by public or private social welfare institutions, courts of law, administrative authorities or legislative bodies, the best interests of the child shall be a primary consideration'. **www.ohchr.org**

If financial or other inducements are offered to participants, such as 'respondents will be entered into a draw to win an MP3 player', the implications of undue pressure to participate must be considered. You should also consider the impact of such coercion on the validity of the results.

You must protect the confidentiality of participants. The British Educational Research Association (BERA) guidelines state that the:

> *confidential and anonymous treatment of participants' data is considered the norm for the conduct of research. Researchers must recognise the participants' entitlement to privacy and must accord them their rights to confidentiality and anonymity, unless they or their guardians or responsible others, specifically and willingly waive that right.* (BERA, 2004, p8)

It is in your interest to obtain such permission in writing through the normal school procedures. You, or more likely your school, will obtain permission from the parents of students under the age of 16. It is important to seek the students' permission and make it explicit that they have the right to freely withdraw from the study at any time. The Association of Internet Researchers (Ess, 2002) has a commitment to ensuring that research on and about the internet is conducted in an ethical and professional manner and suggests that on the permission forms are clear statements about the benefits and outcomes of the research.

When working with students in an online environment (VLE or learning platform) it is most important that no aspect of the study should prejudice the safety or welfare of any student involved; access to the school curriculum should not be impeded; and informed consent should be obtained from school management, staff involved, the students and their parents/ guardians/carers. In practice, your school mentor will conduct much of the liaison and the online environment used in school will ensure that students are safe from intrusion.

'Shibboleth' is any word or phrase that can be used to distinguish members of a group from outsiders. In the context of VLEs, it is associating individuals with particular groups or discussions. Although a school's VLE will be accessible by all students, staff and perhaps parents, systems are in place to ensure only appropriate access is made to individual courses, discussion groups, chat rooms and teaching resources. These can either be based upon the individual – the individual is given a number of permission rights – or it is based upon the facility – the facility lists who is allowed access. It is important that you understand the functionality of the VLE so that you can efficiently ensure that appropriate access is made to the resources and courses you prepare for the system.

A SUMMARY OF **KEY POINTS**

> **Classroom-based research has implications for classroom practice, the usefulness of educational research and professionalism.**

> **Technological developments, particularly those associated with the internet and online resources, are continually occurring and they have an almost immediate impact on classroom practice.**

> **The internet enables easy access to research materials, e-journals and colleague researchers.**

> **The ethical issues associated with classroom-based and online research are important, particularly in the light of the Children Act and Every Child Matters.**

REFERENCES REFERENCES **REFERENCES** REFERENCES **REFERENCES** REFERENCES

BERA (2004) *Revised ethical guidelines for educational research.* Southwell: British Educational Research Association.

Cox, M, Webb, M, Abbott, C, Blakeley, B, Beauchamp, T and Rhodes, V (2003) *ICT in schools research and evaluation series No. 18: ICT and pedagogy.* London: Department for Education and Skills. **www.becta.org.uk/page_documents/research/ict_pedagogy_summary.pdf**

Dawson, C (2002) *Practical research methods.* Oxford: HowTo Books.

Denscombe, M (1998) *The good research guide.* Buckingham: Open University Press.

Ess, C (2002) Ethical decision-making and internet research: Recommendations from the AoIR ethics working committee 27 November 2002. Available online at: **www.aoir.org/reports/ethics.pdf**

Hopkins, D (2004) *A teacher's guide to classroom research* (3rd edn). Maidenhead: Open University Press.

Park, C. (2003) In other (peoples) words: Plagiarism by university students – literature and lessons. *Assessment and Evaluation in Higher Education*, 28 (5): 471–488.

QCA (1999) *Information and communication technology.* London: HMSO.

Soloway, E and Wallace, R (1997) Does the internet support student inquiry? Don't ask. *Communications of the ACM archive,* 40 (5): 11–16. New York: ACM Press. **portal.acm.org**

16
Teaching with newer technologies

By the end of this chapter you should:

- **be aware of the changes arising from government initiatives, including Building Schools for the Future, School Workforce Remodelling and Every Child Matters;**
- **have a means of assessing the potential of new ICT-based resources through considering their affordances;**
- **have an insight into the new technologies you may have to work with in the coming years.**

Professional Standards for QTS

Q1, Q2, Q4, Q6, Q7a, Q8, Q10, Q25a, Q26b, Q27

This chapter primarily addresses the QTS standard relating to the use of e-learning in your teaching and the need for you to take a creative and constructively critical approach towards innovation. By completing the tasks and using the technologies, you may be contributing to the requirements: establishing trusting, supportive and constructive relationships with your students; demonstrating positive attitudes; communicating effectively; making a commitment to collaborative and co-operative learning; identifying and meeting your developing professional needs; personalising learning; assessing learning needs; setting challenging objectives and providing timely, accurate and constructive feedback.

Introduction

As has been noted earlier, the ICT curriculum and pedagogy have had a mere 30 years to develop; there has been little time to rationalise from what we know should be taught to how it should be taught and which methods are best. However, before we have become proficient in teaching with one technology, another technology will appear and pose its pedagogic challenges. With their introduction, many technologies start to dominate ICT practice and teaching and learning in general, and much of what we have learnt about using ICT has to be modified or rejected.

It has been established for some time that there are issues with the physical presence of computers in the classroom and that portable ICT devices do not dominate in the same way (BECTa, 2005). The growing affordability of PDAs and XDAs means that they are more frequently found in schools. These devices can be more readily integrated into classroom use and across the curriculum with the minimum disruption to normal classroom practices.

The new design in schools is beginning to facilitate wireless technologies and greater flexibility in the distribution of computing. The 'Building Schools for the Future' (BSF) programme is the biggest single government investment in improving school buildings for over 50 years. With a strapline 'transforming schools, inspiring learning', the aim is to rebuild or renew every secondary school in England over a period of 10–15 years and to change the educational experience for students and teachers and increase opportunities for lifelong learning for the wider community (DEFRA, 2005, p38).

Exemplar designs have been provided to develop a shared vision of what 'schools for the future' are and to create benchmarks for well-designed schools. They can provide interesting foci for discussions in design and technology (building layout, style, materials, structures), geography (impact upon the environment) and ICT (web design). The online designs are professionally produced and presented by international architectural firms. They can be useful foci for discussions in PSHE (designing a safe learning environment, supporting social interaction) and citizenship (being involved in the decision-making process for education in the near future). The use of ICT is having a positive impact on students' safety and welfare where systems are in place:

- to provide timetables so students can be located at any time during the school day;
- so that attendance can be recorded and analysed to identify patterns of absence and fraudulent registration;
- to immediately inform parents by e-mail, text or phone message if students do not register;
- to track out-of-school pursuits using GPS;
- to enable agencies to share information about students.

PRACTICAL TASK PRACTICAL TASK PRACTICAL TASK PRACTICAL TASK PRACTICAL TASK

Visit the Building Schools for the Future website at www.bsf.gov.uk and follow the 'school workforce' link. Identify how you can contribute to the process of reforming the design of schools.

There are a number of sites showing how architects interpret our needs as teachers. Examples include: www.wilkinsoneyre.com/main.htm and www.mace.co.uk. Do they reflect the ambition of working together to create world-class, twenty-first-century schools – environments which will inspire learning for decades to come and provide exceptional assets for the whole community? (www.bsf. gov.uk/bsf/exemplars.htm)

School Works is an organisation aiming to link the design of school buildings with their impact on teaching, learning, culture and management of those schools. Participation and partnership are at the heart of its approach, connecting those who design and build schools with those who work and learn in them. Try the online game 'Tike & the Missing Mutt'. Tike's dog has disappeared into the local school and she needs to find it quickly. As you travel through the school you meet people and solve problems – raising issues of why schools are organised the way they are and perhaps there is a different way. www.school-works.org/inspiring.asp *Warning:* the School Works game contains flashing images, which may trigger seizures in people with photosensitive epilepsy.

The Extended Schools initiative is also having an impact on the changing nature of schools. No longer will a school be simply be an 8.00 a.m. – 4.00 p.m. building for students but, as with many community schools, there will be a plethora of student services on the same site. This may have an impact upon your subject teaching with adult learners in the classroom, unqualified teachers and lecturers sharing the same teaching space, the inevitable influence of ICT and the provision of blended courses where the classroom-teaching element is just a small part of the learning experience. www.teachernet.gov.uk/wholeschool/extendedschools

The affordances of ICT

This chapter is an opportunity to become familiar with the technologies that are likely to become widespread in their use towards the end of the decade. Associated with each item is an activity that will enable you to have a basic familiarity with the technology. It is also important that when you have the opportunity to use new technologies, you can measure the impact that they might have upon teaching and learning. This affordances checklist is useful.

The affordances of ICT were described (in part) by the TTA in *Higher Standards, Higher Status* (DfEE, 1998).

speed of processing and searching	change timescales	access to experts
automation of functions	remove barriers of distance	easy changes to be made
measurement of events over long or short time intervals	provide access to and control over situations which would normally be outside their everyday experience	enables alternatives to be explored
sequencing and sensing of events with the control of actions	different forms of information	rapid feedback and response
capacity to access and to handle large amounts of information	access to a range of ICT technologies	dynamic feedback and response

Fig. 46. The affordances of ICT

Wiki

A wiki is a collaborative website that users can easily modify via the internet, typically without restriction. A wiki allows anyone, using a web browser, to edit, delete or modify content that has been placed on the site, including the work of other authors. This has been found to work surprisingly well since contributors tend to be more numerous and persistent than vandals and because old versions of pages are always available. Wikipedia is an advanced example of a wiki. Because of its widespread use and popularity, it has taken on an authoritative stance.

PRACTICAL TASK PRACTICAL TASK **PRACTICAL TASK** PRACTICAL TASK PRACTICAL TASK

The first wiki, WikiWikiWeb, is named after the 'Wiki Wiki' line of Chance RT-52 buses in Honolulu International Airport, Hawaii. *Wiki-wiki* means 'fast' in Hawaiian (Wikipedia, 2006). Prove the speed by going to www.wikipedia.org/wiki/Lesson

There are some important questions to be asked about information found in wikis relating to: validity, reliability, reasonableness, provisionality and interactivity.

Look back to the section 'Teaching: high status, high standards' in Chapter 3 for definitions of the words.

Now navigate to the Wikipedia website and investigate the following words: differentiation, assessment, ICT and inclusion.

Based on that experience of Wikipedia and your knowledge of these words, would you be happy to recommend Wikipedia to your students?

Blog

A weblog (also known as blog or web log) is an open-to-all web page that, where permitted, users can amend or add to the information on the log. Blogs often focus on a particular subject, such as food, politics, or local news. Some blogs function as online diaries that can be personal or owned by a small group of contributors. A typical blog combines text, images, and links to other blogs, web pages, and other media. Many blogs do not allow others to contribute but are made by individuals telling their story to the world.

PRACTICAL TASK PRACTICAL TASK **PRACTICAL TASK** PRACTICAL TASK **PRACTICAL TASK**

Navigate to the Blogger website www.blogger.com and take a quick tour. After reading the description of the use of blogs, describe a scenario where you could use a blog as the focus of a topic of work in your subject area. Identify which of the affordances of blogs apply particularly well to your subject area:

- **capacity to access and to handle large amounts of information;**
- **remove barriers of distance;**
- **provide access to situations which would normally be outside their everyday experience;**
- **different forms of information, e.g. video, animation, images;**
- **access to experts;**
- **changes can be made easily;**
- **enables alternatives to be explored;**
- **dynamic feedback and response. (DfEE, 1998, p14)**

Chat rooms

A chat room is a real-time system (also called 'synchronous') based on a website where your text entry is immediately displayed on the screens of everyone else who is accessing the same site. The power of chat rooms is the immediacy of response and potential number of responses. The challenge is that some chat rooms are not limited in access, they are not moderated or they are not monitored, and therefore inappropriate, unreliable, illegal or immoral communications may take place.

A chat room can be as safe as any other online environment providing that it is a closed environment only accessed by use of a username and password. The developing use of learning platforms with their integrated chat rooms means that this has now become an acceptable resource for the classroom and work outside school.

Cathy Richards, a pastoral tutor, writes...

If you are looking for new ways to add variety to your lessons you may wish to think about adding synchronous communication (instantaneous communication such as chat) within your lesson plan. Having spent the past two years specifically looking at the use of chat within the classroom environment I am still amazed at some of the sweeping generalisations that are made with regard to its use. Teachers have told me emphatically that 'chat' can have no place within their teaching environment and that it is totally unsuitable for them whilst having never used the tool before. Sweeping judgements are made about this tool without any practical experience having taken place. Like many other new instruments it has been met, in many instances, by the 'it will never catch on' culture or a positive disregard for its usage. Cathy Richards' doctorate studies investigated how a chat room environment can support pastoral work and emotional literacy. (Richards, 2003, pp23–25)

TECHNICAL TIP

There are many instances when you need to use passwords to access resources on your computer, the school intranet and the internet. It is not advisable to use the same password for everything. In the worst-case scenario you may submit your password to a website that purposefully collects passwords and e-mail addresses to then access your account. In any case, a single password is unlikely to be accepted by every system and then you have the dilemma of deciding on a password for the exceptions. Those are likely to be forgotten.

One approach is to have your own personal system for creating passwords – an example is to reverse the name of the account and add your lucky number to the middle – if the account is Skype and lucky number 75, then the password would be epy75ks. Another approach is to convert some letters to numbers – Skype becomes 5kyp3, baggage becomes 6499493.

You must keep all student data secure. You must protect your desktop from access if that access will give students access to other students' data.

PRACTICAL TASK PRACTICAL TASK PRACTICAL TASK PRACTICAL TASK PRACTICAL TASK

Identify the learning platform that is used in your placement school. Obtain a staff status login and explore the facilities that are used and those that the system could provide to support your teaching and your students' learning. Find out what chat facilities are available and how well you can manage the individuals that enter a discussion that you initiate. With permission of the appropriate staff, initiate a chat session with your students to provide support and feedback.

Chat

Chat systems come in a variety of styles ranging from text-only messaging systems to fully immersive 3D environments. Your students may well be familiar with some chat systems – for instance, many game sites have a chat window running alongside the backgammon, chess or poker environment. Students can build up a relationship by carrying out a sustained conversation with someone over a period. These virtual relationships can be enriching and extending of the online experience. The underlying problem associated with all online communication between people who do not know each other is when the virtual becomes physical.

Remember the 'Know IT All' advice described in Chapter 1 – staying safe on the internet (Childnet, 2005). **www.childnet-int.org/uk/KIA**

Many students, and teachers, chat online. However, they are not necessarily using chat rooms. Chat is essentially a one-to-one communication although some systems allow others to be invited into a conversation. The student will have a limited list of contacts. The software lists those contacts that are currently online; clicking on their name and typing some text sends an 'instant message'. Instant messaging such as Yahoo Messenger, ICQ, MSN, etc., are chat systems; they are not chat rooms. Chat is very much safer because the only people who are aware of you being online are those that you have invited to be on your list. Recently these systems have started to incorporate the ability to chat with multiple people simultaneously, but these are still conversations restricted to the student's list of contacts.

PRACTICAL TASK PRACTICAL TASK **PRACTICAL TASK** PRACTICAL TASK **PRACTICAL TASK**

Arrange with a mentor to be able to talk to a small group of students about their online chat experiences and how they use chat socially.

The *aide-mémoire* for your discussion could be the who–what–when–where–how–why cues.

Chat	Questions
who	who's on your list; what sort of people; how many
how	get them to describe how they log on, identify friends, make new contacts (technical aspects)
when	time of day, days of the week
where	home, school, in private, with friends, with family
why	earning, learning, leisure, friendship
what	the systems used (MSN, Yahoo, etc.)

Fig. 47. Questioning students about chat

Afterwards, carry out a reflection upon your questioning technique.

- **How closed or open were your questions?**
- **Did the students seem to understand the questions?**
- **Did you reinforce good ideas?**
- **Did you give positive or negative feedback?**
- **Did the students have opportunities to ask questions?**

Also, reflect upon their responses and consider what might be the implications for introducing chat into your teaching.

SMS – texting

There is much discussion about the current introduction of mobile telephone technologies into schools. Small Message System (SMS, or texting) is just one of those. The major affordance is motivation – texting is trendy and many students are very proficient. The challenge is that the system is essentially secret and only the two communicators can read the messages. Unlike chat rooms, bulletin boards and e-portfolios, the teacher cannot access in real time and cannot access archives of the conversations.

> *Mobile phones threaten loss of control. Nowadays, the average age of a first-time owner is eight, yet despite their enormous potential as a means of learning and for the exchange of information, mobile phones are banned in most schools. The most popular mass communications device in schools remains the assembly hall – a place where students sit in silence, listening while adults shape their learning experience. This fear of losing control explains why MP3 players, represented by the white knight of the iPod, are under-utilised in schools. They are distrusted even when the only content on them is lectures (the students might turn the volume down).* (McDougall, 2005, p3).

The current versions of XDAs enable screen projection of the telephone display. Perhaps the visual sharing of messages may make the process more open, less prone to abuse through inappropriate (off-task) texting and more focused on reflections, comments and descriptions of the lesson topic.

SMS is also having an impact upon the administrative aspects of the teacher's role. Systems are now available to manage, send and receive secure SMS text messages from your desktop to a mobile phone through web-based applications but can be integrated into your existing school-management software. The affordances of SMS for school and teacher administrative use are:

- **they bridge the digital and social divide where access to a mobile telephone and texting is more frequent than access to a PC and the internet;**
- **text messages are discreet and, by their nature, to the point;**
- **they are inexpensive (of time and money) compared with telephone calls;**
- **the instant nature of sending supporting asynchronous communication;**
- **sending messages to a group of contacts (one-to-many communication);**
- **scheduling a message to go later in the day or week;**
- **tracking delivery of messages.**

With texting has come the dialect or paralanguage of texting. There is a plethora of well-known and locally popular shortcuts to messaging. Called emoticons, they were originally limited to adding emotions to the emotion-free e-mail and ensured that humour was not misinterpreted. The first recorded smiley :-) was sent in 1982 with the explanation that if the message was not a joke then :-(was to be used **research.microsoft.com/~mbj/Smiley/Smiley.html**

:-)	smiling (joke or pleased)
:-(	not happy (unfortunately true)
:'-(	crying (also unfortunately true)
;-)	kidding or teasing (winking)
:-o	surprised
:-D	laughing
:-I	determined
|-O	yawning (bored or stating the obvious)
:-/	sceptical
>:-(or :-||	angry

Fig. 48. Emoticons

The texting dialect is also blessed with acronyms:

AFAIK	As far as I know
ATB	All the best
BRB	be right back
c%d	Could
cul8r	See you later
D or d	The
D8	Date (also Fate, Great, Late, Mate, Wait using 8 phonically)
HHOJ	Ha ha only joking
ILBL8	I'll be late
LOL	Laugh out loud
MbRsd	Embarrassed
NMP	Not my problem
OIC	Oh, I see
PCM	Please call me
PPL	People
RUF2T	Are you free to talk?
SWDYT	So what do you think?
THNQ	Thank you
TTFN	Goodbye ('Ta ta for now')
W8nC	Wait and see
w%d	Would
XOXOX	Hugs and kisses

Fig. 49. Acronyms and abbreviations used in texting

RSS

'Provisionality' is one of the concepts of which students need to be aware. The internet is not a constant – it is continually changing. Examples include websites providing the weather forecast, the arrival times of flights, the currency exchange rates, the cost of components/ ingredients for a project, the world/European/Commonwealth or national records in athletics and so on. These sites are changing frequently, varying from every minute with regard to stocks and shares to every month with regard to OFSTED reports.

Really Simple Syndication or Rich Site Summary (RSS) is a system for keeping up to date with the content of websites. Originally it was designed for syndicating news and the content of news-like sites but it is not just for news. Anything that can be broken down into discrete items can be syndicated via RSS. Once information about each item is in RSS format, an RSS-aware program can check the feed for changes and react to the changes in an appropriate way. You can be aware of the 'recent changes' to your favourite wiki, new downloads from your music provider or the latest from education news from the BBC: **news.-bbc.co.uk/1/hi/help/rss**.

RSS delivers web page material to your computer automatically and your browser or newsreader software alerts you to new arrivals. However, RSS can also be used to trigger the download of multimedia material such as audio files for use on MP3 players called podcasts (see below).

Handheld computers

Handheld computers could bring important benefits to schools, assisting in administration, supporting classroom management and enabling personal and group learning (Perry, 2003). The joint emphasis of use of these new technologies is for managing teachers' work and for teaching and learning. The range and diversity of these devices are immense. You need to be aware that many devices are likely to appear in your school in your early teaching career and you will be expected to accommodate them in your practice.

Drawing from David Perry's work, the advantages of handheld computers need to be exploited to prevent the challenges dominating your use of the devices: 'The most positive indicator at this stage shows that PDAs have considerable potential for making teachers' management and presentation of information more efficient, but there are some conditions necessary for this to be successful' (Perry, 2003, p5).

The advantages of handheld computers (many meeting universal approval in the research study) included:

- **the smallness means that they can always be with you – unlike PCs, which require you to be where they are located and available;**
- **they are personal and so they become your property and are not shared or borrowed – colleagues might ask to use your computer for a moment but they don't ask to borrow a PDA;**
- **they have 'instant-on' – unlike PCs, there is no waiting for an operating system to 'boot up';**
- **they have a much longer battery life than laptop computers;**
- **the quantity of data they could hold appears very high compared to their size;**
- **the ease of synchronisation both manually through docking or infra-ed or automatically through WiFi or GPRS;**

- as a result of synchronisation, the data remain current and reliable;
- the increased functionality, including Microsoft's PocketPC, makes handheld computing a competitor to the laptop computer.

In the research, widespread dislike was expressed for the small screens, the unstable storage leading to lost data (from flat batteries) and the need for new routines to manage the devices effectively. Obviously, a handheld computer cannot be adopted and used without considering and, perhaps, changing other routines. For example, maintaining a good battery-charging regime is important to ensure that the life of the battery is prolonged and the charge/recharge cycle is not shortened.

Concerns were expressed for the ruggedness of the devices for use in school. Again, it is necessary to adopt or change habits of working to ensure the physical security of the device. Theft might be an issue. XDAs are very attractive devices as many operate as a mobile phone as well as a computer. The data they contain and can have access to can be highly confidential and steps need to be taken to password-protect access both to the device and then to the data sets on the device.

Synchronisation can be problematic if it is necessary to synchronise to more than one computer. Online systems like Microsoft Exchange avoid the issue by making a master copy of everything (including calendar, tasks, e-mail and files) on a remote server to which all the other devices synchronise independently.

Training and technical support is an issue in most areas of technology innovation. Always be sensitive to the need to have good support.

PRACTICAL TASK PRACTICAL TASK **PRACTICAL TASK** PRACTICAL TASK **PRACTICAL TASK**

Identify an area of computer use in which you have some competence but need more knowledge or understanding. Arrange, perhaps through your mentor, to have a meeting with a school ICT technician. Discuss issues regarding security of hardware, provision of software for your subject department, monitoring of students' activity (through login facilities), arrangements for passwords and, of course, your personal ICT issue. Try to identify the concerns of the technicians. Also, try to find out how they feel they can support the teachers better.

An overview of the role of PDAs, *Mobile and PDA technologies and their future use in education*, has been prepared by JISC (Anderson and Blackwood, 2004).

Podcast

'Podcast' is both a noun and a verb. A podcast is a file that is downloaded from the internet to your computer, iPod or MP3 player. Podcasting is providing material online for people to download manually or computers to download automatically. The automation is provided by RSS (see above). The term 'podcast' is a combination of 'iPod' (an MP3 player) and 'broadcast'. Podcasts are not limited to audio files but can include video and multimedia presentations. Playback can be on personal computers, MP3 players, PDAs, XDAs and mobile phones.

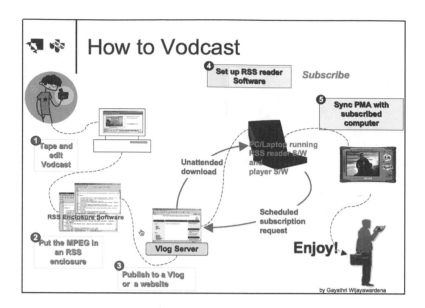

Fig. 50. The creation of a video podcast

The podcast directory is a useful starting point when looking for material to support a lesson:
www.podcast.net

PRACTICAL TASK PRACTICAL TASK PRACTICAL TASK PRACTICAL TASK PRACTICAL TASK

The BBC website is a very useful source of information on podcasting as well as being a good source of educational material in general. For more information on podcasting, use www.bbc.co.uk/radio/downloadtrial

- **Identify a BBC programme of personal interest. Download the MP3 file to your computer, iPod or MP3 player.**

The BBC offer a 'listen again' service. This is different to podcasting where the whole file is sent to your computer and you can then save or copy it to other locations. The 'listen again' service streams the material to your computer and you listen as it arrives. The complete file never exists on your computer. In this way, the owner of the material protects it from being copied. It can only be listened to or, in the case of video, watched.

- ***Learning Curve* is BBC Radio 4's flagship education programme. If it is currently being broadcast, then try the 'listen again' service.**
- **Identify other BBC programmes that support your CPD.** www.bbc.co.uk/learning **and Bitesize are good starting points.**
- **Make a note of the programmes that you have listened to and use the list to provide evidence that you are meeting the Training and Development Agency (TDA) standards.**
- **Is there a programme available from the 'listen again' service that is valuable for your classroom work?**
- **'Vodcasts' (video podcasts) are also becoming available for use with the new generation of video MP4 players.**

GPRS

General Packet Radio Service is always referred to as GPRS. It is a system that is used to establish continuous communication between a handheld computer and the internet using mobile telephone connections. Although using telephone technology, the billing is usually related to the amount of bandwidth used (data downloaded) rather the time of access.

GPRS cards can be inserted into laptop computers, enabling them to be able to access the internet wherever there is a mobile telephone signal. GPRS is a much slower service that the conventional wireless (WiFi) connection but the universal coverage makes it more versatile for off-site activities and communications.

VoIP

Voice over Internet Protocol (VoIP), pronounced 'voyp', is a system of making audio computer-to-computer connections and enabling telephone-like communication to take place. Software is required but, providing both parties have the same software, the connection can be made. Some providers also allow computer-to-landline and computer-to-mobile connection but usually this is chargeable.

In the past, students have handwritten pen-pal letters to students in other countries. Perhaps we will see the day soon when they will now have voice-to-voice conversations across the internet. In his paper on Every Child Matters, Terry Freedman suggests, 'Voice over Internet Protocol and similar technology is used to facilitate easy communications between agencies' to provide a safer environment for students (Freedman, 2006, p8).

FURTHER READING FURTHER READING **FURTHER READING** FURTHER READING
Using wikis in schools: A case study by Lyndsay Grant, Learning Researcher, Futurelab. This paper addresses the potential uses of wikis as learning tools in schools. It places wikis in the context of current relevant literature about collaborative learning, summarising major theories of learning in communities and knowledge-building in networked groups. The use of wikis in school is explored further through a case study in a UK secondary school (Chosen Hill School, Gloucestershire). Available at: **www.futurelab.org.uk/download/ pdfs/research/disc_papers/Wikis_in_Schools.pdf**

14–19 and digital technologies: A review of research and projects is another report from Futurelab written by Chris Davies and colleagues (Davies *et al.*, 2005). It addresses issues related to the use of handheld computers, GPRS, text messaging, chat rooms and weblogs. Available at: **www.futurelab.org.uk/download/pdfs/research/lit_reviews/futurelab_- review_13.pdf**

Teachers of modern foreign languages should read *The potential role of CT in modern foreign languages learning 5–19* by Keri Facer and Martin Owen of Futurelab. They identify a number of key roles that ICTs have the potential to fulfil in MFL teaching and learning, including: increasing motivation to learn languages, enabling language learning across institutions and outside formal educational contexts, offering opportunities for meaningful practice of language in authentic contexts and enabling information and resource sharing between MFL teachers. Available at: **www.futurelab.org.uk/research/discuss/ 03discuss01.htm**

Collaborative learning: Just because you *can*, doesn't mean you *should* is Terry Freedman's thought-provoking analysis of the blind adoption of ICT developments. 'What I am more concerned about is the often uncritical stance of educationalists in relation to these tools. For example, I have read articles which favourably compare Wikipedia to traditional encyclopaedias on the basis of weight, its ability to constantly change, its democratic ethos, and other characteristics. Surely the most important yardstick is accuracy?' (Freedman, 2005)

A SUMMARY OF **KEY POINTS**

> **Technological developments are continually occurring and they have an almost immediate impact upon your work in the classroom, either indirectly through the knowledge and expectation of the students and their parents or directly through government and local initiatives to introduce the technology.**

> **You need to be open to experimenting with new technologies so that you do not miss the opportunity to make your teaching more efficient or more effective.**

> **You must not be swayed by the 'wow factor' of new technologies but ensure that they do deliver, in a cost-effective way, better learning and more efficient administration.**

REFERENCES REFERENCES **REFERENCES** REFERENCES **REFERENCES** REFERENCES

Anderson, P and Blackwood, A (2004) *Mobile and PDA technologies and their future use in education.* JISC Technology and Standards Watch: 04-03. **www.jisc.ac.uk/uploaded_documents/ACF11B0.pdf**

BECTa (2005) *ICT research report on what the research says ICT and classroom organisation in schools.* Coventry: BECTa.

Childnet (2005) *Jenny's Story: An internet safety resource.* London: Childnet International. **www.childnet-int.org/jenny/video.html**

Davies, C, Hayward, G and Lukman, L (2005) *14–19 and digital technologies: A review of research and projects.* Department of Educational Studies, Oxford University. Bristol: Futurelab.

DEFRA (2005) *HM Government. Securing the future – delivering UK sustainable development strategy.* London: The Stationery Office.

DfEE (1998) *Teaching: High status, high standards.* Annex B DfEE Circular 4-98. London: DfEE. **www.dfes.gov.uk/publications/guidanceonthelaw/4_98/annexb.htm**

Freedman, T (2005) *Collaborative learning: Just because you *can*, doesn't mean you *should*.* **www.terry-freedman.org.uk/artman/publish/article_420.php**

Freedman, T (2006) *Every Child Matters: What it means for the ICT teacher.* **terry-freedman.org.uk/artman/publish/article_812.php**

McDougall, S (2005) *One tablet or two? Opportunities for change in educational provision in the next 20 years.* Bristol: Futurelab. **www.futurelab.org.uk/research/discuss/06discuss01.htm**

Perry, D (2003) *Handheld computers (PDAs) in schools report.* Coventry: BECTa. **partners.becta.org.uk/index.php?section=rh&rid=11235**

Richards, C (2003) Chatrooms in the classroom. *InteracTive,* 47: 23–25. Birmingham: Questions Publishing.

Appendix 1
Glossary

Using ICT in teaching has many acronyms, abbreviations and jargon words. This glossary contains definitions associated with ICT and pedagogy.

Automatic functions relating to spreadsheets, models and simulations, changes in output/display in response to changes in input, values or button clicks.

Avatar the persona of a blog or chat that the icon, words, gestures (emoticons) and location suggest.

Blog (web log) web page record of thoughts, views, memories, observations or diary over time of a person or people.

Bluetooth[TM] a wireless technology for communicating between devices – very fast and suitable for audio and video streams of data.

Browser toolbar an extra set of icons/functions to assist browsing.

Bulletin board website to facilitate discussion by users responding to messages left by others (asynchronous).

Calibration usually associated with interactive whiteboards, the reprogramming of the system if the projector has been moved, by pointing at a number of crosses of the screen.

Capacity and range function of ICT to access and to handle large amounts of information; change timescales, or remove barriers of distance; give teachers and students access to and control over situations which would normally be outside their everyday experience.

Chart image based upon discrete data having set formats, e.g. pie, line, bar and scatter.

Chat usually one-to-one synchronous discussion.

Chat room website to facilitate synchronous discussion where contributions by every user can be seen by every other user.

Cloze procedure the presentation of text with strategically selected words blanked out for the students to complete; the students use contextual clues to guess the answer.

Collaborative when students work together to create a shared product or outcome.

Compression process of reducing the size of files for storage and transmission – many files are now automatically saved in compressed format and further compression has no value.

Concept map visual representation of a body of knowledge with a top point and a hierarchical structure below (Novak, 1990).

Co-operative when students work on their own activity but share resources, knowledge or experience.

CPD continuing professional development.

Diagram image constructed of lines and geometric shapes that represents but does not attempt to look exactly the same as what it represents.

Differentiation by grouping dividing the class into groups based upon ability to succeed in the learning objectives of the lesson.

Digital divide the difference of opportunity between those (students) with ready access at home to computers and those that do not have access.

Disenfranchisement as society, including councils, government, teachers and shops, increasingly uses computers for normal provision of information some people will not be able to access basic services, for example, planning department, licensing, course material and discounts.

Docking connecting small devices to larger peripherals; especially applied to connecting a laptop to a conventional keyboard, mouse, screen, printer and network.

Dynamic linking connecting two files so that changing one has an effect upon the output of the other – for example, linking a spreadsheet of addresses to a word processor file to create personalised letters (mail merge).

E-citizenship overarching term referring to online participation in society and participation in an online society.

E-democracy the two-way process between the citizen and another citizen, politician or council.

E-government the one-way process of government services being offered and accessed online.

Electronic portfolio a collection of evidence, usually submitted online, comprised of materials saved in a folder.

E-mail messages sent via the internet.

Enrichment activities that, although in the same topic area, are different to the normal activities of the class or scheme of work; they tend to be more open-ended and challenging to meet the needs of gifted and able students in the class.

Enrichment and extension this phase is often associated with support for gifted and talented students but is also used to describe activities designed for students making the fastest progress through the activities of an ICT lesson; it is an aspect of differentiation.

E-portfolio collection of submitted work that is available online.

Error learner making an accidental mistake.

Errors and misconceptions accidental mistakes and mistakes due to incorrect learning (misunderstanding).

Ethics the rules, regulations, codes of practice and laws that determine correct behaviour.

Exploration making choices and learning from the consequences.

Exposition usually oral, description and explanation of knowledge and concepts using pedagogic strategies.

Extension activities within the same topic area that are in addition to those planned for the majority – often they involve repetition of the task in a slightly different context to reinforce skills, knowledge or understanding.

Feedback output of a system which changes the inputs to the system.

File management organisation of resources on a hard drive, memory stick or internet website to support ease of access and retrieval.

FTP file transfer protocol, the process by which files are placed on the internet (specifically web pages and their supporting resources).

Generic having no specific use but can be used in a wide range of situations; generic software includes word processors, spreadsheets, databases, web browsers and painting/drawing packages.

GPRS General Packet Radio Service, a mobile data service for mobile phones and enables XDAs to access the internet with moderate speed data transfer.

GPS Global Positioning System, a satellite navigation system driven by 30 satellite broadcasts to GPS receivers giving them accurate location data (longitude, latitude and altitude) in any weather, day or night, anywhere on Earth.

Graph image based upon continuous data, with the lower axis usually being number, time or distance.

Gyroscopic describes a mouse that does not need a surface; moving the mouse through the air moves the pointer on the screen; gives independence of location and enables the teacher to mix with the class.

Icon image that represents a concept or (within the graphic user interface of the computer) an action.

Image visual artefact – diagram, picture, icon and symbol.

Information sheet reusable résumé of important ideas – may be retained by the student for revision purposes.

Infrared a means of communicating between computer devices including laptops, mobile phones, XDAs, PDAs, tablet PCs, and printers – now superseded by Bluetooth™ and WiFi.

Interactivity feature of web pages that change in response to text entry and/or clicking on icons (buttons).

Internet reading skills visually scanning documents with the scroll bar, using hypertext links and the navigation icons, tracking back and forth through many pages, coping with material in a non-linear format, changing the format of pages to best suit their needs or the needs of the activity.

Introduction see starters.

Invisibility having information and actions that are not apparent to the user.

Ken Burns effect creating a moving image by zooming into, zooming out or panning across a still image to give focus and interest to a presentation.

Learning platform synonymous with a managed learning environment (MLE), an online environment where teachers can provide learning activities and students can access work, complete assessments and submit work.

Learning style characteristic way in which learners appear to be more successful – visual, auditory or kinaesthetic.

Lesson in my back pocket an activity to occupy the students constructively when the planned lesson becomes impossible; configuratively speaking, it is the preparedness for the inevitable failure of computer hardware or software that is the focus of the lesson.

Mail groups a single e-mail address that send e-mails to a group of subscribed recipients.

Mind-map visual representation of a body of knowledge using shapes and labelled connectors (Buzan, 2000).

Mini-plenary a mini-plenary session occurs during the lesson, often enhancing the teaching by effectively demonstrating techniques and reviewing work done so far.

Misconception see errors and misconceptions.

MLE see learning platform.

Model representation of a real-world situation by variables, formulae and relationships usually in a spreadsheet (also see simulation); enables students to ask 'what if?'.

Network management software Under various names such as NetOp and Ranger, this software enables you to control the screen output on every computer from your own computer; some systems enable you to display a student's screen through the projector.

Online describes resources that require internet connection so that they can be accessed.

Online survey usually based upon a form, a means of data collection.

On-screen represented by a screen image, usually implies only on the student's computer and not online.

Patterns (predicting) seeking patterns either in numbers, events or prose is facilitated by ICT – for example, using a spreadsheet charting feature to create an XY (scatter) chart or a moving-average trend line.

PDA personal digital assistant, usually has e-mail, calendar and some text-processing facilities but varies in sophistication from a simple database and calendar up to a handheld pocket PC computer with synchronisation of files and e-mails to your desktop computer.

PDF file portable document format, a common format of document used on the internet to ensure that the presentation is retained and protected when rendered or printed after download; Adobe Acrobat Reader is a common reader for PDF files.

Pedagogy the skills, knowledge and understanding of the teaching process.

Picture map representation of a body of knowledge or concepts using pictures (photographs, icons, diagrams).

Pixelate image manipulation by which pixel size is increased to hide detail.

Plenary summary of lessons drawing out the key teaching points; can include celebration of students' achievement and setting the context for future learning.

Podcasts multimedia, video and audio resources available online for manual or automatic (RSS) download.

Provisionality being non-permanent, changing over time and in response to changes of input – for example, the ever-changing content of some web pages.

Quiz an interactive presentation of questions and opportunities to answer – the least sophisticated gives feedback to the learner, some give feedback to the teacher and the most sophisticated determines the next learning experience on the basis of the student's performance.

RSS really simple syndication, a system that enables internet users to be informed when changes have been made to specified websites or resources can be automatically downloaded.

Shibboleth open-source system for online resource authentication and authorisation to support the development of personalised online learning spaces for all learners.

Simulation computer representation of a real-life situation.

Situated learning placing the activity in a real/authentic context, making it more relevant.

SMS (text message) Short Message Service – texts sent from mobile phones and XDAs and other handheld devices and even landline telephones and from some websites.

Spider diagram visual representation of a body of knowledge using shapes and labelled connectors.

Starters activities at the start of a lesson to raise cognitive engagement, manage behaviour and/or focus upon a topic.

Symbol shape that has precise meaning.

Trial and improvement a strategy encouraged to help students learn through experience.

URL Uniform Resource Location – the unique address of a web page.

Visual literacy the skills, knowledge and understanding related to images.

Visual stimulation the increased motivation or attention caused by an image.

VLE see learning platforms.

VoIP Voice over Internet Protocol, pronounced 'voyp', a facility to make telephone calls over the internet using dedicated software such as Skype: **www.skype.com**

Walled garden protected environment of limited access to internet sites often provided by local authorities or commercial providers.

WiFi wireless devices, such as computers, mobile phones, PDAs or XDAs connect to the internet through a local access point called a hotspot or through wireless routers in schools or at home, promoting anytime, anywhere learning.

wiki a website that allows users to easily add, remove, or change the content enabling collaborative authoring.

Wireless (RF) see WiFi.

Writing frames a structure that guides the students' writing to ensure that they are able to record, represent or communicate their work or understanding; in science it may include paragraph sub-headings (e.g. apparatus, method, results, analysis, conclusion).

XDA a PDA with mobile phone technology – usually has the following functionality: a megapixel camera, Windows-based software, touch-sensitive display and/or an integral mini-keyboard, e-mail/calendar/notes synchronisation with a PC via Bluetooth, data cable, infrared or by wireless LAN or with an exchange server using GPRS; pocket PC versions of Internet Explorer, Outlook and Windows Media Player; expandable using memory cards – it is also a mobile telephone.

REFERENCES REFERENCES **REFERENCES** REFERENCES **REFERENCES** REFERENCES

Buzan, T (2000) *The mind map book.* London: BBC Publications.

Novak, JD (1990) Concept maps and Vee diagrams: Two metacognitive tools for science and mathematics education. *Instructional Science,* 19: 29–52.

Appendix 2
ICT in your subject

The current and most substantial support for ICT in your curriculum area is the 'ICT Across the Curriculum' pack (ICTAC – pronounced 'ick-tack'). You should obtain a copy of your booklet and poster. The individual booklets can be downloaded from the Standards site: **www.standards.dfes.gov.uk/keystage3/respub/ictac**

In addition to the Secondary Strategy, there are also very good examples of the use of ICT that have arisen from previous initiatives, the National Curriculum and the QCA schemes of work. When you are on placement you may see other good examples of ICT that have arisen from local facilities, the needs of the students or the skills and interests of the teachers. For example, in one school, the model railway club, sponsored by a local firm, provides an interesting and comprehensive example of the use of sensing and control using computers.

ICTAC is one of the four whole-school options your school may have chosen for consultant support from September 2004. The other three options are: AfL – Assessment for Learning, LAC – Literacy Across the Curriculum, or LiL – Leading in Learning. If you are not sure which option your school has chosen, please ask your school Secondary Strategy Manager for further details.

The ICT Across the Curriculum (ICTAC) pack is a set of materials designed to promote the use of ICT across all subjects in schools. It builds on the work of the ICT strand of the National Strategy and the ICT capability that students are bringing to their subject lessons from their ICT lessons. These materials are available to download for all schools and should be used as a whole-school initiative, rather than 'piecemeal', ensuring the ICT capability of students.

You, like qualified teachers, are expected to use computers to make administrative tasks less burdensome and more efficient. This too has greater implications in some subject areas than in others.

The ICT curriculum that is delivered across the curriculum is represented as a pizza. Each 'slice' is a different aspect of handling information (finding things out), communication (exchanging and sharing information) and control and modelling (developing ideas and making things happen). The 'stuffed crust' of the ICT curriculum pizza (reviewing, modifying and evaluating work as it progresses) is a powerful aspect of ensuring that the students' ICT capability has an impact upon their learning and classroom performance.

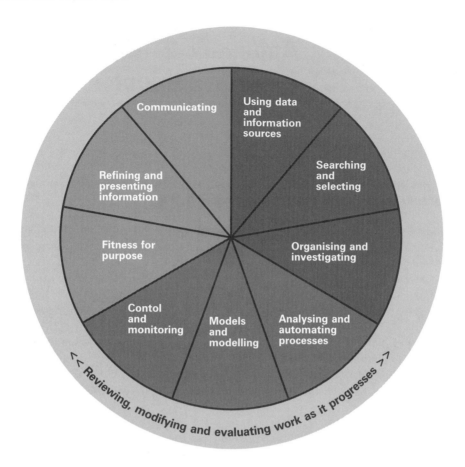

Key to ICT National Curriculum themes:

▶ Finding things out

▶ Developing ideas and making things happen

▶ Exchanging and sharing information

▶ Reviewing, modifying and evaluating work as it progresses

Fig. 51. ICTAC pizza

ICT in English

The teaching of English can make a significant contribution to the ICT capability of students and ICT supports teaching of the four elements of the National Curriculum for English: reading, writing, listening and speaking.

The internet provides an increased diversity in the reading material you can make available to your students. Also, the internet provides the opportunity and need to develop other reading skills, including visually scanning documents with the scroll bar, using hypertext links and the navigation icons and tracking back and forth through many pages that do not necessarily have a linear format. The competent internet reader can also change the format of the viewed pages to best suit their needs or the needs of the activity.

Writing takes many forms and the pervasive use of ICT has brought with it written forms of its own including texting with abbreviations and emoticons, and e-mail with its netiquette. You should be aware that web page writing demands an appreciation of a new structure with the use of hypertext links, standard forms of title and subtitle and common formats of layout. This is a particularly important concept when writing for audiences. The web page layout enables readers with visual impairment to impose their chosen style on the author's work. An important value of the use of ICT in the teaching of English is the motivation impact of publication of the students' work on the intranet and the internet. Also, many students find handwriting and design challenging. Using ICT enables them to express themselves with a high quality of presentation.

New demands are placed upon listening skills. The proliferation of audio blogs, MP3 publishing and podcasting makes listening a more active pursuit, with the ability to fast forward, replay and multitask during the listening process. The range of listening materials has also increased, including listening to written works in the author's own voice.

Speaking and performance opportunities have also increased. Students can now prepare audio presentations and publish to a much wider audience. Their work can be subject to great critical appraisal by peers, teachers and the wider world. Audio blogging and audio chat are becoming popular means of communicating through the spoken word.

ICT supports your work as a teacher. It gives you the opportunity to produce high-quality, professional format, reading and listening materials. Those materials can be easily modified to represent different forms by changing the layout, font and printing. Using a projector can bring reading texts alive with visual images, interactivity and collaborative authoring.

The English National Curriculum makes specific reference to the students' developing ICT skills and understanding of the use of text, pictures and moving images in the presentation of their work. There is a requirement that, as an English teacher, your students are taught to plan, draft, redraft and proofread on the screen of a computer. They should be taught to make full use of presentational devices when presenting polished work. In your training to meet the standards you should ensure you have the ICT skills and are sufficiently competent and confident to teach them.

ICT in mathematics

The teaching of mathematics can make a significant contribution to the ICT capability of students. In particular, mathematics offers opportunities in a wide range of areas of the ICT curriculum, including organising and investigating data, automating functions and developing and exploring models. These reflect the key concepts identified by the Key Stage 3 National Strategy:

- **using data and information sources;**
- **organising and investigating;**
- **analysing and automating processes;**
- **models and modelling.**

Your students should be exploring numerical data in a purposeful way, seeking average, sum, minimum and maximum values and at more advanced levels seeking comparisons, correlations and trends in the data. Identifying bias in the data is an element of this work.

They will need to develop software skills in spreadsheet and database programs. Organising and investigating data include the presentation of results in charting programs following formal analysis using statistical methods. Evaluating the conclusions drawn and the methods used is an element of this work. In your training to meet the standards you should ensure you have the ICT skills and are sufficiently competent and confident to teach them.

Students are expected to create automated processes. The aim of the activities is to increase efficiency and to aid the exploration of mathematical situations. One way in which this is achieved is by creating routines in LOGO to generate 2D shapes. The students then explore the effects of changing different variables. Students in Year 9 may choose to create macros in spreadsheets or may use other automating functions, including nesting procedures in LOGO, to explore a range of mathematical situations. Automation in spreadsheets occurs when variables (cell values) are changed to see the impact upon other cells (results).

The Key Stage 3 Mathematics National Curriculum requires students to experience tasks 'focused on using appropriate ICT [for example, spreadsheets, databases, geometry or graphic packages]'. An important aspect of the requirement is that your students know when it is not appropriate to use a particular form of technology. This ability can only be achieved once they have had a comprehensive experience of ICT and the alternative methods.

Software that you need to have sufficient familiarity with that you can teach the skills and functionality of includes: charting programs, databases, geometry packages, graph plotter, graphic packages, graphical calculators, LOGO and spreadsheets.

ICT in science

The teaching of science can make a significant contribution to the ICT capability of students. In particular, the science curriculum offers you opportunities to use models, sense the environment, search data and present information in your lessons.

Modelling is an important aspect of the ICT curriculum and it provides important strategies for helping students understand scientific concepts and relationships. Students can use ICT to create models and explore understanding by asking 'What if?' questions. They can modify rules and variables to explore the relationships within the model, predict outcomes and test hypotheses. The models can be presented as spreadsheets of data. Alternatively, the numbers can be embedded in multimedia presentations and interactive applications, for example, wave-simulation programs that allow the students to explore amplitude, frequency and direction when combining, passing through a refraction grating or being reflected off a solid surface.

Sensing the environment is an extremely important way in which you can develop the ICT capability of your students. The world is an analogue environment and the computer is a digital device. By considering how sensors work, important scientific concepts can be illustrated. However, at a more fundamental level, with sensing devices and monitoring software students can carry out experiments more successfully. Even simple cooling-curve experiments can be a problem using traditional thermometers if the students become bored or distracted and mistime the readings. Monitoring software can allow the students to carry out other activities during the cooling period. Importantly, the result is a set of data that can be printed as a graph, which motivates and celebrates the work of students who are not necessarily inclined to produce quality work.

When searching the internet for materials, the students need to apply their scientific learning to make value judgements about bias, reliability and appropriateness of the information and data gathered. You need to give them advice and direction. When presenting information gathered from their scientific enquiry, students should consider the audience and use appropriate scientific terminology, avoiding colloquialism and euphemism.

The National Curriculum for science makes many direct references to teaching about and with ICT, including using:

- **data-handling software to create, analyse and evaluate charts and graphs;**
- **databases or spreadsheets to record, analyse and evaluate;**
- **simulation software to explore and model changes or factors;**
- **sensors to record;**
- **the internet to find up-to-date information;**
- **CD-ROM or video technology [to experience dangerous, expensive or distant activities].**

At Key Stage 3, it is a requirement that all students are taught to use data-logging equipment to make observations and measurements. At Key Stage 4, all students should be taught to use ICT sources and tools to collect data from primary and secondary sources (DfES, 2004b).

In science, teaching ICT can make a significant contribution to the effectiveness of presentation and exposition. The use of gooseneck cameras, digital microscopes and CRT displays projected onto the screen means that all the students could easily view the presentations. You should consider how ICT could support your own administrative tasks, including lesson planning, producing and displaying teaching resources, recording student attainment and the evaluation of your lessons and communicating with school colleagues.

ICT in design and technology

The teaching of design and technology can make a significant contribution to the ICT capability of students. In particular, your curriculum offers you opportunities to carry out sustained work on a project involving the design cycle. Students can use ICT to develop, plan and communicate ideas in the same reflective, evaluative and productive environment as they need to meet the ICT requirements of 'developing ideas and making things happen' and 'reviewing, modifying and evaluating work as it progresses'. You, uniquely, can provide opportunities for them to use control technology, computer-aided design and computer-aided manufacture (CAD/CAM).

The National Curriculum for design and technology makes many direct references to teaching about and with ICT including:

- **using spreadsheets to model time and cost;**
- **using CAD software, clip-art libraries, scanners and digital cameras;**
- **using ICT to analyse materials and their properties;**
- **using the internet to obtain information.**

At Key Stage 3, it is a requirement that all students are taught, within the design and technology curriculum, to use ICT as a source of information. All students should be taught to use ICT, particularly CAD, to explore, develop, model and communicate design proposals. They should be taught how to use ICT to design sub-systems and systems (DfEE, 1999, pp136–137). Consequently, for you to meet the standards, you must be able to teach all of those skills, knowledge and concepts.

In design and technology teaching, ICT can make a significant contribution to the effectiveness of presentation and exposition. The use of a single NC (numerical control) lathe, milling or drilling machine can efficiently demonstrate aspects of the curriculum. You should consider how ICT could support your own administrative tasks, including lesson planning, producing and displaying teaching resources, recording student attainment and the evaluation of your lessons and communicating with school colleagues.

ICT in history

The teaching of history can make a significant contribution to the ICT capability of students. In particular, it offers the opportunity for students to search and analyse a vast amount of evidence and opinion. You make the students differentiate between primary and secondary sources and identify bias in accounts.

In history, ICT can make a significant contribution to learning. The students are required to combine information from a variety of sources and then refine it to meet the needs of specific audiences. For example, students can be asked to create a pamphlet to persuade people to join a Tolpuddle demonstration. This sort of activity enables students to organise and present their learning as well as providing a context for students to put themselves in the shoes of people in history.

The visual representation of events and characters from history can have a strong influence upon learning. Using an image search engine you can collate a number of images to illustrate your teaching materials and make them more interesting and motivating. The students can choose from those images that best represent their writing.

In history there are National Curriculum requirements to teach students to select information relevant to enquiry, and the example given is using a spreadsheet or data file of information about an historical event to search and analyse patterns such as mortality rates. The data drawn from all the headstones of a local churchyard can provide a pattern-seeking exercise. Students should be taught how to use ICT to communicate their knowledge and understanding of history (5c).

ICT in geography

The teaching of geography can make a significant contribution to the ICT capability of students in a number of areas, including geographic information systems (GIS), global positioning systems (GPS), mapping, the use of models, sensing and data analysis.

You should be aware of the range of mapping facilities and their potential to support students' understanding of geographical concepts; for example, Google Maps, Streetmap, Digimap, Google Earth, InfoMapper, Memory-Map, Digital Worlds, etc. Each of these offers different opportunities to support learning. The potential of global positioning systems has yet to be realised but when combined with mapping packages such as Memory-Map can enable students to understand the ICT potential in many areas of social and commercial development.

In geography you will use the word 'model' to mean a representation of a concept such as weather systems of the North Atlantic or water flows in different parts of a river system. In ICT the word 'model' means an interactive representation of a real situation. ICT models enable students to ask 'What if?' by changing variables or inputs and seeing the result of those changes. Some of the software is called 'simulation' and includes multimedia, graphics and interactivity, while other examples are based upon a spreadsheet.

In geography, ICT can make a significant contribution to teaching. Readily available software and web pages of maps and visual representations of concepts can be projected for the whole class to see. Video projectors can also enable simulation and spreadsheet models to be presented for whole class collaboration

A weather station can contribute to your students' ICT capability and understanding of computer-based systems. You should take the opportunity to use a weather station when it is presented to you. You should also be aware of the role the geography curriculum contributes to educational for sustainable development, citizenship and education for global citizenship and the contribution ICT makes to those areas.

The National Curriculum for geography makes direct reference to the use of ICT, including: digital cameras in fieldwork; satellite images downloaded from the internet; data-logging using a weather station; presentation software and spreadsheets for analysing data. The economic implications of the use of computers (telecommuting) should also be discussed (Key Stage 3, 6h).

The National Curriculum for geography requires that students are taught to use ICT in developing their geographical skills when:

- **selecting and using secondary sources;**
- **drawing maps and plans;**
- **communicating with others;**
- **developing decision-making skills.**

ICT in modern foreign languages

The teaching of modern foreign languages can make a significant contribution to the ICT capability of your students. Students can use their ICT capability to assist and progress their learning in their language skills and knowledge. ICT can play an important role in helping you to present resources for teaching and carry out your administrative tasks.

ICT can provide you with the media for language development through:

- **using CD-ROM, audio CD and DVD-based material to hear the spoken word;**
- **using digital audio recorders (MP3), audio-recording software and digital video cameras to record, rehearse and perfect speech in the target language;**
- **using presentation software, word processors and multimedia authoring software to enable your learners to present their knowledge, ideas and views;**

- using the internet, CD-ROM and e-books as the source of material that provides 'real' contexts for language development;
- using interactive multimedia and applications to motivate and record your learners' engagement in the curriculum material.

The National Languages Strategy, *Framework for teaching MFL: Years 7, 8 and 9*, reflects on the research that 'ICT is a powerful tool for all learners and enhances the "real-life" factor in MFL study, which often appeals to boys in particular. Research carried out by the DfES shows that achievement is higher across the curriculum where ICT is used – in some subjects by as much as 0.5 of a grade' (DfES, 2003, p151). It continues to state that at Key Stage 4, it was shown that where there was low ICT usage, grades for MFL were lower than predicted.

The National Languages Strategy (Framework of objectives) includes numerous references to the use of ICT to support work on specific objectives. Further information on the use of ICT in MFL can be found in the 'From Framework to classroom' section and Appendix B of the training folder 'Framework for teaching modern foreign languages: Years 7, 8 and 9: the place of information and communication technology'. **www.standards.dfes.gov.uk/ keystage3/downloads/mflfwkdl_70addgui.pdf**

The National Curriculum for modern foreign languages requires that students be taught the techniques for skimming and scanning ICT-based texts. ICT-based resources and texts must be included when teaching about different countries and cultures and when teaching students the knowledge, skills and understanding of the curriculum. The use of e-mail is given as an example of how you might facilitate your students communicating with native speakers and when using the target language for real purposes. To meet the ITT standards, you must be able to teach all of these aspects of ICT-usage.

ICT in art and design

The teaching of art and design can make a significant contribution to the ICT capability of students. Students can use their ICT capability to assist and progress their learning in art and design. ICT can play an important role in helping you to present resources for teaching and carry out your administrative tasks.

ICT can provide the media for artwork:

- using a graphics package to produce a collage of images drawn from a range of electronic sources including scanned and camera images of conventional artwork;
- using a presentation package to present a sequence of images and sounds viewed as a carousel, web page or narrated slide show;
- using a video camera and editing software to produce a film.

The facility of ICT to be able to render images in quick succession means that students can readily compare artistic works, thus supporting analysis and appreciation of form and presentation.

'Art is about expressing feelings and emotions and the human condition. ICT helps us to develop our visual understanding, enabling us to interpret, respond to and work with arrange of visual stimuli to engage and inspire different audiences' (DfES, 2004a). The

ICTAC advice goes on to say that ICT is 'challenging us to rethink the ways in which creativity is developed. It blurs the boundary between traditional art forms by providing opportunities to express ideas in a multi-disciplinary way'. You need to enable students to communicate with, inspire and engage a variety of audiences. Those audiences may be people browsing the internet for artwork.

In art and design there is a National Curriculum requirement to include using a range of materials and processes, including ICT. That use is exemplified by creating print and digital media and using CD-ROMs and electronic sketchbooks to record observations and ideas. The National Curriculum also suggests that students could re-create works of art in a contemporary context and share their work with others via e-mail. A contemporary project might include an audio commentary about an artist's work accompanied by still images of their work. By using a Ken Burns effect, attention is drawn to elements of the images or points made in the audio track. The whole work can be published as a vodcast (video podcast).

ICT in music

The teaching of music can make a significant contribution to the ICT capability of students. Music provides an almost unique opportunity to use a computer to capture external activities (making music on a keyboard) and then manipulate the result to refine and improve. The keywords associated with music and ICT are: sequence, quantise, transpose, notation, MIDI and sound box. You should be familiar with each term and be able to explain them to a group of students.

Sequencing is using software to put together sequences and overlays of sounds, cut and paste to change the order, highlight sections to change the qualities and publish a final product. There are direct parallels with word processing:

- **typing: playing a MIDI keyboard and recording the notes in a sequencer or adding notes to a on-screen stave (standard notation) or adding voices/notes directly onto a sequencer screen.**
- **editing (highlight then copy, cut, paste): highlighting areas of tracks and moving or copying them to other places, deleting sections.**
- **formatting (highlight then apply italic, bold, subscript, etc.): changing the qualities of sections of the music by using a different instrument, voice, tempo, volume or pitch.**
- **transformations (such as text styles, autoformats and themes); changing the qualities of the whole piece of work such as transposing the work to another key.**
- **printing (for draft/redraft or publication): playback for review or performance.**

Quantising is taking real, live, analogue data from the environment and presenting it in a digital format. In the case of music teaching, it is the actions of the students' fingers or mouth on a MIDI instrument being converted to a digital signal and then displayed on standard notation staves or in a sequencer. This is an important aspect of music as well as helping the students understand other applications of ICT that sense the real world and then represent in digital format.

In music, ICT can make a significant contribution to teaching by providing the visual display of music both representing audio patterns, pitch and frequency, but also displaying the standard notation simultaneously with the sound of the notes. Your use of MIDI instruments and a sound box to demonstrate the sounds of different instruments and using own-made CDs and MP3 files, all represent your use of ICT to support your teaching.

In music there are National Curriculum requirements to teach students about ICT-based 'resources, conventions, processes and procedures' in 'selected musical genres, styles and traditions' (4c). They must be taught the knowledge, skills and understanding of music 'using ICT to create, manipulate and refine sounds' (5d).

ICT in physical education

The teaching of physical education can make a significant contribution to the ICT capability of students. In particular, it can introduce students to real-life applications of computers in electronic exercise machines; this raises awareness of their bodies and health. Currently, strong emphasis is being placed upon the use of digital cameras to record and analyse performance; for example, perfecting the technique of an individual's performance or the strategies deployed by a group of players in a team activity. The video recording can be used to celebrate individual performance and exemplify good performance. More sophisticated analysis of video material involves adding control points to the images and then tracking movement frame by frame. Another application of ICT is using sensors to monitor heart rate. (Please note the cautions described in Chapter 6 on health and safety.) It is also suggested by the DfES ICTAC publications that students in PE lessons can also use data collected in class or downloaded from the internet to inform and improve performance.

In the PE subject area, ICT can make a significant contribution to teaching and learning. A laptop and projector give you the opportunity to show sequences of video that demonstrate key concepts that the students need to understand – this may be posture and movement of the individual or strategies and tactics in games play.

The PE National Curriculum makes direct reference to students using heart and pulse-rate monitors and a variety of other measuring and recording devices to collect, analyse and interpret data. Students could use stopwatches and lap recorders linked to data-collection devices to analyse and evaluate performance using, for example, spreadsheets.

You should consider how ICT could support your own administrative tasks, including lesson planning, producing and displaying teaching resources, recording student attainment and the evaluation of your lessons and communicating with school colleagues. An interesting piece of software associated with PE is the recording and display software used for managing a school sports day.

ICT in religious education

The teaching of RE can make a significant contribution to the ICT capability of students. There is a potential for bias and misrepresentation of information about religions. The interpretation of people's motivations and beliefs is prone to prejudice. Being able to detect bias, prejudice and personal position in such information is an important aspect of ICT capability.

In RE, ICT can make a significant contribution to learning by enabling students to examine a large body of knowledge and draw conclusions from the information examined. ICT enables the students to produce high-quality presentations that can promote ideas and motivate readers. They need to understand the consequences of misinformation and the importance of being sensitivities of the audience, for example, making inappropriate representations of Muhammad or Jesus.

There is not a National Curriculum for RE but the QCA, in collaboration with a wide range of faith and belief communities and professional RE associations, has published a non-statutory national framework for religious education (QCA, 2004). It identifies the Key Stage 3 ICT opportunity as: 'pupils could find information on the internet and CD-ROMs and could use e-mail, particularly to share their views on global issues of human rights, social justice and the importance of the environment'. It also states that students could use presentation software, digital video and desktop publishing to express their own beliefs and ideas and use CD-ROMs to experience a virtual visit and video conference to develop their understanding of places of major religious significance.

You should consult the 'locally approved syllabus for Religious Education' to identify the precise ICT requirements in your placement school.

REFERENCES REFERENCES **REFERENCES** REFERENCES **REFERENCES** REFERENCES

DfEE (1999) *The National Curriculum Handbook for secondary teachers in England Key Stages 3 and 4*. London: DfEE.

DfES (2003) *Framework for teaching MFL: Years 7, 8 and 9*. London: Department for Education and Skills.

DfES (2004a) *Key Stage 3 National Strategy ICT across the curriculum. ICT in mathematics*. London: Department for Education and Skills.

DfES (2004b) *The National Curriculum for England: Science*. London: Department for Education and Skills.

QCA (2004) *Religious education.* London: QCA **www.qca.org.uk/9817.html**

Appendix 3
Sample teaching units (STU) for ICT

The sample teaching units form part of a series of resources that illustrate yearly objectives from the *Framework for teaching ICT capability through Years 7, 8 and 9*. The units contain sample lesson plans that you can, if you wish, amend to suit your local circumstances and the needs of your students. Further guidance on using the units is available in the introduction of each document. See **www.standards.dfes.gov.uk/schemes2/secondary_ICT**

The scheme is not statutory; the school can use as much or as little as it wishes and, to some extent, the sequence can be varied. The units are aimed at students who are attaining at levels that are broadly appropriate for their age. It may therefore be necessary to adapt them to meet the students' needs. The DfES also provides advice on 'links with other subjects' section gives information on exploiting links between subjects at **www.standards.dfes.-gov.uk/schemes2/secondary_ICT/links?view=get**

Although the scheme is not statutory for schools to implement, it is a requirement of your training that you are aware of its detail.

QCA reference	STU	YEAR	TITLE	TOPIC
Unit 1	7.1	7	Using ICT	The product is a projected presentation with accompanying speech, with the audience being the class.
Unit 2	7.2	7	Information and presentation	Students are given a real-life context in which they search for, analyse and present data in a traditional database and charting paradigm.
Unit 3	7.3	7	Processing text and images	The product is a paper-based presentation for a particular audience meeting particular style guidelines emphasising draft and re-draft and self-evaluation.
Unit 4	7.4	7	Models – rules and investigations	Based predominantly upon a spreadsheet, the students learn what a model is and how models can be created and applied in real-life situations.
Unit 5	7.5	7	Data – designing structure, capturing and presenting data	Based on the traditional database structure, students capture data through a questionnaire and present the results as charts.
Unit 6	7.6	7	Control – input, process and output	Usually based upon a visual interface (flow chart) rather than commands (programming), students control activities and make them respond to events.
Unit 7	7.7	7	Measuring physical data	Students use sensors to measure physical conditions (analogue) or events (digital) and present the data in graphical and numeric format.
Unit 8	8.1	8	Public information systems	Combines revision of datalogging, sensing and data representation with extensive spreadsheet work and ideas of meeting the needs of the audience.

Unit 9	8.2	8	Publishing on the web	Creating web pages and publishing to an intranet with particular reference to audience and a little HTML work.
Unit 10	8.3	8	Information – reliability, validity and bias	Students introduced to concepts of: content, style, fitness for purpose, fact, opinion, clarity, accessibility, plausibility, criteria to evaluate. Also use of advanced search techniques using Boolean logic.
Unit 11	8.4	8	Models and presenting numeric data	Based upon the use of a spreadsheet (specifically Microsoft Excel) the student explores and creates models based upon simple numeric formula including random number generation.
Unit 12	8.5	8	Systems – integrating applications to find solutions	Covering every aspect of Key Stage 3 ICT, this unit endeavours to integrate the products from a wide range of applications into a single project with the aim of preparing students for less-prescriptive project work.
Unit 13	9.1	9	Control systems	An exemplar case study of an ICT system based on a new water ride in a theme park with keywords of: control, feedback, safety, test, evaluation, sensors, presentation and audience.
Unit 14	9.2	9	Global communication – negotiating and transferring data	An exemplar case study of an ICT system based on a 'remote partner' in another school to collect common, agreed data for a specific topic which is then transferred electronically and merged to form a complete data set and a report on their joint findings.
Unit 15	9.3	9	Systems – managing a project	An exemplar case study of an ICT system based on a front-of-house ticketing system for a theatre with keywords of: project development, systematic, flow chart, design specification, evaluation criteria, time management, problem solving and report summary.

DfES (2003) ICT at Key Stage 3 sample teaching units **www.standards.dfes.gov.uk/ schemes2/secondary_ICT**

DfES (2004) ICT at Key Stage 3. Links with other curriculum areas online **www.standards.dfes.gov.uk/schemes2/secondary_ICT/links?view=get**

Index

Added to the page number 'f' denotes a figure.